WHAT LAWYERS DO... AND HOW TO MAKE THEM WORK FOR YOU

The Official Lawyer's Handbook
White's Law Dictionary

WHAT LAWYERS DO...
AND HOW TO MAKE THEM WORK FOR YOU

DANIEL R. WHITE

E. P. DUTTON | NEW YORK

PUBLISHER'S NOTE: This publication is designed to provide accurate and authoritative information in regard to the subject matter covered. It is sold with the understanding that the publisher is not engaged in rendering legal, accounting, or other professional service. If legal advice or other expert assistance is required, the service of a competent professional person should be sought.

Published in the United States by
E. P. Dutton, a division of NAL Penguin Inc.,
2 Park Avenue, New York, N.Y. 10016.

Library of Congress Cataloging-in-Publication Data
White, D. Robert (Daniel Robert)
What lawyers do—and how to make them work for you.
Includes index.
1. Attorney and client—United States—Popular works.
2. Lawyers—United States—Fees—Popular works.
3. Law—United States—Popular works.   I. Title.
KF311.Z9W48   1987   349.73′068′1   86-19706
          ISBN: 0-525-24478-6   347.300681

Published simultaneously in Canada by
Fitzhenry & Whiteside Limited, Toronto

COBE

DESIGNED BY MARK O'CONNOR

10 9 8 7 6 5 4 3 2 1
First Edition

TO MOM AND CHRISTINE

A Word of Thanks

I didn't write this book completely on my own. I have to take responsibility for any mistakes in it, because that's the way this game is played. But a number of people, lawyers all, helped a lot. I want to implicate them—and thank them—here.

Their ranks include two professors of law, one assistant U.S. attorney, one public defender, and a number of private practitioners. All possess high expertise in one or more of the areas this book discusses. Their wit, liveliness, and sheer intelligence made them delightful to work with, and judging from the low regard in which the legal profession in general is held, I can only assume they don't get out enough.

They are Russell Carter, Barbara Mishkin, Bill Norton, Lisa Robertson, Mark Rochon, David Shipley, David Sokolow, Ben White, Allen Williams, Debbie Young, and Marty Yudkowitz.

Special thanks, also, to Helen Rees, my thoughtful and resourceful agent; John Freund and David Porter, who got me into this, sort of; and Carole DeSanti and Jennifer Josephy, my able editors.

D. R. W.

Contents

WHAT LAWYERS DO...
AND HOW TO
MAKE THEM
WORK FOR
YOU

1. What *Do* Lawyers Do?

It is hard to say whether the doctors of law or divinity have made the greater advance in the lucrative business of mystery. EDMUND BURKE
(1729–1797)

Of all the decisions I've made in my life, becoming a lawyer was definitely one of them. MARTIN J. YUDKOWITZ
(1954–)

What lawyers do, if nothing else, is take money from you. Or—the same thing—they send you bills, outrageously big ones, which you invariably pay because you have no idea of what they'll do to you if you don't. (Worse, you have a very good idea of what they'll do, such as tie you up in a room and read their briefs to you.)

I should explain something. I have high regard for a number of lawyers, including my brother, my father, one grandfather, one aunt, two uncles, two great-uncles, and various cousins— fine people all. If I were ever in trouble in Hopkinsville, Kentucky, I'd run to the law firm of White & White (my cousin

Pollard and his son Lee) in a second. Like many of my law school classmates, they're helpful, straight-shooting folks.*

So don't get me wrong. I don't mean to imply that lawyers are universally dollar-hungry. The fact is, law schools place a fair bit of emphasis on helping the helpless, defending the defenseless—in general, doing good. Which pays beans. And more than a few law students absorb more than a bit of this ethic.

Then again, there's no denying that plenty of lawyers are in it for what sociologists refer to as "the money." And even the altruists charge hefty fees, because their good hearts don't spare them the cost of offices, law books, secretaries, paralegals, typewriters, photocopiers, and, if they're to command any respect at all, briefcases and speaker phones.

Which gets us back to this book's title and the invariable tendency of lawyers to shift money from your pocket to theirs. Perform a wallet biopsy on you—without anesthetic. The point of this book is to help you keep this sort of redistribution of wealth at a minimum, while getting from lawyers neither less *nor more* than you need.

To be sure, there's more at stake in understanding the law than money. There's staying out of jail, for example. And staying *in* your apartment, if your landlord is trying to evict you. There's getting out of your marriage, if you're determined to do so, as painlessly as possible. And making sure your property will go where you want it to go when you go where all of us are going sooner or later. This book touches all these bases while showing you how, if consulting a lawyer is unavoidable, to keep your legal fees at a minimum.

This book doesn't attempt to turn you into a lawyer. There are already plenty of lawyers—although not so many, mind you,

---

*One of the most successful of all these lawyers is my aunt Mary. I mention this to make the point that plenty of lawyers are female, notwithstanding that my occasional use of the pronoun *he* where no particular gender is called for by the context may suggest that every lawyer, judge, or prosecutor is male, even if he isn't. Our language's lack of gender-neutral pronouns engenders in me what the writer Roy Blount, Jr., calls Pronoun Guilt. I have tried to avoid using any pronoun at all where I could do so without verbal histrionics or leaving a space in the sentence. Otherwise I apologize for not knowing what to do about it.

that every American can have his own. We have to learn to share.

It does show you how to handle a number of things that you might have thought only a lawyer could handle. In situations where you really ought to get some measure of input from a lawyer, it discusses what kind of lawyer you should hire, including when it's okay to go with a low-priced general practitioner, and when you need a high-priced specialist. In situations where only the latter will do, this book discusses the law in the area, so you won't be flying blind. You don't have to be at your lawyer's mercy, the way you are with your doctor or car mechanic.

Think of how comforting it is to be able to tell a taxi driver the names of a few streets along the way to your destination, even though you may not know the entire route. It reduces his natural temptation to take you from La Guardia to Manhattan, say, via Cleveland. Just so, the more you know about what your lawyer is supposed to be doing for you, or at least the more your lawyer *thinks* you know about what he's supposed to be doing for you, the better off you are.

The best way to use lawyers is to use them as little as possible.

This isn't to say you shouldn't hire someone else to take care of the unpleasant chores of life just because you're physically capable of taking care of them on your own. If you hate cleaning your rain gutters, hire somebody with a ladder to clean them for you. If you hate emptying your cat box, hire somebody with a strong stomach to empty it for you (or get rid of your cat). That's what money is for.

But if you're interested in conserving your money—a primary assumption of this book—you should hire a *lawyer* for a given chore when only a lawyer can handle it (or can handle it better than anyone else). Why hire a lawyer to unclog your sink or even help you prepare your tax return when you can get a plumber or an accountant to do the same work for less? The critical consideration here is that a lawyer charges higher fees than anyone else, except maybe a doctor. (And you shouldn't have any trouble distinguishing the two; if he tells you to take your clothes off in his office, he's probably a doctor.)

Make no mistake: You shouldn't plan on getting through life without *ever* hiring a lawyer, even if by luck or daring you've managed to avoid it so far. It's advisable, if not critical, to hire one to prepare your will, for example, or to assist you in your divorce, or to look over the papers if you're buying or selling a house. These are bread-and-butter areas of the law.

There are other situations, moreover, in which you should *absolutely, positively* hire a lawyer—if you're involved in any matter having to do with a lot of money, for example, or you're in a dispute with someone who has hired his own lawyer.

The former point covers a lot of situations. Suppose you're buying a new house. The price is way up there—$300,000, say. This won't be the first house you'll have owned; in fact, it'll be the fourth. Up to now you've always let your husband's brother Al, a real estate broker, represent you in the transactions, and Al's work has always been fine, as far as you can tell. But this deal is bigger than any of the others. You're sinking your life's savings into it. Maybe, it occurs to you one day, you should bring in a lawyer.

Your instincts are excellent. Indeed, they're consistent with what I hereby offer as the first of White's Irregular Rules:

> Where there's a lot of money at stake,
> hire a lawyer.

Why?

Because where there's a lot of money at stake, you want to make dead solid certain the matter is handled properly from a legal perspective. And only a lawyer can do that.

Suppose you want to leave everything you own to your daughter. (This would call for about as simple a will as there is.) You're not rich, but between your house, which is fully paid for, and your life insurance policy, the total is an amount you enjoy contemplating. You've found a write-your-own-will handbook for your state, and you're confident that everything in it is accurate. In these circumstances, couldn't you produce a workable will on your own, without making what amounts to a charitable contribution to a lawyer? Maybe. *Probably.* But if there's a lot of money at stake, why risk it?

There's a cost-benefit/risk analysis to be performed here. The chances of something going wrong might be small, but if for a comparatively small sum you can enlist the expertise of a good lawyer, thereby reducing the chances to virtually zero, isn't the expenditure justified?

Consider the other situation mentioned above in which it's imperative that you hire a lawyer, namely, when you're in a dispute with someone who has hired his own lawyer. Here I offer the second of White's Irregular Rules:

Never go one-on-one in court against a lawyer.

It's not a fair fight. You might be smarter than Albert Einstein, and the opposing lawyer dumber than a municipal bureaucrat. But he (the lawyer) is bound to know tricks, procedural maneuvers, that are nearly impossible for a layperson to combat. The presiding judge may help you out a bit, even as he chides you for wasting his time by coming into court without a lawyer. But he won't research the law for you, write your briefs for you, or raise arguments that you haven't come up with on your own.

There's another reason you shouldn't go one-on-one against a lawyer in court. It probably wouldn't really be one-on-one, but more like three-on-one, or five-on-one. A senior partner at a law firm is like a general in an army, and how many generals so much as cross the street without their aides, adjutants, and other courtiers? Law firm partners, especially those at sizable firms, have junior partners, associates, clerks, paralegals, and night-shift secretaries—a small army capable of firing off briefs, motions, and memoranda with machine-gun-like speed and devastation.

Courts (with the exception of one special court, discussed below) are no place for a layperson unaccompanied by a lawyer. Think of them as R-rated movies, and of yourself as under seventeen— a babe in arms.

Suppose you want to sue someone who owes you money. You think, The debt couldn't be clearer. I have a signed contract to prove it, and witnesses to back me up. How can I lose?

Your spunk is laudable, if not your naïveté. What if the opposing lawyer moves to dismiss the case "for lack of subject matter jurisdiction"? What if he alleges that you lack "standing" to sue? What if he countersues you on a theory of *respondeat superior*? These things have nothing to do with who's right or wrong, but they could leave your case dead in the road, like a possum run over by a cement truck.

What's the exception to the above-mentioned rule about staying out of court without a lawyer? The various courts in each state usually include a *small-claims court* (often referred to by lawyers as the "small-change court"). In a small-claims court you can generally get along fine without a lawyer.

Each state has its own rules—this makes places like North Dakota feel important—but the basic idea of a small-claims court is to provide a forum for the resolution of disputes involving so little money that it's not worth anyone's while to hire a lawyer. Suppose the *jurisdictional limit* of the small-claims court in your state is $750. (It might be twice that.) This means the most you can ever win there is $750. If someone owes you $2,000, you can sue him in the small-claims court, but (1) you won't get more than $750, even if the judge agrees that the defendant ought to pay you $2,000, and (2) you can't thereafter go to some other court and sue for the remaining $1,250. In some states you can appeal a small-claims court's decision against you, but otherwise the matter is at an end.

To get a small-claims case rolling, usually all you have to do is fill out a standard complaint form and file it. If there's a filing fee, it's probably in the neighborhood of ten dollars. Your case will be set for a few weeks after the filing of your complaint, at which time you simply show up and explain to the judge what happened. For details of the procedures in your state, call the court itself (look in the phone book under *state* courts); it can surely supply you with forms and explanatory materials. You should also contact a national consumer organization called HALT (an acronym for Help Abolish Legal Tyranny), and order its helpful manual titled *Small Claims Court*. (HALT is located at 319 F Street, N.W., Suite 300, Washington, D.C. 20004 (202/347-9600). It publishes a number of law-related manuals, which are available without charge to its members. The minimum membership fee is now fifteen dollars.)

Even in the comparatively loose, nontechnical context of

small-claims courts, evidence is critical. Be sure to bring with you the dry cleaner's receipt for the suit you're saying they ruined, the photographs you took of your neighbor's tree after it fell on your garage, the mechanic who inspected your car and said it must have been defective when you bought it. The judge may announce his decision immediately after considering all the evidence, or he may mail you something in writing a week or month later.

As for representation, you're free to bring along a lawyer. He won't be able to help you as much in the small-claims court as he might elsewhere, however, because the process is supposed to be informal. Small-claims court judges don't like seeing hired guns run roughshod over justice with their usual procedural maneuvering and technical arguments.

Note that if the party you're suing is a corporation, it may *have* to be represented by a lawyer; this is simply the rule in some states. The downside of this rule is that you'll be doing battle against a lawyer. The upside, and it's a substantial one, is that the stakes of the case are automatically higher for your opponent than for you. For example, because small-claims court proceedings more often than not involve waiting around all day for your case to be called, your opponent could be out $500 in legal fees before the case even gets to a judge.

Don't get the idea that a corporation will automatically roll over and play dead if you sue it in small-claims court. Sizable corporations often spend several thousands of dollars fighting lawsuits that involve only a fraction of that amount, just to prevent anyone from getting that idea. Still, if your claim is plausible, the added expense a corporation may face in legal fees could definitely help promote a settlement favorable to you.

This book discusses ten fundamental areas of the law, each selected on the likelihood—indeed, the near certainty—that ordinary people will need information about that area sooner or later. Securities law, antitrust law, maritime law—you could live ten or twelve happy, fruitful lives without the slightest knowledge of these subjects. (I plan to try, starting the next time around.) But wills, taxes, housing, insurance, divorce—you'd have to be

Robinson Crusoe to get by without knowing something about most of these areas.

Chapter 7's discussion of the law of copyright might seem somewhat off the beaten path. Since the publication of my first book, however, I've encountered a striking number of people poking their heads out of the artistic closet, confessing the existence of original songs, poems, novels, paintings, and screenplays, most produced in absolute secrecy. The human craving for self-expression appears powerful—only slightly less so than the fear of self-exposure. If you've ever contemplated subjecting the product of your artistic efforts to the scrutiny of an audience wider (but surely no less forgiving) than your dark-of-night imaginings, this chapter should prove useful.

A major topic not addressed is so-called products liability, which involves suing a retailer, wholesaler, or manufacturer—somebody in the chain of supply—when a product that ought to be safe turns out not to be safe. The reason this topic isn't addressed is simple: Suppose you're watching the news one night and your Sony television explodes, shooting lethal pieces of glass in every direction. Or you pop open a Coca-Cola one afternoon only to find someone's thumb in it. You can't sue Sony or Coca-Cola on your own. Those are giant corporations, represented by the highest-priced, best-equipped, most aggressive lawyers money can buy. You wouldn't stand a chance. Recall the second of White's Irregular Rules:

Never go one-on-one in court against a lawyer.

How do you go about finding a lawyer, especially when you need a really good one? Let your fingers do the walking? Answer a television ad for some huckster whose office consists of the back seat of his '72 Vette (*Chevette*, that is) or the pay telephone booth at the Exxon station across from the courthouse?

It's tempting to go into a lengthy discussion of the pros and cons of various methods, but the fact is, it's a matter of common sense. You should find a lawyer the same way you would a doctor—and do you throw a dart at the yellow pages when it comes to the person who's going to remove your adenoids?

A referral is your best bet, preferably a referral from another lawyer, ideally a referral from another two or three lawyers—to ensure that the first lawyer hasn't referred you to someone whose primary virtue is his willingness to remember the favor and send other business to the first lawyer later on. This happens a lot.

For nuts-and-bolts advice on referrals, interviews, and written agreements with lawyers, HALT, the consumer organization mentioned above, publishes a helpful manual titled *Shopping for a Lawyer*. Also, the American Bar Association (1155 East 60th Street, Chicago, IL 60637, 312/947-3685) publishes a *Directory of Lawyer Referral Services*, which lists organized lawyer referral services around the country. Although these services generally won't "recommend" a specific lawyer or comment on anyone's professional competence, they're better than the yellow pages, because their lists include not only the names and numbers of most lawyers in town, but also the types of matters each lawyer is willing to handle. Thus, if you're looking for a lawyer to advise you on a specialized area of the law—for example, tax, divorce, real estate, or bankruptcy—one of these services can get you started in your search.

In interviewing a lawyer, don't be shy. Lawyers, like barbers and chimney sweeps, are simply businesspeople with a service to sell. Of the various questions you should ask any lawyer you're considering hiring, three merit special emphasis:

• *Will you handle my matter personally?* Your matter won't necessarily suffer if your lawyer delegates the work on it to his partners or associates; these people may be more competent than he is. Still, you have every right to know his plans along these lines, as well as to meet and form your own opinion of the people who'll actually be doing the work.

• *How will you determine my fee?* A given lawyer may charge by the hour, the quarter-hour, or even the six-minute unit. He may charge a fixed fee for the particular service you want (attending a house closing, for example), or a percentage of anything he wins for you in court. Whatever, find out in advance. And get him to identify every possible expense that might be charged to you.

• *How often will you bill me?* You want your lawyer to bill you as often as possible (monthly billing is probably the norm), so you can keep an eye on his expenses and monitor what, if anything, is happening in your case. Insist that he itemize his bills, so you can be sure you're paying for *legal* work, rather than theater tickets or obedience training for his dog.

The question of how to go about finding a lawyer brings us to the third of White's Irregular Rules:

Who your lawyer is matters.

In a better world, justice wouldn't turn on something as arbitrary as the quality of the lawyer you happen to be able to locate and afford. No lawyer in his right mind will tell you, however, that a lazy, stupid, or poorly trained lawyer can't doom you—in the litigation context, by losing a winnable case; in the business context, by giving away the store.

Consider an all-too-common story. A husband and wife are getting divorced, not amicably. Each sets out to find a lawyer. The husband, a prominent businessman, consults his colleagues, through whom he tracks down and hires the finest divorce lawyer in the state. The wife, a traditional homemaker, consults her friends—other homemakers. Eventually she ends up hiring a third-rate lawyer whose main experience is in landlord-tenant disputes.

Predictably, the husband's lawyer runs roughshod over the wife's lawyer. The wife ends up receiving a fraction of the money she needs, deserves, and, but for her choice of lawyers, would have received. Now she's fifty-five, alone, and broke.

The moral: Who your lawyer is matters—a lot.

Suppose you're the wife in the situation above. Suppose also that your lawyer, in addition to being no match for your husband's lawyer, was downright negligent in handling your case. He failed to interview key witnesses before the trial, missed the deadline for replying to important pretrial motions, divulged your confidences to people outside his office, made lewd and suggestive remarks to you on several occasions, and showed up at one hearing with alcohol on his breath (offering none to you).

What do you do?

At one extreme, you sit back in silence and take it. At the

other extreme, you hire a second lawyer to sue the first one for malpractice. The latter is hardly an unheard-of step; in 1985, according to insurance industry statistics, malpractice suits were filed against one out of every eighteen lawyers in the country. Given facts as extreme as the ones just described, you'd be more than justified in suing, and more than likely to win.

Intermediate steps include firing your lawyer, complaining to the grievance committee of the local bar association, or both. As for complaining to the grievance committee, keep in mind that a lawyer charged with professional misconduct could suffer censure, probation, suspension, or even disbarment. Hence, he has every incentive to turn on you, portraying you as ignorant, unbalanced, paranoid, promiscuous, and prone to acts against nature.

Still, complaining might be the right thing to do, both for yourself and for this shyster's future clients. If this is the course you choose, call any lawyer or the local bar association. Many bar associations publish descriptions of the process. New York's Committee on Professional Discipline, for example, puts out a pamphlet titled, with admirable directness, "How to Complain About Professional Misconduct by Lawyers." HALT also puts out a useful manual titled *Using a Lawyer . . . And What to Do If Things Go Wrong.*

As for firing your lawyer, unless you're at the critical stage of a trial or some other matter, it's hardly an extreme step. It may cost you something, in that the next lawyer you hire may have to re-cover some of the ground covered by your first lawyer, but if it's worth it to you, do it.

It can't be overemphasized that lawyers are simply businesspeople with a service to sell. As is true for doctors, secretaries, stockbrokers, stable cleaners, and every other group, some lawyers are competent, and some aren't. Passing a bar exam guarantees little—certainly not competence; every literate primate in the country could pull it off sooner or later. The bottom line: Don't *assume* a lawyer knows what he's doing, just because he's a lawyer. If you're not happy with his work (keeping in mind that the best lawyer in the world can't rewrite facts), get rid of him. There are lots more where he came from.

*   *   *

A word on nomenclature. This book refers in various contexts to three types of congregations of lawyers: *big firms, little firms,* and *clinics.*

*Firms,** big and little, constitute the traditional mode of legal organization. Typically consisting of "partners" at the top and "associates" at the bottom, they comprise the bulk of all lawyerdom.

Big firms, by which I mean those consisting of, say, forty lawyers or more (and some have grown to more than four hundred in recent years), generally reside in large cities and do most of their work for large corporations and wealthy individuals. Although exceptions spring readily to mind, they tend to be rich, expensive, and staffed with the best lawyers—specialists in their fields.

By *little firms,* I mean those consisting of, say, forty lawyers or fewer, including solo practitioners. Little firms tend to be less expensive than big firms, partly because little firms tend to have fewer high-priced specialists. By no means, however, should you assume without asking that a lawyer in a little firm charges reasonable rates.

Clinics are the low-cost, multioffice operations you often see advertised on television. Hyatt Legal Services, which has offices all over the country, is the largest and probably best known. These operations call themselves *firms,* and there's no particular reason they shouldn't, but it's important to distinguish them from traditional firms, given the bulk-process, quick-and-dirty nature of the services they provide. *Clinic* is a serviceable if somewhat arbitrary term.

In providing basic legal counsel to people with basic legal needs, clinics play a useful role. But know their limitations. You go to a McDonald's for hamburger, not filet mignon. For the same reason, you should go to a clinic for advice on simple, low-stakes problems, not sophisticated law.

---

*"*Firm*—an assemblage of lawyers, similar to a 'pride' of lions, 'gaggle' of geese, 'school' of sharks, or 'bunch' of bananas, although sharks also frequently congregate in firms (as do a few bananas)." *White's Law Dictionary* (1985)

2. Family Law— From Dating to Divorce

Living Together •
Prenuptial Contracts •
Divorce and Mediation •
Marriage and Property •
Child Custody and Support •

It is a maxim that husband and wife should never have it in their power to hang one another. GEORGE FARQUHAR
(1678–1707)

Is not marriage an open question, when it is alleged, from the beginning of the world, that such as are in the institution wish to get out; and such as are out wish to get in? RALPH WALDO EMERSON
(1803–1882)

Marriage is a serious thing—something you don't want to do more than three or four times in your life. MARTIN J. YUDKOWITZ
(1954–   )

LIVING TOGETHER

Relations between the sexes are too important to be influenced by romance. Too much is at stake.

Suppose you let a friend move in with you for a while. You're a rich insurance salesman, and she's a talented but struggling artist. She needs a place to crash, and you have a second bedroom no one is using. You charge no rent. She, out of gratitude, cleans up around the place and occasionally cooks dinner. Eventually a spark of romance ignites, and soon you find, as before, that you have a second bedroom no one is using.

After two years of semi-bliss, the two of you begin to fight. She moves out. A month later you find yourself being sued for *palimony*. Surprised?

What are the legal obligations between two people in such a nontraditional, more-than-dating-but-less-than-married relationship? What if you meet someone at a party and invite her to stay over for a single evening—are you legally obliged to buy her brunch the next day?

Things aren't as easy as they used to be, when the only question was, do we get married or not? Now you have a smorgasbord of options, which can be lumped together under the rubric of *cohabitation* or, less clinical sounding, *living together*. And people are taking advantage of these options. In 1984, according to the Census Bureau, there were some two *million* unmarried-couple households in America, almost four times the number in 1970.

Let me set some parameters on what I'm talking about. All relationships fall on a continuum, from dating, at the tame end, to marriage, at the other end. Here I'm talking about something in-between. By *living together*, I don't mean a mere coed roommate situation involving no more intimacy than your occasionally finding the other person's underwear in your washing machine.

Neither do I mean *common-law marriage*, which, although it doesn't involve such rituals as a blood test and formal vows, *is* a marriage. In the few states that still recognize common-law marriage (thirteen, at last count), the law requires that the two people view themselves as actually married and hold themselves out to the public as married.

If you decide to move in with your boyfriend or girlfriend, your parents or friends might ask, why stop there? Why not go all the way and get married?

To you, a more appropriate question might be, why am I going *this* far? Fair enough. But there may come a time when you're a little farther along on the continuum, when the idea of getting . . . you know, doing the "M" thing . . . seems less outrageous.

There are at least five objective, economic advantages to being married (or disadvantages to not being married). Knowing these may come in handy if your live-in partner ever says to you, "Why get married? We'll always love each other. There's no point."

1. *Joint income-tax returns.* You and your friend can't file a joint income-tax return if you aren't married. If one of you has an income and the other doesn't, being married can substantially reduce your income tax. (On the other hand, in view of the much discussed "marriage penalty," which can amount to thousands of dollars if the two of you have equal incomes and are in sufficiently high tax brackets, tax considerations may weigh *against* marriage. This yields, among other things, an incentive to marry in January rather than December, since your marital status on December 31 is controlling for the entire year.)

2. *Protection of the house.* As discussed more extensively below, a husband and wife may in many states hold their house in a form of joint ownership known as a *tenancy by the entirety.* A primary feature of this form of ownership is that creditors can't get at the house to satisfy the debts of either *individual* spouse. This form of ownership isn't available to live-in partners.

3. *Inheritance.* In many states a surviving spouse is legally guaranteed a substantial portion, perhaps a third or more, of the property of a deceased spouse, even if the will of the deceased spouse attempts to give the survivor nothing (see Chapter 10, "Wills"). A live-in partner enjoys no such inheritance rights.

4. *Insurance and other benefits.* Depending on where you live, how you make your living, and perhaps other things, your spouse is usually entitled to certain benefits—insurance, social security, pension payments, worker's compensation—*based on the marital relationship.* A live-in partner is usually entitled to no such benefits.

5. *Child support.* A child's father is required to contribute to the child's support, regardless of whether he's married to the mother. But could you, the child's mother, prove the identity of the father? The law presumes your *husband* to be the father of children you conceive during your marriage, unless he can prove otherwise—which is rarely easy. No such presumption applies to a live-in partner.

Palimony

A bigger consideration than any of the above—one you should force yourself to take into account before moving in with someone—is, what happens if you part?

In the typical yuppie cohabitation—two young, self-supporting professionals who split all expenses down the middle—very little happens if they part. They divide up their emotionally significant possessions—the ferns, the wines, the Cuisinarts—and go their own ways.

The tougher situation involves a relationship akin to a traditional marriage. Here one person, usually the woman, has given up her career (or declined to pursue one) and assumed the role of a homemaker. To characterize the arrangement in commercial terms, the couple has put into operation a two-part, ongoing transaction: (1) current domestic services in exchange for current economic support, and (2) a forgone opportunity to pursue a career in exchange for *future* economic support.

The last of these elements, future economic support, is the usual sticking point. This was the heart of the dispute between actor Lee Marvin and Michelle Triola Marvin, who lived together in a traditional, marriage-type relationship for some seven years. Michelle claimed in her suit for palimony* that she and Lee had an express contract—oral, not written, but that's valid, *if* there's proof that the words were in fact spoken. Under this contract, according to Michelle, (1) she agreed to give up her singing career and take care of Lee, and (2) Lee agreed to support her for the rest of her life and share with her the ownership of any property they might acquire.

Not surprisingly, Lee replied (in paraphrase), "Contract? What contract? If I'd wanted to be on the hook for life, I'd have married her. If she had pressed me to sign a contract, I'd have said, 'Look, there's a *reason* we're not married. Who wants those kinds of obligations?' " (Also, at least for the first two years they lived together, Lee was still married to someone else.)

---

*This is not a legal term; it was coined by the press, as was *galimony*, which first surfaced when Marilyn Barnett sued tennis star Billie Jean King for economic support allegedly promised in the course of their lesbian affair. We still await an appropriate label for suits by men against men.

This is hard to reply to. Indeed, the court ultimately held that Michelle hadn't proved the existence of a contract.

Marvin v. *Marvin* is still the preeminent case on palimony, and it broke some important ground. First, the California Supreme Court said that if Michelle could prove she had an actual contract with Lee, she could prevail. The court rejected the argument that such a contract, since its terms presumably included sex, came impermissibly close to a contract for prostitution.

The court mentioned several other legal theories under which one might obtain palimony. (You always need a theory.) These theories, in addition to that of "express oral contract" (Michelle's theory), include:

Implied contract. Even though the two of you never shook hands and explicitly said, "We hereby agree . . . ," there was a genuine understanding between you.

Quantum meruit (Latin for "as much as he [or she] deserves"—dangerous turf for most of us). Even though there was no real contract between the parties, one party (Michelle) provided valuable services, the other party (Lee) knew she expected something in return, and it just wouldn't be fair not to give the former something for her efforts.

Significantly, the California Supreme Court rejected the once commonly applied rule that services performed in connection with cohabitation are presumed to be a gift. The court said it should be presumed that the parties intended to "deal fairly with each other." In other words, if you launder enough underwear, you're entitled to more in return than an occasional "Thanks, Babe."

Overall, *Marvin* could be viewed as good for palimony claims. But don't jump to the conclusion that cohabitation is now risk-free for the economically dependent party.

For one thing, despite what Californians may tell you, there are other states in this country. Some may choose to follow the liberal *Marvin* rule, some may not.

Suppose you've lived with a man for eighteen years, paid more than half the cost of the home in which you both live, and performed all the traditional duties of a housewife. Then things sour. Having heard about palimony claims, you decide your case is a winner.

If the year were 1977 and you lived in Georgia, you would hear the Georgia Supreme Court describe your arrangement as "immoral," as it threw you out on your ear. This makes no sense, of course. Given the divorce statistics these days—according to the U.S. Department of Health and Human Services, half the couples obtaining divorces in 1982 had been married fewer than seven years—someone who stays in a serious relationship for eighteen years deserves a citation for uncommon fidelity.

Even if you live in California, the fact that a court can no longer throw out your palimony suit on the ground that it involves prostitution doesn't mean you're sure to win. You still have to prove the existence of facts supporting your claim.

Could you prove the existence of an express contract, or at least an implied one? Could you rebut your live-in partner's argument that if the two of you had wanted to incur marriage-type obligations, you were fully capable of finding your way to the justice of the peace? Michelle Marvin couldn't.

The bottom line is that a palimony claim is a crapshoot. Under any of the theories described above, your chances are less than fifty-fifty.

Cohabitation Contracts

There's one legal theory that wasn't argued in *Marvin*. Michelle's position was that she and Lee had an *oral* contract. To this Lee responded that if they had wanted a contract, why wouldn't they have put it in writing?

This is the very question you should ask yourself if you're living with someone: Why not put the terms of your agreement in writing?

The answer is that it's unromantic. It's worse than that—it's *anti*romantic.

Besides, the way cohabitation comes about often doesn't lend itself to a written agreement. The process tends to be gradual, commencing with an occasional overnighter and, as one party starts leaving underwear and a toothbrush at the home of

the other, expanding slowly into a routine. Only over time, perhaps spurred by something as mundane as the expiration of
someone's lease, does the arrangement take on the status of full
cohabitation.

"Sign a cohabitation contract?" you ask. "Why, we haven't
even figured out where to plant my begonias. Maybe later, if
we decide this situation is going to last."

Nevertheless, in certain circumstances you really should insist on a cohabitation contract, romance be damned:

• You're giving up a career.

• You're not exactly giving up a career, but you're reaching
an age that would make it hard to start a career that you would
otherwise have been interested in pursuing.

• You're about to move somewhere with your live-in partner
that you wouldn't dream of moving to on your own.

• You're planning to have children.

In any of these circumstances, because you're giving up or
at least putting at risk your economic security, you're more than
entitled to some assurances in return.

Cohabitation contracts can cut in either direction, *eliminating*
postbreakup obligations (palimony) as well as imposing them.
Suppose you're not a traditional homemaker, but a high-pow-
ered executive with a diploma from a well-known business school.
Your concern isn't that you'll be left penniless when the bloom
is off your rose, but rather that you'll find yourself financially
on the hook to that sexy but somewhat slippery actor you've
been supporting, with no clear benefits for yourself other than
the occasional TV dinners it took him four months to learn to
thaw.

Fine. Include in your cohabitation contract any terms you
want, although the more money is at stake, the more careful
you need to be about drafting the thing. Courts closely scrutinize
contracts between people who are intimately involved, recognizing the vulnerability of an infatuated lover to fraud and unscrupulous self-dealing by the object of his or her attentions.

INTEGRATION OF COHABITANTS' FINANCES

Various circumstances in addition to those mentioned above call for some kind of cohabitation contract, even if it's just a single paragraph scribbled out in longhand. One such circumstance is that in which you and your live-in partner take some substantial step toward integration of your finances.

I don't mean just buying a VCR together or subscribing jointly to *The Wall Street Journal*. I mean taking on some major obligation that you couldn't (or wouldn't want to) handle on your own. The question you should ask yourself in such circumstances is, would you be up that well-known creek in a chicken-wire boat if your live-in partner were to vanish tomorrow?

Suppose you and your live-in partner are considering buying a house together. What if, in the event of a breakup, neither of you wants to stay in it—do you sell it, or rent it? If you decide to sell it, what if the two of you can't agree on a fair price? Or you can agree on that, but the real estate market is currently depressed, and one of you needs money quickly and wants to take whatever it will bring? All these questions involve a good bit of money, so you'd be well advised to put something in writing.

OBTAINING A COHABITATION CONTRACT

Cohabitation contracts are no more complicated than pre-nuptial contracts, but less common. Hence, you'd probably be better off getting one not from a bulk-process lawyer at a giant clinic, but instead from a family-law specialist at a traditional firm. Depending on your lawyer's rates and the complexity of what you want, a cohabitation contract could cost anywhere from $300 to $2,500. Generally you should be able to get one for well under $1,000.

If you're skilled with words and at asking the sort of "what if" questions mentioned above in connection with joint ownership of a house, you might be able to write your own cohabitation contract. Here, as everywhere, however, recall the first of White's Irregular Rules:

Where there's a lot of money at stake,
hire a lawyer.

A reasonable model contract appears in *Marriage and Family Law Agreements* (1984), by Samuel Green and John Long (Shepard's/McGraw-Hill, P.O. Box 1235, Colorado Springs, CO 80901. You can buy your own copy of this book for approximately seventy dollars or simply borrow one from a local law library). Just fill in the blanks and delete the paragraphs that don't apply to you.

PRENUPTIAL CONTRACTS

The joys of being single, you may have concluded, are overrated. You're ready now to take the plunge. Maybe this isn't your first plunge. (According to the Census Bureau, over 85 percent of divorced people remarry, usually within five years.)

Novice or veteran, you should give some thought to a prenuptial contract. Even the strongest proponent of these contracts might balk when it comes to actually signing one, but a salutary purpose is served just by sitting down with your fiancé and discussing the provisions each of you might think of including.

A prenuptial contract is a document in which you and your fiancé—not your *spouse*; you have to execute this document *before* getting married—set forth ground rules for your marriage or its dissolution. It could be thought of as the flip side of a cohabitation contract: The point of a prenuptial contract is usually to *eliminate* obligations that the law would otherwise supply.

The classic example of someone in search of a prenuptial contract is a wealthy older man embarking on his second marriage who wants to see most of his estate go to his children by his first marriage, rather than to his second wife (whose motives in marrying him he may suspect).

What would happen to this man's wealth in the absence of a prenuptial contract? If he predeceased his second wife, she would almost definitely get one-third or more, even if his will attempted to leave her nothing (see Chapter 10, "Wills"). If the marriage ended in divorce, a judge might let the man keep most of what he had accumulated before the second marriage; but because of his wealth, the second wife would probably receive considerable alimony.

There are countless things you can address in a prenuptial contract. If you're Catholic and your fiancé is Jewish, you might want to agree on the religion in which the kids will be raised, or whether the household will be kept kosher. If either of you works for a large corporation that frequently asks its employees to move to other cities, you might want to agree on where you'll live, or where you *won't* live. A New York couple agreed that they would submit to marital counseling for six months before either of them could file for divorce. A Philadelphia couple agreed that the husband could keep his electric train set in the event of divorce.

Is a prenuptial contract a good idea? Sure. A contract is a good idea whenever there's a lot at stake. Divorce in this country is epidemic (over one million per year for the last decade). And every marriage that doesn't end in divorce ends in death. Seriously.

Enforceability

Not every form of prenuptial contract will be smilingly enforced in court. Some will be completely ignored. Why?

Suppose you're the beautiful actress Kathleen Turner. A huge number of men would happily sign anything you put before them (including a veal cutlet), most without examining it. The law, more attuned to reality than people suspect, understands that love is blind. Just as a court won't enforce a contract you signed when you were drunk, neither will it enforce an unreasonable contract you signed when you were in love.

What's reasonable? It depends on the judge. But to maximize your prenuptial contract's chances of being enforced, you should observe two rules: (1) make sure the contract *looks* reasonable, and (2) make sure it *is* reasonable.

1. *"Looking* reasonable." Making a prenuptial contract look reasonable requires, first, having it examined by a lawyer representing your fiancé. This lawyer can't be your cousin, your company's in-house counsel, or someone otherwise connected to you. Get the lawyer to sign the actual contract, acknowledging that he has reviewed it and advised your fiancé on it.

The look of reasonableness requires, second, disclosing to your fiancé all relevant data about yourself, especially financial data. Your contract is doomed if a judge learns that when your fiancé agreed to accept $20,000 in the event of a divorce, she had no idea you were worth fifty times that much.

Finally, the look of reasonableness requires setting forth any facts or circumstances tending to refute the notion that you're in a position, economically or psychologically, to take advantage of your fiancé. Imagine yourself as a judge looking at a prenuptial agreement between a fifty-year-old war-hardened businessman and a blushing home economics major right out of finishing school. You're instinctively concerned for the home ec major, and you'll use any excuse you can find to protect her.

2. *"Being* reasonable."* Judges don't like seeing indigents on the street when they drive home at night. Hence their willingness to ignore a prenuptial contract that treats one spouse harshly, such as by leaving him no means of support.

What constitutes harsh treatment depends, of course, on the circumstances. If your spouse has a lucrative job as a radiologist, he's clearly capable of supporting himself without help from you (although there may be an open question as to whether he can support himself in the life-style to which your riches accustomed him). If, on the other hand, your spouse hasn't a nickel of his own and is utterly without marketable skills, the chances that a judge will enforce a prenuptial contract that leaves him high and dry are nil.

The key, then, is not to cut your fiancé off completely. Plan to leave him *something*—the more, the better, ideally enough to support him in a style comparable to the one he enjoyed with you.

Sex

Suppose you're a woman of normal urges. (Okay, maybe a little greater than normal, but still on the bell curve for mammals.) Your fiancé, on the other hand, has all the lust of a hibernating bear, and, like a bear, goes inactive for prolonged periods. Not for any particular reason. "I just don't feel like it" is his usual refrain.

Judges don't like cases raising this kind of problem. It embarrasses them.

If you're married, you're legally entitled to sexual relations of a normal kind and with normal frequency (with your spouse). So courts have repeatedly held.

What do you consider "normal"? Would you care to have that opinion discussed on the national news?

Now you know why judges don't like these cases.

Because you can already divorce your spouse if he or she isn't forthcoming within the "normal" range, there's no point in addressing the subject in a prenuptial contract. And a judge won't enforce a provision for something "abnormal," as a man from Louisiana found in his suit to enforce a prenuptial contract restricting intercourse to once a week. (He argued that his wife had breached the contract by seeking coitus thrice daily.) Best to leave it alone.

Obtaining a Prenuptial Contract

The points above about obtaining a cohabitation contract apply as well to obtaining a prenuptial contract, including the availability of a good model in *Marriage and Family Law Agreements,* by Green & Long. Be wary of drafting your own prenuptial contract, however.

The reason is that so much is at stake. Although cohabitation is usually a temporary status, marriage tends to be long-term. Also, marriage is vastly harder to undo. If you do draft your own prenuptial contract, at least get a lawyer to look it over for glaring holes or violations of local laws, including those regarding witnesses, manner of execution, and other formalities. Perhaps one of your friends who's a lawyer will draft a prenuptial contract for you as a wedding present (although then you might have to invite the stiff to the reception).

DIVORCE AND MEDIATION

Ask any divorced friend what he considers the worst time of his life. If he doesn't grimace, shake his head ruefully, and mutter something about his horrible divorce, it's only because he's trying to banish the entire episode from his memory.

Nothing I can say here will make your divorce pleasant. There are definitely steps you can take, however, to minimize the trauma and expense.

"No-Fault" Divorce

In old movies, one hears a common refrain sung by married men to their paramours: "You know I love you, but my wife won't give me a divorce." As recently as the late 1960s, this was a plausible if disingenuous explanation for failing to alter the status quo.

Merely wanting out of a marriage wasn't enough. You (the married man) had to persuade a court that your spouse was somehow "at fault"—for example, that she had beat you, cheated on you, or wouldn't have sex with you. In the eyes of the state, marriage was too sacred to be allowed to dissolve for lesser reasons. Society would crumble.

How, then, could your spouse "give" you a divorce? By filing for divorce herself, making allegations that you would happily concede. Why would she be willing to help you out in this manner (in addition to the fact that being married to you was no treat)? Because you would have agreed to a generous property division and heavy alimony.

Blackmail? No doubt she and her lawyer preferred to think of it as a quid pro quo. In any event, how else was a middle-aged homemaker with several children and no marketable skills to get by?

Times have changed. California passed the first *no-fault* divorce law in 1970, and since then every state except South Dakota (where the law may change even as this book goes to press) has passed some version. Under the no-fault system, your spouse doesn't have to have done something "wrong"; you can get a divorce for "irreconcilable differences" or "irretrievable marital breakdown" (the terminology varies from state to state). It may be enough that you and your spouse have simply lived apart for some period, such as a year. (Eighteen states, by one recent count, have adopted no-fault divorce in its purest form. Most of the rest, "fault-option" states, permit no-fault divorce if certain conditions are met.)

Enlightened?

To my mind, yes. *No-fault* may be an inapt term because usually there's plenty of fault. But in the fragile, open-nerved world of a foundering relationship, where a look or gesture barely perceptible to the other dinner guests can constitute a hard psychological shot, determining who did what to whom, and in what order, is frequently impossible:

"He flattened my soufflé."

"She deserved it for running over my golf clubs."

"That wouldn't have happened if you'd been more sensitive in bed."

"How am I supposed to be sensitive when you're always doing . . . you-know-what?"

The problem is that nonfaulting homemakers, because they can no longer "withhold" divorce, are deprived of the leverage they once had. In theory this shouldn't affect the economic terms of breakups, because divorce courts should award homemakers sufficient property and alimony regardless of the absence of a determination of fault. But it doesn't seem to work that way. This is possibly because no-fault proceedings often afford judges no opportunity to learn of the offenses committed by faulting spouses. It may also be because judges, still overwhelmingly male, believe that homemakers, still overwhelmingly female, just don't need or deserve the kinds of sums they could once exact from their philandering mates. In any event, the well-documented fact is that on average, homemakers—usually women—get substantially less than they used to.

Contested or "Fault" Divorce

No-fault means what it says: Nobody is at fault, or at least fault is deemed irrelevant. Hence, the judge in a no-fault divorce proceeding often won't listen (and may even be statutorily prohibited from listening) to the colorful slurs you and your spouse came prepared to hurl at each other.

In a *fault* divorce, on the other hand, people can and do level the most sordid accusations imaginable.

What are they fighting over? Two things: kids and money. (I'm lumping the house, cars, and bank accounts under the category of "money.") If the parties don't disagree on these things, a judge will tell them to get lost. He isn't interested in serving as an umpire on debates over who never listens to whom, whose relatives are more psychotic, or any of the other things married couples find to fight about when something else is really on their minds.

To be sure, vicious fights can also occur in the no-fault context. How?

First, many states allow or even require judges in no-fault proceedings to receive evidence regarding fault and take it into account in awarding property and alimony. Second, even in states with different rules, the parties can often find ways of getting fault-related issues before the court. The wife's infidelity comes out as the husband's lawyer attempts to show that she isn't fit to receive custody of the kids. The husband's tendency to violence comes out as the wife's lawyer attempts to show that she needs additional money to repair her broken ribs.

Whatever the context, fault or no-fault, would it really be all that bad? Picture yourself on the witness stand as your spouse's lawyer grills you:

"Did you ever stay late at the office?"
"Sure. I'm a diligent worker."

"Were you there alone?"

"Not always."

"Was your secretary ever there?"

"Uh, sometimes."

"Is your secretary of the opposite sex?"

"As whom?"

"You."

"Yes, but what does that . . ."

"Did the two of you ever go out to dinner?"

"Well, usually we just sent out for sandwiches."

"*Usually?*"

This can get on your nerves.

It may be that you're prepared for a fight, even spoiling for one. In a few instances, such as where your spouse represents a genuine threat to the children, there may be no alternative. Nevertheless, I would emphasize a point that your own lawyer should attempt to make clear but that you may have trouble appreciating because of the somnolence you experience every time he opens his mouth: Divorce litigation is a miserable experience.

Who among us has done *nothing* that he or she would not cringe to see revealed to the world? How would you like to wake up one morning to a breakfast of sunny-side ups and a multi-column story detailing your darkest secrets—your sex life, your bowel habits, what really happened to your dog—on the front page of a national newspaper? Everything that happens in court becomes a matter of public record, freely available to scandal-hungry reporters. Keep in mind that if you had nothing embarrassing in your past (or nothing that could be made to *look* embarrassing), your spouse's lawyer would be begging to settle.

Minimizing the Role of Lawyers

Once you and your spouse have decided to part, you have, as already indicated, two basic issues to resolve: Who gets the kids, and who gets the money?

To resolve these issues, you have two basic alternatives: You can resolve them yourselves, or you can have someone else resolve them for you. The first alternative is clearly preferable: It saves money, it's quicker, it saves money, it keeps your private affairs private, it saves money.

I therefore offer the fourth of White's Irregular Rules:

Handle your divorce as far as possible *without* lawyers.

I don't naïvely assume, nor should you, that negotiations with your soon-to-be-former spouse will be easy. But what are the chances that hiring a lawyer will improve the situation? Your hope, of course, is that by hiring a lawyer, you'll ultimately get a bigger cut of the financial pie. But the only thing you can be absolutely sure of is that your lawyer's fee will reduce the size of the pie.

It's like the old shtetl tale of two men contending over the rightful ownership of a cow, one pulling on its head, the other pulling on its tail—and the lawyer milking the beast all the while.

Keep in mind that if your negotiations with your spouse break down, you can always call the lawyers in later. They aren't going anywhere.

To be sure, there are several situations in which you should definitely consult a lawyer, and quickly:

• Your spouse has hired a lawyer.

• There's a huge amount of money at stake.

• You're so distraught that you may make decisions you'll rue later on.

• You suspect you or your children are in physical danger.

• You suspect your spouse is about to flee to another state, where the authorities in your state can't get at him.

The last four of these situations are extreme. As for the first, think of it like nuclear war: You both lose if either of you pushes the button, so there's no benefit in being the one to push it first.

Later, after all major decisions have been made but before anything has been signed or filed, it wouldn't be a bad idea for each of you to consult a lawyer, just to be sure you haven't overlooked anything big. *But don't make calling a lawyer your first step.*

The Mechanics of Getting Divorced

Obtaining an *uncontested divorce*, that is, one in which there are no legal disputes between you and your almost ex-spouse, is probably simpler and less anxiety-producing than buying a house. You file a petition with the local divorce court (possibly attaching a settlement agreement that describes what you're doing with the house and other property), hang out for a while (most jurisdictions impose a waiting period, usually ranging between thirty days and a year), and then submit a request for a final decree of divorce. Some states require you to make a brief appearance in court, where a judge asks if you know what you're doing and if anybody is forcing you into this against your will.

Where is the local divorce court? What exactly does the divorce petition have to say? Is a settlement agreement required? How long must you wait?

You might be able to find the answers just by calling the local divorce court or bar association. Perhaps a regular bookstore carries (or could order for you) a manual of the local rules and procedures. You could even call one of the lawyers listed in the yellow pages, who'll probably chat with you a while in hopes of getting you as a client.

Then again, you may decide that the several hundred dollars a low-priced lawyer would charge to handle the scut work for you is worth the price, like paying someone to fertilize your lawn.

Note that you and your spouse could hire one lawyer between you. A lawyer presented with a request for dual representation might tell you (correctly) that he isn't supposed to represent two people with adverse interests. Then he might suggest (halfheartedly) that one of you get a different lawyer. If the two of you have already ironed out the substantive issues, however, and all you want him to do is draw up the papers and file them in the proper place, there's no real problem, and eventually he'll go along.

BEWARE

You and your almost ex-husband have resolved all the who-gets-what issues on your own. Nothing remains but to find a lawyer to make the divorce happen. You set up an appointment with one. You're taking care of this end of things, because your husband is busy playing golf. Typical.

The lawyer listens thoughtfully as you describe the terms you and your husband have agreed on. Then he says, "You know, you deserve better." Too true, you think. "And," the lawyer adds, "I could get it for you."

Clang! Clang! Clang!

Bells, sirens, and red flashing lights should go off in your mind. The last thing you need right now is to have a lawyer dragging you into litigation.

Do you deserve more than you and your husband have agreed on? Without question.

Would you *like* more? Of course.

But your husband undoubtedly feels the same way. If the arrangement you and he have hammered out is one you can contemplate without nausea, stick with it. This isn't to say you shouldn't hear your lawyer out; his professional opinion is what you're paying for. But much of the time it's more important that a divorce be concluded than that it be concluded perfectly. Your question to yourself now shouldn't be, "Is this deal the best I could possibly get?" It should be, "Is this deal one I can live with?"

Divorce Lawyers

Perhaps I sound hostile to divorce lawyers (who invariably refer to themselves as "matrimonial lawyers" or "family lawyers"). Not at all. A wise and sensitive one can provide immeasurable comfort. But how many wise and sensitive people are there in the world, and what are the chances that someone you find through the yellow pages will be one of them?

Divorce lawyers aren't ogres, but their primary concern—for themselves and for you—is cash. This is how they've been trained to think. It's how most people think.

Recognize that there are limits on what you can expect from your divorce lawyer, as nice as it would be to find one who combines all the qualities of lawyer, minister, psychotherapist, indulgent grandparent, and loyal dog.

When your lemon of a car breaks down, you look to the garage mechanic for technical aid, not emotional support and spiritual guidance. For the same reasons, when your lemon of a marriage breaks down, resist viewing your lawyer as anything but a mechanic wearing pinstripes and a tie.

What kind of lawyer should you get to handle your divorce? An uncontested divorce is so simple that you might as well go to one of the giant legal clinics or otherwise shop around for a rock-bottom price. (Before hiring any lawyer, pin him down about the *total* cost of the divorce, including filing fees and any contingencies that could require additional sums.)

A contested divorce is more complicated and involves higher stakes. For that you want a specialist in divorce law. Be aware that a first-class divorce lawyer charges as much as any other kind of lawyer and that divorce-related litigation can be as time-consuming and expensive as any other litigation.

Three Points on the Mandatory Waiting Period

1. You may be galled at the thought of having to wait six months or a year for your divorce to become final. You're an adult. You don't need the government telling you to cool off and spend a year of your life thinking it over.

Perhaps your reasons go further: You're itching to get re-married, which of course you can't do until your divorce is final.

If your state maintains a traditional fault system of divorce alongside its no-fault system, and if your spouse has committed vile acts that entitle you to a divorce under the fault system, you may be able to bypass the waiting period by moving forward on that front. It's far from certain this will speed things up, given the snail's pace of most litigation, but a lawyer in your area should be able to tell you how long the fault process normally takes.

2. As long as you're talking to a lawyer, ask about the local rules on predivorce dating. In some jurisdictions, striking up an

intimate relationship before your divorce becomes final could constitute, at least technically, the crime of adultery. Are you supposed to sit home every Saturday night for a year? No way? Still, it wouldn't hurt to find out just how discreet you need to be.

3. There's one possible benefit connected with the pre-divorce waiting period. Suppose you and your separated spouse maintain an amicable relationship. The memories are mixed, but you're still capable of cooperating for mutual gain. If together the two of you could save several thousand dollars by filing a joint income-tax return—permissible until your divorce becomes final—why not postpone the legal severance indefinitely?

Mediation

Today there exists a highly regarded alternative to the expensive public brawling we call litigation. This alternative appears in a multiplicity of incarnations, which travel together under the rubric *mediation*.

What goes on in mediation? Techniques vary, but the basic idea is that you and your spouse sit down with someone knowledgeable about the legal and psychological aspects of marital breakups, and together the three of you hammer out an arrangement that you and your spouse can live with. Mediation is thus as appealing for what it *doesn't* involve—harassment with legal papers, a public trial, *lawyers*—as for what it does involve.

A mediator has no power to issue a binding decision. He serves as a facilitator, *not* a judge.

Often mediators are social workers or psychologists. Sometimes they're ministers, occasionally lawyers (although the lawyers don't act *as lawyers*, that is, as representatives of one side against the other). Mediators who aren't lawyers frequently maintain a roster of lawyers available for consultation, because there are always legal aspects to a divorce. Mediation recognizes, however, that the psychological aspects of divorce are no less deserving of attention than the legal.

Most mediators, including lawyers who serve as mediators, have had special training in conflict resolution. Don't get the idea, however, that mediation is a touchy-feely encounter-group experience in which some California guru makes you chant mantras and eat granola. Good mediators are down-to-earth problem solvers who happen to recognize that divorce is painful.

Mediators usually work by the hour, charging roughly the standard rate in the area for psychologists, lawyers, social workers—whatever your mediator happens to be. A ballpark total for a divorce is $1,000 ($100 per hour times ten hours), perhaps less if you and your spouse don't go to bat against each other on every possible issue. Spouses can split the fee, but even if one of you were to pay the entire tab individually, the cost would come to a fraction of what you'd pay a lawyer to do battle for you in court.

Keep in mind that by signing up for mediation you don't commit yourself to anything except the mediator's hourly rate. You can walk out at any time. Also, you're free to consult a lawyer (even if your mediator is himself a lawyer) before signing anything; most mediators will actually encourage this.

How do you find a mediator? Check your yellow pages, consult a lawyer or social worker, or call the local family court. You could also write or call one of the following (not an exhaustive list):

1. The Special Committee on Alternative Dispute Resolution of the American Bar Association, Suite 200, 1800 M Street, N.W., Washington, DC 20036-5886 (202/331-2258). The Special Committee publishes a directory of mediation programs around the country, some connected with prestigious law schools.

2. The National Center for Mediation Education, Suite 3F, 2083 West Street, Annapolis, MD 21401 (301/261-8445).

3. The Academy of Family Mediators, P.O. Box 4686, Greenwich, CT 06830 (203/629-8049).

4. The American Arbitration Association (AAA), 140 West 51st Street, New York, NY 10020 (212/484-4000). Request the AAA's brochure "Family Mediation Rules." You might also order, through the AAA or a regular bookstore, a book by Robert Coulson, president of the AAA, called *Fighting Fair—Family Mediation Will Work for You* (1983), 196 pp., $14.95.

A Word on "Quickie" Divorces

Everyone has heard of couples who fly to Nevada, Mexico, the Virgin Islands, or some other reportedly easygoing jurisdiction for what lawyers euphemistically refer to as *migratory* divorces.

Are these legal? In some instances.

Advisable? Almost invariably not.

You shouldn't get tricky in this area without a good reason. And there's no *good* reason for moving that quickly on something as significant as your divorce. Is it really vital that you marry your secretary next week? Mightn't the delay save you from yourself?

As for legality, if you and your spouse act *jointly* in getting a divorce in another state, it will probably stand up in your home state, simply because a court there won't let either of you come in later and challenge something you were a party to. You'll complicate your life beyond telling, however, if you try to pull this off unilaterally. Although another state in which you've actually established roots (become "domiciled") may be willing to declare you single, it can't affect the property or alimony rights of your nonparticipating spouse in another state.

This is especially true if the court that declares you single is outside the United States. A unilateral divorce decree from Mexico or Haiti will get you laughed out of an American court.

MARRIAGE AND PROPERTY

There are two property-related questions you should think about in connection with marriage: (1) What, if anything, should you do with your property upon getting married? and (2) What is likely to happen to your property if your marriage dissolves?

The Joint Tenancy

Given that every marriage entails at least the possibility of divorce—and with divorce, division of property—it's far from crazy to view marriage as a threat to your property. There's a better way to look at marriage, however: It can *save* your property.

Suppose you and your spouse own a valuable piece of real estate. If the place is held in your name alone, your individual creditors can take it from you—the whole thing—even though your spouse helped pay for it.

If you and your spouse hold the place as *tenants in common*— a form of co-ownership—your individual creditors can't take the whole thing, but they can force a quick sale of it and take your share of the proceeds.

If, however, you and your spouse hold the place as *tenants by the entirety*, your individual creditors can't take any of it (not unless your spouse, too, is in their debt—which is why shrewd lenders typically require spouses to cosign loan documents).

There's no magic in this. A tenancy by the entirety is permitted in most states, often with respect to some forms of personal property—cars and bank accounts, for example—as well as with respect to real estate. (This arrangement also offers certain benefits with respect to avoiding probate. See Chapter 10, "Wills.")

Putting property in a tenancy by the entirety raises two problems. First, if you later want to sell the property, you can't— not without the consent of your spouse, who owns it as much as you do.

Second, if you should predecease your spouse, he'll become the 100 percent owner of the property, even though you may have wanted to leave it to your children by your first marriage, or to some Buddhist monks you met while hiking in Nepal. The *right of survivorship* that characterizes any joint tenancy means the entire place goes to whichever of you outlives the other— an inflexible rule that leads some estate planners to oppose placing property in joint ownership.

Who Gets What in a Divorce

If you and your spouse can't decide for yourselves who should get what share of your property, a court will grudgingly decide for you. What you'd like to know in advance is, what will the court decide?

All anyone can say is, who knows? But I offer the following points to discourage wild fantasies by either of you about how you're likely to fare in court.

To the homemaker. Assume you're female and that yours has been the traditional role: the faithful homemaker. Assume that your spouse is male and that his has also been the traditional role: the faithless slime. Everyone including your husband's mother agrees that you deserve every penny he now owns or will ever come by. What he's offering, however, is somewhat less.

Before charging into court with the confidence of a Baptist holding four aces, keep in mind that a court can't order your husband to give you money he doesn't have. Johnny Carson's wives get millions, but Johnny Carson *has* millions.

Moreover, whether your husband is rich or poor, a court *won't* order him to give you everything—probably not even half. Consider, for example, the experience under the divorce law of New York, which, like the laws of most other states, directs judges to make "equitable" (not necessarily meaning *equal*) divisions of marital property. Before its recent (1986) amendment, that law directed judges to calculate spousal maintenance on the basis of the dependent spouse's postdivorce "reasonable needs." According to one report, the average division of marital property under this standard yielded approximately 70 percent to the husband and 30 percent to the wife—this under a law that was passed in 1980 to replace an older law considered unfair to women!

The 1986 amendment to New York's law eliminated the "reasonable needs" language. Now that law directs judges to focus on the dependent spouse's predivorce "standard of living" and to take into account the presumably limited earning capacity that results from passing up a career or higher education. How women will fare under this new law remains to be seen.

*   *   *

To the breadwinner. Don't assume, by virtue of the preceding points, that you'll be able to run the divorce gauntlet painlessly. Your wife may not get as much your conduct would, in a better world, entitle her to, but she'll get a lot. The pie from which the judge will cut her slice includes (with the possible exception of property acquired through gift or inheritance) *all* property acquired during the marriage, *regardless* of whose name it's held in.

Child Support, Alimony, and Property Division

There are three types of divorce-related transfers: (1) child support, (2) alimony, and (3) division of marital property. In theory each of these matters is decided separately, but whatever a court takes out of one pot obviously reduces what's left in the others.

1. *Child support*. A judge will award as much child support as he thinks the child in question "needs." Does a child "need" to go to prep school? If so, does that prep school "need" to be Groton or Phillips Andover? Maybe. In determining need, a judge will look at the parents' ability to pay, how they've been raising the child up to the time of the divorce, and anything else that's required by local law or that the parties can persuade him is relevant.

It's hard to overstate how serious the law is about child support. If you go bankrupt, you'll still owe child support. If your former wife takes your children to Tahiti, you'll still owe child support. If the man your former wife marries in Tahiti is a billionaire, you may get off the hook for alimony, but you'll still owe child support.

2. *Alimony*. The overwhelming majority of divorces are granted without alimony. In many cases both spouses are just too poor; they have no substantial resources now, nor realistic prospects of acquiring any. In other cases both spouses are self-supporting, so alimony is neither needed nor requested. In yet other cases, the marriage has lasted only a year or two, so neither spouse can claim to have put so much into it as to deserve anything out of it.

Where alimony is deserved, and usually given, is the traditional breadwinner/homemaker situation: The parties have been married a long time, the homemaker has given up any significant shot at a nondomestic career, and without alimony the home-maker would suffer a dramatic decline in life-style.

The factors a court will take into account in awarding ali-mony include: need (as with child support, a relative term); ability to pay; the comparative fault of the parties (in some ju-risdictions); and anything else the court feels like taking into account on the day in question.

In almost every jurisdiction, alimony obligations terminate (either automatically or upon application to the court) when the recipient remarries. Alimony may also terminate if the recipient "moves in" with someone—a point worth addressing carefully in any separation agreement.

Actor Marlon Brando's separation agreement defined "re-marriage" to include "*appearing* to maintain a marital relationship with any person." Marlon was less than eager to support his ex-wife's boyfriends. A California court ruled that this provision did not unreasonably restrict the former Mrs. Brando's social life, because it was worded so as not to apply to "one-night stands."

3. *Property division.* In most states a judge is legally author-ized to divide *marital property*, that is, property the spouses have accumulated during marriage, in any manner he thinks "equi-table." What sort of division is a given judge likely to think equitable? Who knows? A lawyer who has seen him in action may have some ideas. The big question today isn't who *gets* marital property, but rather, what *is* marital property?

Suppose you and your boyfriend, Michael, get married one nice spring day in 1971. At the time, you're teaching school in New York. You have a bachelor's degree and a temporary teach-ing certificate, but you'll have to put in eighteen more months of study to get your permanent certificate. Michael teaches, too. He has completed only three and a half years of college, but he's attending night school to get his degree, taking pre-med courses.

Michael applies to medical school in Guadalajara, Mexico, and gets in. You agree to move there with him, postponing the work necessary for your permanent certificate. The two of you move south of the border in 1973. In Mexico, while Michael studies, you scrounge up various teaching and tutorial positions to pay the rent and keep him supplied with tongue depressors. In 1976 the two of you return to New York so Michael can complete his last two semesters of medical school there. You resume your former teaching position, still without the necessary background for a permanent certificate. You continue in this position for several more years.

In late 1980 Michael receives his license to practice medicine. It's about time, you think. Two months later, your marriage almost a decade old, Michael sues for divorce. It's safe to say you're miffed.

Pretty clearly, you should get all the property. There's only one problem: *What* property? You and Michael don't own anything except a few sticks of furniture beaten to kindling by your incessant moving from city to city. All you really have to show for your years of sacrifice is a medical license—*Michael's* medical license.

Is it possible to pin a price tag on such a thing? If so, would a court ever deem it a form of marital property to be divided between parting spouses?

Yes, and yes.

The case just described is essentially true. On the day after Christmas 1985, New York's highest court ruled that Michael O'Brien's medical license constitutes marital property within the meaning of New York's domestic relations law, and therefore that license is subject to "equitable division" with his ex-wife, Loretta.

The trial court in that case found that Loretta had given up her own educational and career opportunities to promote those of her husband. Through her work while Michael was studying and training, she had contributed 76 percent of their joint income (exclusive of one student loan obtained by Michael) during their marriage. The court rejected Michael's contention that Loretta was entitled to no more than (a) "rehabilitative maintenance," or (b) the equivalent of her "direct financial contributions."

How to value a professional degree? Loretta's expert witness compared the average income of a college graduate with that of a general surgeon (what Michael planned to become) over the twenty-two-year period between when Michael's residency training would end and when he would reach the age of sixty-five. Taking into account inflation and other factors, the expert reached a valuation of $472,000. The court said Loretta was entitled to 40 percent of this amount, or $188,000, to be paid in eleven annual installments.

New York isn't the only state to have addressed the issues raised by the O'Brien case. In Michigan a wife received part of the value of her husband's law degree. In Washington state, a wife received part of the value of her husband's dentistry license. Other states have come down the other way, holding that an advanced degree or a professional license does *not* constitute marital property to be divided between parting spouses. By last count the score was even—six states for, six states against.

Tax Issues and Who-Gets-What in a Divorce

One clear benefit of resolving your who-gets-what issues out of court is that it affords you an opportunity to do something for yourself that no court will do for you: perform sophisticated tax planning in the course of making your decisions.

One example: Although alimony is supposed to be reported as taxable income by the person who receives it, and may be deducted by the person who pays it, neither point is true with respect to child support. Now, assume that you're the breadwinner in your marriage, and that you and your almost ex-wife have agreed that you'll pay her a fixed monthly sum to cover alimony and child support. How much of that sum constitutes alimony, and how much child support? Half and half? If your tax bracket is high and hers is low, it's advantageous for you to allocate as much as possible to alimony (as much, that is, as your tax lawyer or accountant says you can).

Why would your wife go along with this, since the reverse allocation is better for her? Because you'll make it up to her with *more* alimony, or in some other way—not by doing anything illegal, but just by taking advantage of legitimate opportunities to retain for yourself as much as Uncle Sam allows.

Another example: Assume your husband received custody of your child, but because his taxable income is minimal, the dependency exemption on the federal income tax return is worthless to him. You, on the other hand, have lots of taxable income and could make good use of the exemption. Under rules that became effective in 1985, he can allocate the exemption to you, the noncustodial parent. (Again, he'd do this only for a suitable quid pro quo.)

A pragmatic tip: IRS rules require that a custodial parent seeking to make such an allocation execute a written waiver, which the noncustodial parent must attach to her tax return. You can take advantage of this requirement by making your waiver effective for only one year at a time, so you'll have something to withhold the next year if your former wife fails to keep up with her child support payments.

CHILD CUSTODY AND SUPPORT

Custody

The who-gets-the-kids question—perhaps nowhere else in the law will you find so great a contrast between the ease of articulating a rule and the difficulty of applying it.

The easily articulated rule is: The children go to whichever parent will take best care of them.

In determining who will take best care of them, a judge considers everything the parties bring to his attention, as well as everything he can think of on his own: who has the most money, who has shown the greatest interest in the children, whom the children seem to like the most—you name it.

Support

Like the answer to who gets the kids, the answer to who *supports* them is easily articulated: You do, if they're yours. Your spouse has to help, but nothing he or she does, or fails to do, can affect your support obligation.

How long must you support them? It varies from state to state—usually until the age of majority, but conceivably longer if they're for some reason unable to look after themselves at that time.

Child Support and "Illegitimacy"

Unmarried motherhood: Uneducated women endure it; Hollywood starlets flaunt it; lesbians hail it; mid-career professional women cautiously consider it.

There's no question that the mothers of "illegitimate" children have a legal duty to support such children. But what about the fathers? Are there legal consequences associated with the male's biologically essential, if socially casual, role in the creative act?

Suppose you're a male who came of age in the 1960s, when feminists were taking hard shots at you and every other member of your loutish gender. You were always an open-minded person, and after being told a thousand times that throughout history men have selfishly failed to bear their share of the responsibility for avoiding pregnancies out of wedlock, you came to agree. So you began, whenever you found yourself on the verge of consummating your passions with a new lover, to ask The Question: "Are you protected?" This put your liberal conscience at ease and, at least for a while, earned you points as a sensitive, modern male.

A decade or so passes, and you're still asking The Question. One day, however, you get a novel response. The woman says something along the lines of, "You think I'd risk getting pregnant by you? What kind of arrogant jerk would ask such a question?"

Your lust in abeyance, you ponder: Don't I have a stake in knowing if she's protected?

Yes! If a woman bears your child, you'll have a legal obligation to support it, regardless of the circumstances of the conception. So if you want to keep asking The Question, ask away. Anyone who says you don't have a stake in knowing the answer doesn't know the law.

3. Taxes

Obtaining Tax Advice •

Dealing with the Internal Revenue Service •

Estate Planning •

To tax and to please, no more than to love and to be wise, is not given to men. EDMUND BURKE (1729–1797)

The income tax has made more liars out of the American people than golf has. WILL ROGERS
(1879–1935)

Estate lawyers never die. They just smell that way.

MARTIN J. YUDKOWITZ
(1954–   )

The big question regarding taxes is how to avoid them. Tax avoidance shouldn't be your number-one priority in life—for guidance on that, read Freud. But it should definitely rank somewhere in your top three or four.

As evidence of the national consensus on the legitimacy of tax avoidance, I cite the repletion of the best-seller lists each spring with tax guides bearing titles such as *Saving Income Tax, Pay Less Tax Legally,* and *How to Catch Uncle Sam Bending Over.*

The first part of this chapter, "Obtaining Tax Advice," discusses the use of these guides, and then the four basic sources of personal, or one-on-one, tax advice—a subject rendered more important than ever by the extensive revision and complexification (my own term) of the tax laws in 1986. The second part, "Dealing with the Internal Revenue Service," discusses audits and other circumstances in which you might find yourself in direct contact with the IRS (or "Service" —an ironic term). The third part, "Estate Planning," discusses the disposition of your property upon your death.

OBTAINING TAX ADVICE

The Tax Guides

Have you ever glanced at one of the tax guides in a bookstore or supermarket and thought, To hell with it. This is twenty times bigger than what the IRS sent me. I'm not out to master the whole tax code?

An understandable response.

But most tax guides carry a huge amount of valuable information. Moreover, written and cross-checked by experts, they're unquestionably more reliable than the average low-priced tax preparer. The guides are easier to use, admittedly, if you already have a little familiarity with taxes, but that's not essential. Just don't let yourself be intimidated by their size and countless cross-references to things nobody has ever heard of.

A bigger question than whether you ought to try any tax guide at all is *which* guide should you try first?

Here's a tip almost guaranteed to save you eight to ten dollars, as well as a trip to the bookstore: The IRS puts out a booklet called *Publication 17—Your Federal Income Tax*. This booklet is free—which, as Jack Benny said, can never hurt. According to a 1985 *Consumer Reports* review of six popular tax guides, *Publication 17* is roughly as good as any of the commercially published guides, although it's less aggressive than they are in steering you to tax-saving tips.

The Tax Reform Act of 1986 (which could also be called the "Accountants' and Tax Lawyers' Full-Employment Act") will necessitate heavy revision of *Publication 17*, as well as all the commercially published guides. (Note that the IRS will be releasing, in addition to the revised *Publication 17*, separate materials describing the changes in the law.) How well a guide dealt with the old law doesn't necessarily indicate how well it will deal with the new law, but in the absence of any other basis for selection, the comparative merits of the guides' earlier incarnations deserve at least some consideration.

Consumer Reports gave the top nod to Barry Steiner's *Pay Less Tax Legally*. It gave second place to *J. K. Lasser's Your Income Tax Guide*, the oldest of the bunch. I wouldn't buy (or *have bought*) either of these, however, without looking at the popular *Arthur Young Tax Guide*, which is published by the nationally prominent accounting firm whose name it bears. This guide includes a number of major IRS forms, which at the eleventh hour could be a lifesaver. (Presumably because of its comparatively recent vintage, it wasn't included in the *Consumer Reports* review.)

Individual Tax Advice

What kind of person stoops to paying for personal advice on his tax return? An intellectual jellyfish who is too intimidated by a Form 1040 to take a stab at it, even with the aid of a several-hundred-page tax guide?

Yes.

But also countless others.

One legal self-help book advises, "Never do your taxes yourself (unless you happen to be an accountant or tax attorney)." This goes too far. I "do" my own tax return each year, and no one seeking either to compliment or insult me has ever called me an accountant or a tax attorney.

True, most accountants probably prepare their own returns. They know the tax code, they like numbers, and most important, they can operate desk calculators with one hand. But countless tax lawyers routinely pay others for help. My brother the tax lawyer, who graduated with honors from Harvard Law School, has an accountant prepare his tax return. So does Mortimer Caplin, a Washington, D.C., tax lawyer who served as commissioner of the IRS from 1961 to 1964 and who reportedly bills clients at $300 per hour. Randolph Thrower, another former IRS

commissioner (1969–1971), says he hasn't prepared his own return "for years."

According to the IRS, some 44 percent of all people filing
individual tax returns in 1984 got paid help. As the examples
above indicate, this figure includes people of above-average tax
sophistication and wealth. Also, the Service estimates that of the
people who itemized deductions on their returns (presumably
those with the most going on financially), a much greater share—
between 60 and 70 percent—paid for help. The bottom line is,
paying for personal tax help is nothing to blush about.

Should *you* pay for personal help? Here, as everywhere, there's
a cost-benefit analysis to be performed. Note that the cost of any
form of tax help is tax deductible (assuming, under the new tax
law, that the total of your miscellaneous itemized deductions
exceeds 2 percent of your adjusted gross income).

The cost of personal tax help depends, not surprisingly, on
what kind you get. There are four basic sources of commercially
available help: (1) the giant, bulk-process tax "clinics," (2) "enrolled agents," (3) certified public accountants, and (4) tax lawyers. The costs of these range from cheap, to moderately expensive,
to very expensive, to I-assume-you're-joking. (The IRS's free tax
service, used by millions of people each year, is discussed in
"Dealing with the Internal Revenue Service," below.)

TAX CLINICS

By *clinic* I mean any of the giant, bulk-process, mass-ad-
vertised operations that offer low-cost, no-frills service and cater
primarily to people with modest incomes and extremely limited
knowledge of financial matters. Well-known examples are Ben-
eficial Tax Center, H&R Block, and Household Finance Center,
all national chains with offices listed in the yellow pages. These
are the McDonald's of tax services—quick, efficient, impersonal,
occasionally surly, not bad for the price.

The last of these features, the price, is the primary virtue of
a clinic. Preparation of a simple return—for example, one involving a few routine deductions and no income other than
wages set forth on a Form W-2—may cost less than fifty dollars.

Unlike the other tax advice sources discussed below, many clinics charge not by the hour but on the basis of the number of IRS forms required, the overall number of entries on those forms, or similar factors.

Your entire visit to a clinic may last no longer than an hour. You're in the office the whole time, answering questions as necessary. You don't need an appointment, although the closer you get to April 15, the tougher it may be to get in without one.

As little as I generally care for chain operations, the big clinics have been around for a good while and aren't going anywhere. This means two things: First, you'll have someone to go after if they botch your return. Second, if you have to respond to an IRS inquiry or, God forbid, visit an IRS office for an audit, someone from the chain will be available to help you prepare your response or, in the latter case, accompany you to the IRS office—a standard part of any tax-return preparer's job.

The downside of going to a clinic is just what you'd think: You get what you pay for. The large chains say some of their tax preparers are CPAs or "enrolled agents" (discussed below), but most aren't. Because only a handful of states impose any restrictions in this area, anybody with a pencil and a pocket calculator can go into the business. Employees of the large chains receive some kind of training, but usually it's minimal—maybe a week of full-time study, or the equivalent. One of my college roommates worked as a tax return preparer in a clinic—*while in college*—to pick up beer money.

The tax-return preparers at clinics prepare your tax return. Period. They don't offer tax-planning tips for the rest of the year except in the most incidental manner, and few of them (recall my roommate) will be available for consultation later on. Also, there are legal limits on the extent to which a clinic can assist you with an IRS audit or audit appeal, unless it happens to be able to supply you with someone qualified as a CPA, enrolled agent, or lawyer, which it may not be able to do.

The matter of who can do what for you in the event of an audit is a bit complicated. The average tax-return preparer from a clinic (someone who is not one of the three types just mentioned) is permitted to *accompany* you in responding to an IRS inquiry about your return, but not to *represent* you in the way

that a lawyer, CPA, or enrolled agent might, presenting substantive legal arguments on your behalf. All he can do in an
audit is explain how your return was prepared and then shut
up unless addressed by the audit examiner.

The tax-return preparer who actually signed your return
may, with a notarized power of attorney or equivalent author-
ization from you, perform a limited representation function before the IRS if you aren't able to appear (or choose not to), but
(1) that individual might not be around when you need him,
and (2) he's permitted to perform this function only at the *audit
echelons* of the IRS, that is, at a meeting with an audit examiner
(the first step) and at one level of appeal from there, a conference
with a supervisor (the second step). He can't argue on your
behalf at the next level of appeal, the Office of Appeals (the top
level within the Service) or at the next level of appeal after that
(which takes you outside the Service), the U.S. Tax Court, Claims
Court, or District Court. Technically, anyone who can pass the
Tax Court exam is allowed to represent clients there (lawyers
alone are exempt from this requirement), but this exam is so
rigorous that few CPAs, fewer enrolled agents, and virtually no
clinic tax-return preparers pass it or even take it.

The bottom line on tax clinics? If your finances are simple
and you're a little short on funds at the moment—some "moments" seem to last forever—give a clinic a try.

ENROLLED AGENTS

Anyone considering going to a tax clinic should also consider
hiring a little-known breed of tax animal called an *enrolled agent*
(meaning "enrolled" to represent clients before the IRS). With
respect to fees, credentials, and authority to represent clients
before the IRS, enrolled agents fall somewhere between clinic
tax-return preparers, on the one hand, and CPAs and lawyers,
on the other.

There are two ways one can become an enrolled agent: (1)
continuous work for five years in a tax-interpretation branch of
the IRS, or (2) passing a rigorous two-day exam given by the
IRS. Either credential marks one as far better qualified than the
average tax return preparer at a clinic. Although seldom if ever

licensed to take cases beyond the IRS to the Tax Court, enrolled agents are, like CPAs and lawyers, permitted to represent clients all the way to the top of the IRS itself, which is farther than you'll probably ever want or need to go.

Hourly rates for enrolled agents vary a good bit, but a ball-park figure is sixty dollars per hour. You can find an enrolled agent by checking the yellow pages under "Tax Return Preparation" or by contacting the National Association of Enrolled Agents, 5410 Grosvenor Lane, Bethesda, MD (800/424-4339 or 301/897-8702).

I recommend speaking with several enrolled agents before actually hiring one, both to ascertain the range of rates in your area and to confirm that the people in question really are enrolled agents. You may have to press hard on the latter point. My own calls to the offices of several "tax experts" indicate that the average secretary has no idea whether his boss is an enrolled agent, and in some instances the "expert" himself won't understand the question.

CPAS

Certified Public Accountants are genuine professionals. Like lawyers, CPAs have undergone extensive training and passed a notoriously hard set of exams.

Not everyone trained in accounting is a CPA, and not every CPA is directly involved in tax work. But you're as safe as you can get—note that I don't say "safe"—in assuming that a tax-trained CPA possesses a lot of helpful knowledge.

CPA firms, like mouthwashes, come in small, medium, and economy sizes—except the economy sizes aren't necessarily economical. The giant national firms, some with literally hundreds of members, command the most prestige and charge the highest rates. They also claim, probably with some justification, to employ the best people.

The rates at the large firms, notably the "Big Eight" firms such as Peat Marwick Mitchell & Company or Arthur Andersen & Company, range from, say, $40 to $200 per hour, depending on the credentials and seniority of the individuals doing the work. As at a large law firm, a young drone with a low rate usually performs the time-consuming grunt work, while a senior partner reviews the work, signs the papers, and schmoozes with the client.

Can you save money by going to a smaller firm? Probably, but it's not certain. Lots of solo and small-firm practitioners started their careers at the big firms and continue to charge comparable rates. Moreover, because they don't have a vast proletariat of comparatively cheap drones under their command, their costs may actually be higher.

Should you hire a CPA to prepare your return? *Just* to prepare your return? If your finances are simple, hiring a CPA might be overkill. On the other hand, if your finances are moderately challenging, at least to you, and you wouldn't mind picking up a few tax pointers, go with a CPA. Plenty of people consider several hundred dollars a small price to pay just to have someone spare them the labor of tallying their medical expenses, charitable donations, stock transactions, itemized deductions, and so on.

What CPAs really boast of offering, and what you should really go to them for, is long-term tax and financial *planning.* A good CPA will help you organize your personal finances, offering advice on whether you're paying too much interest on your mortgage, how much life insurance you should own, what kinds of investments might serve you best (at least from a tax standpoint), and how you might reduce your future tax liability. Moreover, he'll provide advice not just at tax time but throughout the year.

What's the relationship between CPAs and lawyers? Socially, they get along just fine. Lawyers like having CPAs around, because they view CPAs as the only professionals more boring than themselves. (CPAs, in turn, look down on actuaries.)

A number of CPAs *are* lawyers, or at least attended law school. But they aren't permitted to represent you *as* lawyers; they're legally required to go one way or the other. No one's business card or letterhead proclaims him to be both a CPA and a lawyer.

So CPAs don't practice law? They do it every day, interpreting laws, predicting court and agency decisions, making "legal" judgments for clients. An *opinion letter* prepared by a CPA discusses judicial decisions, congressional reports, Treasury regulations, IRS revenue rulings—you wouldn't know except for the letterhead that it wasn't prepared by a lawyer.

The same is true in reverse. Lawyers who fill out tax returns or perform mathematical calculations for their clients are clearly practicing "accounting."

This is a controversial subject and a source of tension between the two professions. Each categorically denies poaching on the other's turf. Hogwash. There's simply an overlap of the two fields, and there's nothing to be done about it.

Which profession offers superior tax expertise? For the nuts-and-bolts work of filling out tax returns, even most lawyers would agree that CPAs are your better bet, if for no other reason than that they do it more often.

For financial planning, which includes but isn't limited to *tax* planning, the answer is the same. Top tax lawyers of course have tremendous financial savvy, but you should at least start with a CPA. Not only do CPAs charge lower rates than tax lawyers do (and the discussion could end right there), but also it's generally accepted that CPAs spend more time acquiring and providing "financial," as opposed to purely "legal," expertise.

Hiring a CPA. Plenty of CPAs are listed in the yellow pages, but the best way to find one is through references. Try to get references from people who earn their living the same way you do, because a CPA with experience in your specialized area— medicine or small business, say—is bound to have picked up some things a generalist hasn't.

It's not only reasonable but advisable that you ask about billing rates. Rarely will CPAs commit themselves to a fixed price for a project of any size, but you're definitely entitled to a rough estimate of the time likely to be required—for example, fifteen hours by a drone and five hours by a gray eminence.

Ask whether the people who perform your work will be available for consultation throughout the year. Ask whether the firm has any program for apprising clients of significant tax developments. Ask about the firm's computer capabilities, the turnover rate of their personnel, when they go on vacation (and where)—anything you can think of.

A word of warning: Don't confuse CPAs with CFPs, or Certified Financial Planners. CFPs may have received some kind of specialized training, but that training doesn't include tax-return preparation. Any CFP who claims otherwise is yanking your chain.

In 1985, the International Association for Financial Planning, the largest U.S. association of financial planners, awarded a certificate suitable for framing to one Boris "Bo" Regaard of Tampa, Florida. The certificate identified Bo as a certified financial planner and as an IAFP member. It omitted that Bo is part poodle and part schnauzer—in short, a dog.

TAX LAWYERS

If my advice about CPAs is valid, and if, as is true, the average tax lawyer charges more than the average CPA, why would you ever want to hire a tax lawyer?

For starters, if you've committed tax fraud or, just about as bad, somebody at the IRS or Justice Department thinks you have, you *need* a lawyer. Lawyers alone are legally permitted to represent you in virtually any of the courts in which you might find yourself defending against those kinds of charges. Also, lawyers alone understand criminal law and criminal procedure.

Even if no one is alleging activities of a criminal nature, your tax problems may be serious enough that only a lawyer will do. Tax *disputes*—fights with the IRS—are best handled by lawyers. Again, lawyers alone are permitted to represent you in most of the courts to which you might appeal your case following an adverse ruling by the IRS. Also, the presence of a lawyer armed with cases and rulings that he appears prepared to file in court can inspire a healthy concern on the part of an IRS examiner as to whether, in hounding you, he's about to involve the Service in a prolonged, potentially losing battle.

Another important benefit to having your tax disputes handled by a lawyer involves the protection afforded by the well-known "lawyer-client privilege," as well as by the more obscure "work-product rule."

In a nutshell, the *lawyer-client privilege* protects confidential statements, spoken or written, by you to your lawyer. (For this purpose, think of your lawyer's office as a priest's confessional, if you can.) In partial contrast, the *work-product rule* protects memoranda and other documents that were (a) prepared by your lawyer (b) in anticipation of litigation and (c) contain the lawyer's opinions, mental impressions, and legal theories. (For this purpose, think of your lawyer as a football coach with a game plan, which he's of course permitted to keep absolutely secret from the opposing side.)

Don't dwell too much on the complicated issue of what is and what isn't protected by these doctrines, although one point regarding the lawyer-client privilege is worth noting: The privilege doesn't protect communications that weren't originally intended to be "confidential."

Suppose your lawyer is a personal friend. You mention something to him out loud at a dinner party one evening, or in a crowded locker room. Months or years later you realize that your statement is legally damaging. Thank God for the lawyer-client privilege, you think.

Not so fast. You're going to be hard put to persuade a court later that your statement in either of these situations was intended to be confidential, and hence should be protected by the lawyer-client privilege.

The moral? If you want to say something confidential to your lawyer, say it *to your lawyer*—and to no one else.

Now, the lawyer-client privilege and the work-product rule don't protect absolutely everything. But they protect a lot. And any protection at all is more than you'll get if the only person in your corner besides yourself is your CPA (although some states now have laws establishing an accountant-client privilege).

What you need to ask yourself is, how much is such protection likely to be worth to you?

Only a tiny fraction of all returns gets audited—in fiscal 1985, for example, the figure was 1.3 percent of the 99.4 million individual returns filed. Moreover, only a tiny fraction of the returns that get audited end up in litigation; most people throw in the towel and accept the auditor's initial findings. Finally, only a fraction of the people whose returns end up in litigation want or need to prevent disclosure of their records to the IRS. We're getting to low numbers here.

Still, plenty of people, especially wealthy people and those involved in sophisticated business ventures, have a big stake in keeping the Service's hands off their private letters and memoranda regarding tax planning. There's nothing shady about this. In countless situations there's no clear answer as to what the tax law requires, so lawyers and clients spend long hours considering alternative tax strategies, noting the strengths and weaknesses—not to say illegalities—of each. And once a given strategy is chosen, they have a legitimate stake in not disclosing to the IRS the documents they've prepared revealing their personal views on its strengths and weaknesses—especially its weaknesses.

Are your own records so "delicate" that they warrant hiring a lawyer to help you keep them beyond the long arm of the law? Only you and your lawyer can say.

There are additional reasons, unrelated to litigation and preventing disclosure of information, that you might want a lawyer instead of a CPA. A lawyer knows the law respecting partnerships and corporations—obviously vital for persons involved in business. A lawyer knows the law respecting divorce, which can rewrite your financial story from beginning to end. A lawyer knows the law respecting wills, trusts, and estates—the keys to ongoing life for your money and your memory (don't think the two aren't related). A lawyer knows the law respecting charitable foundations, which anybody with a ton of money and an ounce of heart should consider at some stage of the game.

This isn't to say a CPA knows nothing about these areas. But having approached them exclusively from the tax perspective, if at all, he knows them to a comparatively limited degree.

Does that affect you? Perhaps not if your involvement in such areas is either so marginal or so simple and straightforward that legal expertise isn't necessary. But keep two points in mind.

First, if there's a lot of money at stake, your involvement isn't "marginal"—by definition. It probably isn't simple and straightforward, either.

Second, in a tremendous number of situations, you *have* to

have a lawyer. No one else is capable of papering over the plan or project. While CPAs prepare tax returns, along with memoranda and opinion letters addressing related tax issues, that's it (for your purposes). If a CPA advises you to get a will or set up a trust, partnership, corporation, charitable foundation, or anything else, he'll have to send you to a lawyer to obtain the documents.

If you're going to have to hire a lawyer to prepare virtually every document, the question shifts from "Why pay for a lawyer?" to "Why bother with a CPA?" (except perhaps for the bare task of preparing your return).

The answer? Two heads (even bald, bespectacled ones) are better than one. If tax lawyers know lots of things CPAs don't know, CPAs often know things lawyers don't know. The fact is, people employ both CPAs and tax lawyers for related projects all the time, often putting them together in the same room. Usually only sophisticated, high-stakes tax matters warrant such double attention, but if you want it, don't worry that for some reason it's taboo. Lawyers and CPAs are hired guns; there's very little they won't do for a price—in the middle of Times Square at high noon.

Hiring a tax lawyer. The guidelines listed above for hiring a CPA apply as well to hiring a tax lawyer, except that given the uniquely specialized nature of tax work, extra care in the hiring process is appropriate. Regarding location, you shouldn't be concerned if the tax lawyer you want happens to live in another city. Tax work lends itself to a national practice, the rules being pretty much the same everywhere. For this reason, I'm tempted to refer everyone to my brother in Atlanta, except that it seems as if he's doing most of the country's tax work already.

Tax lawyers tend to charge the highest rates in an already high-charging profession. How do they get away with it?

Tax is as arcane and demanding a specialty as exists in the law. Mastering the tax code probably requires more time—and more intelligence—than any other area. A saying in the profession is that tax lawyers never go hungry, because so few people want to do their work—or can.

DEALING WITH THE INTERNAL REVENUE SERVICE

It's not by chance that the Internal Revenue Service is often referred to as the *Infernal* Revenue Service. You instinctively fear and dislike it, the way you instinctively fear and dislike anyone trying to take your money.

Some people aren't content just to curse and mutter. IRS agents have begun to encounter assaults and threats of violence in such numbers that the Service now marks certain taxpayer files "PDT," meaning "potentially dangerous taxpayer." Most such problems arise in the collection context, as IRS agents confiscate cars and other property to enforce tax judgments, but who among us doesn't think murderous thoughts when contemplating an audit?

IRS Tax Advice

The IRS offers two types of tax assistance by telephone: Tele-Tax, which provides recorded information on some 150 topics, and a regular call-in service that puts you in touch with a human, roughly speaking. Each is listed in the yellow pages and in the Forms and Instructions booklet that comes with your Form 1040. The IRS also maintains a number of walk-in tax assistance offices, which are worth knowing about if you'd rather kill time standing in line downtown rather than sitting on hold at home.

How reliable are these services? The Tele-Tax recordings are probably accurate as far as they go. As for the regular call-in service (and this applies as well to the walk-in service), to characterize it as "uneven" is to flatter it, as everyone who has ever tested it agrees.

On a question of any difficulty, a single call is likely to yield erroneous information; multiple calls are likely to yield erroneous *conflicting* information. According to a 1986 survey by Congress' General Accounting Office, the IRS's phone service improved from the preceding year. For questions involving more than general answers and references, its accuracy rate rose all the way to 63 percent. In other words, over one-third of the information provided was just plain wrong—in a good year.

The "expertise" of the people who staff the IRS telephones is far below that of accountants and tax lawyers. This isn't surprising, since the IRS people may have received as little as several weeks of training. Their willingness to speak authoritatively on complex issues assures you of little but that they're alive and reached the office before you called.

"What do I care if they're right or wrong?" you may ask. "Once they've given me an answer, aren't they bound by it?"

No. As the IRS's Forms and Instructions booklet itself confesses (in tiny print and somewhat obliquely), "If we do make an error, you are still responsible for the payment of the correct tax"—"correct" meaning whatever the statutes and regulations say, not what a part-time federal employee says. (The Service's informal responses to general inquiries should be distinguished from its "private-letter rulings," which address fully elucidated fact situations and usually emanate from authoritative sources within the IRS. *These* rulings are considered binding on the Service, at least with respect to the specific taxpayers involved. You need a lawyer or CPA to prepare the request for a private-letter ruling. The preparation costs could easily amount to several thousand dollars.)

IRS Audits

The big question with respect to audits, as with respect to taxes themselves, is how to avoid them—and for the same reason: Both make you poorer. When paying taxes, of course, you're dead solid certain to end up poorer, whereas when getting audited, according to IRS statistics, there's only about a 78 percent chance you'll end up poorer, and about a 7 percent chance you'll end up richer. Who wants to play those odds?

FILE A RETURN

The primary rule for staying out of trouble with the IRS is: *File a return.* If this sounds obvious, good. Plenty of people, including the current mayor of Chicago, are less informed.

Filing is always better than not filing, even if you dread an audit so badly it makes your hair hurt. First, not filing renders you guilty of a criminal offense that could land you in jail, whereas the worst that could happen as a result of filing (absent fraud or the like) is that you'll owe more money. Second, filing triggers the running of the statute of limitations. Generally the IRS has only three years to come after you for more money, whereas if you don't file at all they have literally forever. Third, so tiny a percentage of all filings receive in-depth IRS review that you probably won't get audited even if you deserve to be.

What if you don't owe any money? What if the IRS owes *you* money? It doesn't matter. Unless you're someone's dependent or a lot poorer than you probably are if you're reading this book (a gross income of around $5,000, depending on the year, is the cutoff point for an unmarried person under sixty-five), you have to file. So file.

FILING EXTENSIONS

It has been said that of life's two certainties, taxes are the only one for which you can get an automatic extension. Not true. What you can get an automatic extension for is your tax *return*.

If April 15 rolls around and you know you're not going to be able to complete and file a return on time, don't assume that you'd better not file at all, lest you signal the IRS that you've committed the sin of procrastination. They don't shoot people for that.

File a Form 4868, "Application for Automatic Extension of Time to File U.S. Individual Income Tax Return," which gives you four extra months to put together your return. This doesn't give you any extra time to pay your *tax*; you have to estimate it and send it in with your Form 4868 by April 15. If your estimation turns out to be lower than your actual tax obligation, you'll owe interest on the difference. If your estimation is off by more than 10 percent, you'll owe interest plus a penalty.

You can request an extension even beyond the automatic four-month period. The Service will deny such a request, however, unless you can come up with a real good reason.

In most areas of the law, if you keep your nose clean, nobody will bother you. In the tax area, you can calculate your liability perfectly and still get audited.

How does the IRS decide which returns to audit? It admits that there can be an element of sheer chance. Under the Service's Taxpayer Compliance Measurement Program, a few returns are selected for audit at random. Hence the concept of "audit roulette."

It's not pure roulette, however. The IRS makes no bones about being in the business of maximizing revenue—which means, presumably, that it concentrates on the returns of the rich.

The Service also keeps an eye out for conflicts between the information it receives from different sources. Thus, if you think your year-end statement from someone such as your banker or broker is mistaken, you should either (1) take care of the problem *before* filing your return, (2) explain the mistake on your return, or (3) simply accept the mistaken calculation. Simply to claim something different is to ask for an audit.

Finally, the Service zeroes in on returns bearing "red flags." Red flags consist of items out of the ordinary, as well as ordinary items in extraordinary quantities, such as unusually high medical expenses or charitable donations. (What's "unusually high" is measured by the average figures for persons in your income group.) Other red flags consist of items particularly susceptible to abuse, such as home offices and casualty losses.

Seldom, as a practical matter, is there any good way to avoid red-flag items. If you do give an unusual amount of money to charity, you should certainly deduct it all. I don't plan to give up my home office deductions just because the IRS views such deductions with suspicion.

Occasionally, on the other hand, you do have some maneuvering room, such as in the *percentage* of the rent you deduct as the cost of your home office ("Yes, sir, I know seventy-five percent seems high, but I sleep in my closet and use the bedroom for meetings with clients"), or the *level* of your valuation of stolen property ("Absolutely, ma'am, that was an original Ming Dynasty umbrella stand").

With respect to any claim involving an element of discretion, I hereby offer the fifth of White's Irregular Rules:

Don't be a hog.

There's nothing wrong with giving yourself the benefit of a reasonable doubt, perhaps even being a little aggressive, such as by claiming 20 percent rather than 15 percent of your rent as the cost of your home office, or by valuing the stolen property at $2,500 rather than $2,300. The IRS is fishing for whales, not guppies. But resist hoggery. The Service will spot it, be irritated by it, and fight hard to nail you for it.

One modest step you can take to reduce the odds of your being audited is to include with your return a letter or memorandum explaining anything extraordinary. Don't be deterred by the fact that there's no space for an explanation on the standard form.

A NOTE ON DOMESTIC HELP

If you're a typical yuppie or perhaps half of a two-job couple, you probably employ a cook, housekeeper, baby-sitter, or the like. If so, you can get yourself audited or otherwise in trouble with the law by failing to pay any of the four taxes that may be due in connection with such employment.

• *Social Security.* If you pay an employee as little as $50 in any calendar quarter, you're liable for the Social Security tax. Currently the rate of this tax (due quarterly, with Form 942) is 14.3 percent on the first $39,600 of wages. Your alternatives for handling this obligation are either (1) to pay half the amount yourself and deduct the other half from your employee's paycheck or (2) to pay the entire amount yourself (in which case you have to report half the amount as taxable income to the employee).

Note that however much your compliance with these rules benefits an employee in the long run, there's a good chance, especially if this employee is used to being paid in cash, that he'll object to your filing anything that gives the authorities an accurate picture of his finances.

• *Federal income tax.* You can withhold this tax for your employee or not, as you wish. Either way, assuming you meet the $50-per-quarter threshold that triggers the Social Security tax, you have to file with the Social Security Administration (*not* with the IRS) a Form W-2 indicating the amount of your employee's compensation. The W-2 for any year is due annually, by the end of February of the following year, but you have to give your employee a copy of it a month earlier, that is, by the end of January of the following year. If you employ two or more persons you also have to file a W-3 with their W-2s.

• *Unemployment tax.* If you pay an employee $1,000 or more in any calendar quarter, you—and you alone—are liable for the federal unemployment tax. This is due annually, with Form 940, by January 31 of the following year. Currently the rate of this tax is 6.2 percent of the first $7,000 of compensation, but because you can claim a credit of up to 5.4 percent for any *state* unemployment insurance you pay, the effective rate of the federal tax may come to just .8 percent.

• *Workers compensation.* Many states require employers to pay for workers compensation coverage for employees who work a certain minimum amount—say, thirty hours per week.

WHAT HAPPENS IN AN AUDIT

You're a good person. You pay your debts and keep your promises. You floss nightly and fear God. Why, then, did you find an audit notice in your mailbox today?

Relax. Unless you've done something truly appalling, the worst they can do is take some more of your money. They can't kill you. And if they do, they can't eat you.

Note at the outset that an audit is different from pounding yourself on the foot with a hammer: An audit has no element of voluntariness. In particular, you have to answer any questions the examiner asks and provide any records he requests. The Service has statutory authority to compel you, your spouse, your employer, your banker, your broker, and anyone else to turn over anything that "might" throw light on the correctness of your return.

There are three types of audits. In ascending order of intrusiveness, these are:

1. *Letter audits.* Roughly 10 percent of all audits consist of nothing more than a letter from the IRS asking you to document something on your return—for example, to provide a photocopy of a check written to a charity. If you have the proof, send it in. If not, get ready to explain why not, or to pay more tax.

2. *Office audits.* The most common form of audit, comprising roughly 75 percent of all audits, consists of a meeting with an IRS examiner at the examiner's office. (Since you'll be dealing with this person face-to-face, it may be worth noting that the term *examiner* is generic for either of two types of IRS auditors, "tax auditors" and "revenue agents." The latter tend to be better credentialed, higher paid, and used for more complicated tasks, such as the "field audits" described below.)

An office audit commences with a notice "advising" you to appear at a specified place and time (not unlike the way a police officer "advises" you to "pull over"). You can either show up then or call and request a more convenient time.

What will the examiner want to talk about? Usually the notice will give you some indication, such as "all medical expenses" or "all sources of income." If the notice is silent in this respect, call and ask.

What should you wear to an office audit? There's no merit in appearing before an examiner looking too affluent. Examiners are trained to sniff out evidence of unreported income. Besides, they're no less likely than the rest of the world to resent people who earn more than they do.

Why not see if your old Timex won't keep time for one day as well as your gold Rolex? Why not get one last wearing out of that frayed coat you were about to use to clean the cat box?

There's no requirement that you appear personally for a desk audit or, for that matter, a field audit. In either case you can usually choose to be represented (rather than merely accompanied) by a lawyer, CPA, enrolled agent, or the person who signed your return as its preparer. However, unless the subject of the audit isn't you but your company, in which case the examiner might actually prefer to deal with your chief financial officer rather than you, why insult the examiner by failing to show a personal interest in what he does for a living?

3. *Field audits.* A field audit usually involves a visit by an examiner to your home or office. Although the main idea is to spare you the burden of transporting voluminous records to an IRS office, another purpose may be to enable a revenue agent to sniff around on location. Unlike an office audit, which is comparatively perfunctory, a field audit is usually so extensive (and burdensome) that in most instances it commences with a phone call to discuss questions of location and time.

AUDITS AND TAXPAYER RECORDS

What records will you need for your audit?

All of them.

Check stubs, canceled checks, deposit slips, charge slips, theater tickets, airline tickets, every kind of receipt known to modern civilization. Your appointment calendar. Letters from your doctor, broker, banker, bookie, and insurance adjuster. Legal judgments for and against you. Previous returns for years that might be relevant.

Is it hard to assemble all your financial records? No harder than matching your socks in a darkroom. Note that it's not just a matter of throwing them (your records, not your socks) into a suitcase and walking out the door. You have to assemble them, organize them, compare them to the figures on your returns, and then come up with an explanation for the disparities.

As for records you definitely don't have, consider this ingenious measure: Get them. You obviously can't self-generate the actual receipts for meals or tickets you bought last year, but for anything you paid for by credit card, you can probably obtain some kind of documentation from the card issuer. Similarly, with a simple phone call or letter you can probably obtain old brokerage and bank records, the latter including invaluable lists of checks. Your doctor's office probably maintains records of medical payments going back several years. And for a nominal fee the IRS will provide copies of your old returns.

*   *   *

A *Wall Street Journal* reporter wrote of being required in the course of his audit to explain every deposit in every one of his accounts—checking, savings, money market, brokerage. Could you explain every entry in your checkbook?

Good records are the key to surviving an audit. So *keep good records.*

It's as simple as that—and as difficult, or why do so many people have such sloppy records? I describe my own record-keeping system below, to stimulate your thinking. (It's adequacy has never been tested in an audit.) If you like any parts of it, they're yours.

Inspired by the reporter's story mentioned above, I scribble in my bankbook, money-market records, IRA records, and stock lists the source(s) of funds for any deposit or purchase. I keep separate lists—by hand, on a yellow legal pad—of medical expenses, business expenses, charitable contributions, and income. Each entry on these lists indicates the nature, date, and amount of the outlay in question, as well as whether that outlay was by check or otherwise; and, if otherwise, whether I kept a receipt. All receipts I do have I staple together, one on top of the other, in chronological order. I update the lists every week or two, depending on when I start to notice receipts piling up in my wallet. (Note that travel and entertainment expenses require especially detailed records; a canceled check or credit card receipt isn't enough. Also, there are new and often burdensome requirements for substantiating charitable donations of property with a claimed value of $500 or more. If the claimed value exceeds $5,000, a special appraisal is required.)

How long should you hold on to your records? For underpayments of tax and various other offenses, the statute of limitations runs six years from the filing of your return. You should hold on to all your records at least that long. You should also hold on to any records, however old, that bear on current or potential future tax liabilities, such as your divorce decree (showing your alimony obligations) or your house purchase documents (showing your mortgage interest obligations).

For a few especially serious offenses, such as fraud, there may be no limitations period at all. For this reason you might do well to keep your records for a full decade before yielding to the temptation to deposit them in your circular file—along with old coffee grounds, eggshells, and used kitty litter. How much space can a few years' worth of records take?

AFTER YOUR AUDIT

The odds are seven to ten that your audit will result in your owing the government money, and worse than that if yours is a field audit rather than a letter or an office audit. If you do end up owing money, you have three options: (1) pay, be happy you didn't end up owing more than you did, and forget about it— the course chosen by the overwhelming majority of auditees; (2) pay, and then fight about it; or (3) refuse to pay, and then fight about it.

If you take either of the last two courses, you can fight about it all the way to the top of the IRS—which you should definitely do before going still higher, that is, before going to the courts. Your chances within the IRS are probably better than in the courts, both because the process in the former context involves *negotiation* with IRS officials, rather than formal litigation against them, and because the IRS much prefers to settle cases (which it does approximately 80 percent of the time) rather than fight them out in the courts. No doubt the IRS is spurred in its settlement negotiations by the prospect of having to pay the legal fees of taxpayers who "substantially prevail."

If you lose within the IRS, you can appeal to one of three courts: the U.S. Tax Court (if you didn't pay) or either the U.S. District Court or the U.S. Claims Court (if you did pay). There's an element of arbitrariness as to which course you follow in this unnecessarily complex system, but each court is somewhat different (for example, the District Court offers a trial by jury). From any of these courts you can attempt to carry your case up two more levels all the way to the U.S. Supreme Court, although that Court, which is hard enough to reach in any event, has a well-established disinclination to get involved in the tax area.

Unless you're just fighting to vindicate a principle—for reasons perhaps best understood by Freud, people get unusually riled in their dealings with the government—you shouldn't plan on appealing to any of these courts without a lawyer. The only alternative to being represented by a lawyer is being represented by yourself (neither a CPA nor anyone else is legally permitted to represent you in court), and the issues at that advanced stage will generally be too complex for any layperson to have a realistic chance of prevailing against an experienced IRS official.

If you're thinking about going into court alone—and about half of the taxpayers who sue in the Tax Court don't have lawyers—keep in mind three things: (1) Your chances of prevailing are best if you're disputing factual issues, such as the substantiation of deductions, rather than purely legal issues; (2) the Tax Court offers a simplified system for *small claims,* defined as those involving less than $10,000. The filing fee under this system is $10; and (3) the Tax Court can slap you with a civil penalty for filing what it considers a frivolous lawsuit. In 1985 it assessed penalties averaging $3,600 against 543 claimants.

Within the IRS, the need for representation—whether by a lawyer, a CPA, or an enrolled agent—is somewhat less than in the courts. At all levels of the Service, including the top (the Appeals Office), the procedures are sufficiently informal and well explained in various publications that you won't feel as hopelessly lost as you might in the judicial labyrinth. Still, winning at the Appeals Office requires persuading it to overrule the decision of one of its own auditors and/or that auditor's supervisor—and what are a layperson's chances of doing that?

One pointer: If, at the end of an office audit, the examiner rules against you, don't storm out ranting about moronic federal bureaucrats and your intention to take the damn case all the way to Oliver Wendell Holmes or whoever is running the show these days at the Supreme Court. Ask for a conference with the examiner's supervisor then and there. Often you'll be permitted to take this informal type of appeal immediately; the examiner will just walk down the hall and ask if his supervisor is back from lunch (it's 3:00 P.M.) and has a few minutes to listen to fairy tales from another taxpayer with an out-of-season tan claiming his trip to Acapulco was medically required.

IRS Mistakes and Delays

Mistakes by the IRS in dealing with your filed return are virtually impossible to avenge. The Service is a Kafkaesque bureaucracy—impenetrable, unresponsive, at once monolithic and utterly divided against itself.

What do you do if you fail to receive a refund you know you have coming? (Suppose, to add insult to penury, you receive instead an obviously mistaken notice of additional taxes owed.)

Call the IRS. Then write them (by certified mail, making sure to include your social security number). Then call again. Then write again. And again and again.

Your next step is to try to contact the nearest office of the Service's self-touted Problem Resolution Program (PRP), which purports to help taxpayers with purely administrative snafus. The PRP considers itself a last resort and will accept inquiries only after you've attempted to resolve your problem through conventional approaches for several weeks—or several months (the figure you get depends on whom you talk to).

It appears that the way to reach the PRP is to call the main IRS number in your area and swear to whoever answers that you've spent a prolonged period attempting to resolve your problem by correspondence. (Ask this person what he believes the requisite period of correspondence to be, and whatever he says, insist you've been at it twice that long—which eventually you will have been.) Then offer him anything he wants if he'll have someone from the PRP call you. (Don't bother saying "at his convenience." That's understood.)

This may or may not work. It can't hurt. Nothing can hurt. Try contacting the national head of the PRP, Jack Petrie (or his successor), 1111 Constitution Avenue, N.W., Washington, DC 20224 (202/566-6475).

To say the least, this process is severely frustrating. I offer you what comfort there may be in a saying that frequently appears in the offices of tax practitioners: *Illegitimi Non Carborundum*—Don't let the bastards wear you down.

ESTATE PLANNING

Your *estate* is whatever property you don't take with you when you die. (Most of the property you own at death will fall into this category.)

Why "plan" for it?

Because you won't be around later to say what should become of it. At that stage the most you'll be able to do is watch from Above as others put into effect (or fail to put into effect) the orders you issued in your will and related documents.

Estate planning involves, then, figuring out what kinds of orders you want to give regarding your property. It also involves maximizing the amount of property that's yours to give orders about.

Two considerations traditionally dictate the kinds of orders you might want to give: first, whom you want to get your property when you die; second, avoidance (or postponement) of taxes, especially the federal estate and gift taxes, although the federal income tax also plays a significant if indirect role. These two considerations are interrelated, for the simple reason that the less you give Uncle Sam, the more is left over for everyone else.

The key to having a lot of property left after you die is to *have* a lot of property *before* you die. You laugh. Good investing and thriftiness constitute excellent, although by no means independently sufficient, forms of estate planning.

Accumulating wealth in this life isn't the only means of providing for your survivors. Even the poorest beggar can leave behind a mountain of mammon through the device of life insurance. On the other hand, depending on your circumstances, life insurance may not represent a good investment. If the premiums deplete valuable and appreciating assets, for example, your beneficiaries might be better off if you left the money where it is.

What's the point? That sound estate planning involves more than arranging for the disposition of your assets once you're gone; it also involves intelligent management of your assets while you're still around.

The following discussion addresses the two main legal topics (as opposed to the myriad *financial* topics) involved in estate planning: (1) federal estate and gift taxes (sometimes referred to as *death taxes*)* and (2) devices for disposing of your estate.

The Federal Estate and Gift Taxes

Avoidance of the federal estate tax is to some extent a rich person's game, because no tax is due on estates of less than $600,000, which meets most people's definition of *rich*. This is an essential point: If your worth at death is $600,000 or less, your executor won't even have to file an estate-tax return.

To say this is not at all to say that people with less than $600,000 should forget about the estate tax. Suppose your sister's accumulated wealth totals $600,000. If you leave her your estate of $599,999—or, for that matter, $599—you'll put *her* over the $600,000 threshold, resulting in what lawyers refer to as *estate overload*.

Note another essential point, this one dealing with the relation of the gift tax to the estate tax: Until you get into truly gigantic gifts (or numerous comparatively small gifts), *you don't actually pay a gift tax at the time of a gift*. The $600,000 exemption is in fact a *unified credit* against *both* your estate tax *and* any gift-tax obligations you've accumulated over your lifetime. The two taxes operate in conjunction—which makes sense: Gifts are gifts, whether given while you're alive or later. In most cases the gift tax is paid at the same time as the estate tax, namely, after you die.

Unless you're the kind of friend I dream about, and you make me a gift in one year that exceeds the $10,000 annual gift tax exclusion *plus* the $600,000 exemption level, for a total of $610,000, you simply file an "informational" gift-tax return in the year of a gift and then let your executor worry about the rest, namely, whether the *final* total—the sum of (1) your taxable estate plus (2) the excess of all your gifts over $10,000 in any year—exceeds $600,000.

---

*Some states have their own death taxes, including both a *local estate tax* and an *inheritance tax*. The former is a miniature version of the federal estate tax, the latter a comparatively small tax imposed on the *recipient* of gifts from a deceased.

*   *   *

Even if your riches far exceed $600,000, you might be able to escape the federal estate tax by one or more of the following devices (in conjunction with the $600,000 exemption):

• *The unlimited charitable deduction.* If you own, say, $5,600,000, you can leave $5,000,000 (or more) to some charity, thereby avoiding any estate tax whatsoever. Any less would leave your estate with more than the exempt $600,000, and some estate tax would then be due (unless you simultaneously took advantage of other estate tax-avoidance devices).

• *The unlimited marital deduction.* If you own $5,600,000, you could leave $5,000,000 (or more) to your spouse. For these purposes, he's treated the same as a charity (the way you always thought of him). This, too, would enable you to avoid any estate tax.

• *Shrewd planning.* What constitutes "shrewd planning"? Consider the $1,200,000 in cash you were planning to leave your beloved wife. You have a heart condition and are certain to predecease her, by your calculation (and hers).

A shrewd tax lawyer would look down the road, however, and consider what will happen to all that money when your *wife* dies. He would point out that she'll suffer from "estate overload" because—think about it—you won't be around to afford her the same marital deduction that she afforded you. Uncle Sam stands to make a bundle.

Leave her only *half* the $1,200,000, the shrewd tax lawyer might propose. (That part, of course, falls within the unlimited marital deduction.) Put the remaining $600,000, which falls within the standard estate exemption, into a *bypass trust*, with the income from the trust to go to your wife for as long as she lives, and the principal to go upon her death to your niece, your alma mater—anywhere but to Uncle Sam. That $600,000 in trust, or whatever is left of it when your wife dies, won't be treated as belonging to her for federal estate-tax purposes.

Another example of shrewd planning: Take advantage, to the extent consistent with your own needs and resources, of one or more of the four devices for avoiding probate discussed in Chapter 10, "Wills," namely gifts, life insurance, joint ownership of property, and trusts. Avoiding probate and avoiding taxes are two different things, but anything you take out of your estate for purposes of avoiding probate will also, if properly handled, escape the estate tax.

It's critical to note here that the estate and gift taxes constitute an enormous iceberg, the mere tip of which is delineated above. While the countless hidden complexities of these taxes may or may not bear on your personal situation, you should give a tax lawyer a chance to think about it.

Devices for Disposing of Your Estate

The ideas above relate to the goal of minimizing your estate-tax liability. You should think about them whatever the size of your estate, but especially if it's likely to exceed the $600,000 exemption level. Two other goals merit your consideration, regardless of the size of your estate: (1) disposing of your estate in the manner most to your liking, and (2) minimizing your current income tax.

The basic device for disposing of your estate is your will. Simplest and most obvious of the ways to dispose of property through your will is to give it to somebody outright: "I leave all my property to Rodney Beegle."

You can get trickier than that, however. You can create and bestow upon someone what's called a *life interest:* "I leave my farm to Rodney Beegle *for the duration of his life,* and *upon his death* to my godson Max."

You can give someone a *contingent* or *executory* interest: "I leave my farm to Rodney Beegle, but *if* Rodney marries Irene Vonk, then the farm should go to my godson Max."

You can give someone a *power of appointment* (meaning a power to give property away): "I leave my farm to Rodney Beegle for life, and upon Rodney's death, to such persons as Rodney in his will appoints." You could add to this, "If Rodney fails to appoint anyone, then to my godson Max or to such persons as Max may choose to appoint."

The idea underlying powers of appointment is to enable you to give someone authority to distribute your property in the light of future events. If you're an Oklahoma oil millionaire, you might leave your property to your wife with a power to appoint the property upon her death "To whichever of our children seems most likely to attend college—the overeducated peckerwood will need it."

TRUSTS

Life interests, powers of appointment, and other standard devices found in wills can also be utilized in conjunction with trusts. Suppose your son is inexperienced in financial matters and would be hard put to figure out what to do with the $1 million stock portfolio you're considering leaving him. Put the stock in a trust, to be managed by, say, a bank trust department, with the income to go to your son on a monthly basis. You're worried that in an emergency he might need to dip into the principal? Include a provision authorizing the trustee to dip into the principal as he believes necessary for your son's maintenance and support, taking into account your son's other sources of income. As for what happens to the principal when your son dies, give him a power of appointment. Or make that decision for yourself, spelling it out in the trust agreement.

Note that you can make a trust revocable or irrevocable. If you make it irrevocable, it's out of your hands forever, which is good and bad: bad, in that you lose control of it; good, in that, if properly structured, it won't be considered a part of your estate when you die.

On the other hand, if you make the trust revocable, the principal *isn't* out of your hands forever, which is good and bad, too: bad, in that it will be considered a part of your estate when you die; good, in that if you set up the trust a few years before your mind goes the way of your hair—down the drain—you'll have an opportunity to observe how the trustee manages the stock (or real estate, or whatever). If he starts investing in revival versions of the Ford Edsel, you can cut him off at the pass.

Trusts offer significant benefits with respect to children and disabled people. Suppose you and your wife die, leaving behind a young daughter and a good bit of money. Absent other arrangements, some court will appoint a guardian to look after your daughter and your money until your daughter comes of age. There are alternatives to leaving such matters to a court, however.

As for your daughter, your will can name someone to serve as her guardian. As for your money, you can put it (through your will or otherwise) in a trust for your daughter's care and support. This way, both the guardian (named in your will) and the trustee would be people of *your* choosing, presumably people you know and trust. Also, neither would have to incur expenses of the sort that someone appointed by a court would typically have to incur, such as the cost of a bond to ensure faithful performance of his duties.

Don't bet the ranch that cause for concern about your daughter's welfare will miraculously vanish when she reaches legal adulthood. Suppose she suffers from Moonie tendencies, or occasional uncontrollable urges to rove airports wearing bed sheets and soliciting "donations" in exchange for leaflets charting the path to salvation. You're sure she'll come around eventually, but you aren't sure whether "eventually" will be sooner or later.

The solution might be to set up a *spendthrift trust*, which would direct the trustee to periodically release limited sums of money to your daughter, but would preclude her from selling, assigning, or losing by legal judgment any portion of the trust money that hadn't yet been released. Thus, she couldn't donate the trust principal to her cult leader, nor could she lose it to some creditor, such as the Rolls-Royce dealer from whom she picked up a set of wheels to carry her guru around between sermons on materialism.

An alternative means of achieving the same goal would be to set up a *discretionary trust*, giving the trustee sole authority over how and when to release the trust money. He could release it immediately, or he could hold it indefinitely. He could condition its release on your daughter's joining the Junior League or some other, more socially acceptable cult.

Just as any trust can be revocable or irrevocable, it can also be *inter vivos*—set up while you're alive—or *testamentary*—set up when you're not alive, through your will. The latter is fine, especially if you don't like the idea of cashing in even one chip until your last card has been played. But the former offers at least two advantages:

1. *Confidentiality.* Unlike a testamentary trust, which as a part of your will becomes a matter of public record during probate, an *inter vivos* trust can remain a complete secret from everyone (except its trustee) forever.

Suppose you want to leave certain of your cousins more money than others, but you don't want the latter group to know they're getting shortchanged. Put half of your stock portfolio, say, in an *inter vivos* trust, with the income to go to you for your life and the principal to go to the favored cousins upon your death. The disfavored group will never see the trust agreement and hence never know exactly what became of the bulk of your wealth.

Another option would be to set up an *inter vivos* trust with only nominal funding and then include a "pour-over" clause in your will, channeling, say, half the value of your estate into the trust. People reading your will would be able to see that a portion of your wealth was going somewhere other than to them, but not having access to the trust agreement, they wouldn't know where.

2. *Income-tax savings.* While few people really need the level of confidentiality just mentioned, everybody wants to save on income tax—perhaps the *inter vivos* trust's primary function. To illustrate, if your income puts you in a high marginal tax bracket, and your young daughter doesn't play professional tennis, model postage stamp–size swimsuits for *Sports Illustrated*, or otherwise earn twenty times more than you do, you might want to transfer money to her in trust today, thereby rendering the income from that money taxable to her rather than to you—and hence taxable at *her* marginal and typically much lower tax rate.

Giving her the money outright, instead of in trust, would serve the same purpose, as well as remove it from your taxable estate. But that would also place the money in the hands of someone whose youthful judgment might induce her to spend it on alcohol, gambling, or fast cars—or else squander it.

In order to achieve the desired income-tax benefit, the *inter vivos* trust property must be genuinely out of your possession and control. This means the trust has to be irrevocable. It also means you can't retain a *reversionary interest* in the trust property, that is, you can't provide for the return of the property to yourself at any time.

The rules weren't always so stringent. Previous to the 1986 tax-law changes, you *could* retain a reversionary interest in the trust property and still receive the income-tax benefit. The popular *Clifford trust*, for example, was required by federal law to last only ten years and a day. During this period the income from the trust principal would go to, and be taxed to, your daughter, but thereafter the principal plus any accumulated capital gains would return to you. Today, new tax-avoidance devices will have to be found.

TRUSTS AND CHARITABLE GIVING

Are your healthy mercenary drives sometimes interrupted, however momentarily and inexplicably, by impulses that your detractors would describe as "decent," even "philanthropic"?

Suppose you're thinking of leaving your IBM stock to Harvard. Good. The value of the stock would be deducted from your estate for purposes of the federal estate tax.

But a more profitable alternative might be to set up a *charitable remainder trust*. Under this arrangement, you give the stock to the trust today, thus receiving a charitable deduction for *this year*. (It seems fair to say that savings while you're alive are preferable to savings when you're dead.) You provide for the income on the stock to go to yourself for the rest of your life, thus avoiding the sacrifice of current income that an outright gift would entail, and provide for the stock itself to go to Harvard upon your death.

Not a bad deal.

Do Your Family a Favor

One last idea involving estate planning, sort of.

What would your estate consist of if you were to give up the ghost today? Suppose the answer is: a checking account, a savings account, a money-market fund, an IRA, several stock investments, some life insurance proceeds, one real estate limited partnership, a condo, and part ownership of a cabin outside of town. You can recite the entire list by memory.

Can anyone *else*? Would the FBI itself have trouble tracking it all down in your absence?

Do everybody a favor. Make a list of your assets, identifying not only all of the above, but also the names of your broker, your accountant, and anyone who owes you money. Also, list your liabilities, including—why not?—your major charge card accounts.

Ideally, you should give a copy of this list to your lawyer or a trusted friend. At the least, stick it in an obvious place in your file cabinet, such as in a folder marked "Finances."

No one will laugh at you for this. Your lawyer will think you're smart. The trusted friend will think you're a great guy— especially if he stands to get a portion of the assets that he'll now be able to locate when your time comes.

4. Housing

House Buying and Selling •
Landlord-Tenant Law •

I have heard of a man who had a mind to sell his house, and therefore carried a piece of brick in his pocket, which he showed as a pattern to encourage purchasers.   JONATHAN SWIFT
(1667–1745)

"She was only a real estate agent,
But she sure showed me a lot."
Country & western lyrics,

MARTIN J. YUDKOWITZ
(1954–   )

HOUSE BUYING AND SELLING

As painful as it is for a lawyer to admit this about anything, the key considerations in buying and selling a house aren't legal, but economic or commercial. Consider some of the basic tasks involved in buying a house:

• Finding one you like. For this the best person to consult is a real estate broker or agent.

• Obtaining suitable financing. For this your best bet is a mortgage broker or clearinghouse, especially since neither usually charges for its services.

• Determining how much you can afford. Often the real question here isn't how much you can afford, but how much a

78

lender *thinks* you can afford. Only you and it can determine the answer to that.

• Getting a house appraised and inspected. These are technical tasks, which only professional appraisers and inspectors are capable of performing.

All these tasks lie beyond the expertise of the average lawyer, even the average real estate lawyer. To be sure, a competent practitioner could probably *find out* most of what an expert on these subjects should be able to tell you; and no doubt he'd be willing to, for the right price. (For the right price he'd mow your lawn.) But assuming you're interested in getting the job done economically, as well as competently, hiring a lawyer could be a bad move.

Buying a House—The Sequence of Events

Make no mistake: A lawyer can provide valuable services to someone buying (or selling) a house. Before considering at what point in the sequence of events it might be wise to bring a lawyer into the picture, however, you need to understand what the sequence of events typically is.

Buying a house has much in common with getting married. Consider both processes from their earliest stages: A house hunt commences with casual, open-minded investigation of what's out there: you review classified ads in newspapers, cruise through attractive neighborhoods, maybe check out a few places mentioned by friends. This is not unlike playing the field socially: you review personal ads in newspapers, cruise through singles' bars, maybe get set up on a few blind dates.

Eventually you find a house you really like, not necessarily one you want to live in forever, but one that should do for a while. The parallels to finding someone who'll marry you are obvious.

At some point you make a bid on the house. Like your bid for your true love's hand in marriage, it falls somewhat short of what the other side had in mind. (Both bids result in sleepless nights as you await the reply, but only your bid on the house carries a deadline—typically several days or a week—for a response.) If either bid is accepted, you experience elation, followed by severe anxiety—have you made a terrible mistake? In both contexts you find comfort in the knowledge that nothing is yet carved in stone—or executed in ink.

Serious negotiations commence. Does the washer-dryer stay with the house? Termites (and next-door neighbors) have showed their ugly faces—who's going to pay to get rid of them? The *closing costs* will come to well over $5,000—what's an appropriate allocation? (Note that the broker's fee is traditionally paid by the seller, and the cost of the "title search," discussed below, is traditionally paid by the buyer. Items like fuel oil, property tax, and school tax are usually prorated on the basis of when the closing takes place.)

These postacceptance negotiations in the housing context are analogous to the postacceptance negotiations in the marriage context. Who's going to pay for the wedding? Will either or both of you change your names? Will you have kids, and will you care if some of them turn out to be of another race?

The next step is producing a contract of sale. Responsibility for coming up with at least a first draft—which often involves little more than filling in the blanks on a standard form—generally falls to the seller.

You and the seller sign the contract of sale as soon as it's ready. You don't await the final stage of the process—the "settlement," or "closing"—which may be several months away. Signing the contract of sale, like buying your fiancée a diamond ring and arranging a meeting of the prospective parents-in-law, means you're committed. Stuck. No easy exit.

Does execution of the contract of sale mean the deal is 100 percent certain? Hardly, although neither you nor the seller can now walk away from it on a whim. Just as the wedding is contingent upon satisfactory blood tests, the house deal is contingent upon, among other things, your ability to qualify for a loan, the seller's ability to produce clear title to the house, and the results of your expert's inspection of the house.

Immediately upon signing the contract of sale is when you submit your formal application for a loan. (Most banks won't even accept a loan application unaccompanied by a signed contract.) Because obtaining loan approval from a bank can easily take six weeks, you need to be ready to spring into action when the time comes. Start your search for a loan at the same time you start your search for a house—even earlier, to give you an idea of how much money you'll have to spend.

Similarly, immediately upon signing the contract of sale—better yet, even earlier—is when you should hire a professional inspector to check for subtle but significant flaws in the house—the absence of a roof, for example. (You're likely to notice the absence of a floor yourself.) A ballpark figure for such an inspection is $200. Anyone can advertise himself as a house inspector, so require references, and check for professional affiliations, such as the American Society of Home Inspectors.

Now the grand, if somewhat gratuitous, finale: the closing. Like a wedding, this event isn't *wholly* devoid of legal significance, but neither is it half as important as all the fuss surrounding it suggests.

For the closing, everyone gathers in one room—you, the seller, the lender, your lawyers (if you have such), and a representative from the title company. You introduce yourselves and then, if no one knows any card tricks or plays a musical instrument, commence signing and exchanging documents. Orchestrating the affair is a *closing agent*, who may be a lawyer, broker, representative from the title company—it varies from place to place.

The center ring events are as follows:

• You sign the promissory note ("I, Horton Tuttle, promise to pay back the bank's loan, plus interest"), mortgage agreement, and related papers—possibly several copies of each, except you should be careful to sign only *one* promissory note—and hand them to the lender.

• The lender hands you a check for the amount of the loan, possibly minus various fees and expenses. (Take along a number of blank checks, in case the lender requires you to pay each of these fees and expenses separately. And make sure you have at least $2,000 in your checking account.)

• The seller signs the deed to the house and hands it to you.

• You hand the deed to the title company for recording at the appropriate city or county office.

• You endorse the lender's check over to the seller.

*   *   *

At the conclusion, you have the property, the seller has the money, and the lender has your life.

Note that a closing typically involves a number of other documents, maybe as many as fifteen. Don't let this scare you, as it does many people at their first closing. You pick up an unfamiliar document and say, "What's this?" A stranger wearing cheap cologne says, "Don't worry about it. Just sign it." This makes you uncomfortable, life having taught you that when a stranger says not to worry about something, that's a good time to start worrying about it. Reflexively your hand creeps back to confirm the presence of your wallet.

Your instincts are sound. Feel free to ask about anything you don't understand. The stranger may be right—the document you're looking at probably isn't worth worrying about—but ignore him. You don't have to live with him, the way you do with your house and your mortgage.

Be aware that closing practices vary greatly from state to state, and even within states. Sometimes the entire process is handled by mail, through an *escrow agent,* who acts as a sort of clearinghouse, receiving and distributing money and documents in accordance with the contract of sale.

The Role of Lawyers

At what point in the above-described scenario might it be wise for you to bring a lawyer into the picture? You'll get as many different answers to this question as the number of people you ask—unless the people you ask are real estate brokers, who'll unanimously contend that you needn't bring a lawyer into the picture at all, since brokers selflessly look after the interests of everyone—the buyer, the buyer's dog, the seller, the seller's parakeet, and everyone the buyer and seller have ever met or heard of.

This contention is something you could spread on your lawn to make grass grow. As discussed below, brokers work for themselves.

There are three basic points in the course of buying a house at which it might be a good idea to bring in a lawyer. First (working backward), you might bring one in at the very end, to accompany you to the closing. His role there would be to make sure you sign only what you're supposed to sign, get everything you're supposed to get, and, in general, walk out with your pockets unpicked.

Second, you might bring in a lawyer slightly earlier, possibly just a day or two earlier, to review all the papers in advance of the closing. Having done that, he could then attend the closing or not, depending on whether he thinks it's necessary and whether you're willing to pay the price for his time.

Third, you might bring in a lawyer right after your bid is accepted, when negotiations on the contract of sale are about to commence. His role at this stage would be to negotiate on your behalf, or at least review the course of your own negotiations. If you want him involved to the maximum possible extent, he could also negotiate with the lender regarding the terms of your loan. Then, as described above, he could review all the papers before the closing, attend the closing to make sure everything goes as it should, and, finally, stop by your new house to polish the floors and clean the windows before you move in.

As for the benefit of having a lawyer involved at all, that depends. Are you legally and financially sophisticated? Can you trust the other parties? Is this your first closing? How much money is at stake?

Regarding this last point, recall the first of White's Irregular Rules:

> Where there's a lot of money at stake,
> hire a lawyer.

"In what house purchase," you ask, "is there *not* a lot of money at stake?" Good point. Whether the sale price is $60,000 or five times that, no doubt it will feel like a lot to whoever is paying it.

The bottom line? One has to conclude that so much is at stake in buying any house that getting a lawyer involved, at least to some extent, is a good idea. You can hire a competent lawyer to review your papers just before the closing—the second alternative described above—for perhaps $300. (Lawyers' rates in this area vary a good bit. Shop around.)

How about earlier—do you need a lawyer to negotiate the contract of sale? In some circumstances, absolutely. If there's a lawyer on the other side, for example, you should get one, too, to make it a fair fight. Never negotiate one-on-one with someone who has substantially more technical knowledge and negotiating experience than you have. The answer is the same if the deal is sufficiently unusual that it's not possible to use standard forms, so that lots of original drafting is required.

What if the seller hasn't hired a lawyer, and form documents are sufficient to do the deal—*then* do you need a lawyer to handle the negotiations on the contract of sale? Again, it depends. Can you be as tough a negotiator as you'd want your lawyer to be? Are you willing to put in the time necessary to master all the contractual mumbo-jumbo? Does the seller strike you as reasonable and scrupulous? (Keep in mind, if this is your first real estate transaction, that it has to be at least the seller's second.)

Possibly you'll be spared having to decide what tasks it's worthwhile to pay your lawyer to perform. Many lawyers, rather than charging an hourly rate for their services, charge a flat fee—ranging from $300 to over $1,000—for handling a house purchase from beginning to end. No doubt these lawyers would like to earn their fees with as little work as possible, but most will perform any reasonable service you request. (Confirm this before hiring anyone.)

As for the closing itself, for approximately $300 you can hire a lawyer simply to accompany you to it, doing nothing beforehand and nothing afterward. There's no consensus on whether it's important to have a lawyer present at the closing. Some people experienced in the real estate area say it is; some say it isn't.

If a closing consisted of no more than signing and exchanging papers, your lawyer's role would consist of no more than handing you a pen whenever your turn came to sign something. Typically, though, much of the paperwork that should have been completed long before the closing isn't completed until the closing itself. Hence, there's room for error up to the last minute—in allocating charges, in *computing* charges, in tying up loose ends generally. This is why it's good to have a lawyer present.

What Kind of Lawyer?

Suppose you've decided you want a lawyer to represent you at some stage of buying or selling a house. Fine. But unless you're looking at a house in the half-million-dollar range, avoid the big firms. You'll be paying exorbitant rates for expertise you don't need and can't use. House buying and selling isn't among the most intellectually demanding areas of the law. The smarter your lawyer, the better off you are, but you should place less emphasis on that sort of credential and more on aggressiveness and experience in the area.

A lawyer's experience should be easy enough to find out about—ask. Specifically, ask how many real estate transactions he has worked on in the past year. The number needn't be in the triple figures, but it shouldn't be a single figure, either. Also, request references. As for his aggressiveness, you'll have to go with your instincts, but references might be helpful there, too.

If the house you're looking at is comparatively inexpensive—under $80,000, say—and the deal has no unusual wrinkles, you might be fine with a lawyer from one of the legal clinics. Otherwise, try to find someone at a small firm—fewer than ten lawyers, say—or even a solo practitioner. Generalizations are risky, but that's as good a way as any to maximize your chances of finding a lawyer with both reasonable rates and a respectable, if not dazzling, level of competence.

Nine Critical Tips

Set forth below are nine tips or suggestions, knowledge of which could save you more than a little money, and more than a few headaches. I offer these partly to demonstrate from another angle the commercial, as opposed to legal, nature of the key considerations in buying a house. Mainly, though, I just wanted you to know them.

1. *Where brokers interests lie (and why brokers lie)*. Always keep in mind that the nice broker who shows you a house and unqualifiedly recommends it to you doesn't work for you. He doesn't care if you overpay. Indeed, since the size of his commission

(usually 6 percent) reflects the size of the purchase price, he *wants* you to overpay.

Does this mean he works for the seller? Sort of—the seller pays his commission (and then passes the cost on to you). But unlike someone working for a flat fee or an hourly rate, a broker gets no money unless the deal goes through. Hence, it's in his financial interest to *make* the deal go through. Brokers will give you a thousand reasons why this isn't so, asserting without blushing that, darn it, their own bank accounts couldn't be farther from their minds. Apparently they think P. T. ("There's a sucker born every minute") Barnum was conservative in his estimates.

2. *Exclusive listings.* If you're selling your house and willing to list it exclusively with a given broker (the advantage of which is that the broker may give you a break on his commission), don't commit yourself to this arrangement indefinitely. You want to be able, if the broker doesn't come up with a buyer in a month or two, to switch to *non*exclusive listings with several brokers. Also, your exclusive listing arrangement should provide, with respect to people who've already looked at the house, that no broker's commission will be paid if one of these people buys.

3. *The negotiability of broker's commissions.* A broker's commission is as negotiable as anything else—not only its size, but also who pays it. If you and the party on the other side of a house deal are only a few thousand dollars apart, getting the broker to reduce his commission by a percentage point or two could make all the difference.

4. *Coordinating the sale of your old house and the purchase of your new.* Try to condition the sale of your old house on your ability to locate a new one; you don't want to find yourself with nowhere to sleep for several months. Similarly, don't commit to buying a new house until your old one is sold; you don't want to be under pressure to sell your old one quickly and perhaps too cheaply, and you certainly don't want to find yourself with two lawns to mow each weekend.

5. *The size of the down payment.* If you're buying a house, it might be in your interest to make a large enough down payment—from 20 to 30 percent, depending on where you live—

to avoid having to buy mortgage insurance, which typically costs around half a percentage point, or $500 on a $100,000 house. On the other hand, if mortgage insurance isn't required (or, perhaps, even if it is), it might make economic sense for you to put down the smallest amount possible in order to maximize your *leverage*, that is, to allow you the biggest possible investment with the smallest possible commitment of your own funds. The less you put into the house, the more you have available to invest else- where. (Note that almost never will you be allowed to put down less than 5 percent, and usually 10 or 20 percent will be required.)

6. *Joint responsibility for a mortgage.* If you and a friend take out a mortgage together, each of you will be responsible for the entire amount, not just half.

7. *Binder agreements.* Whether you're the prospective buyer or seller of a house, resist signing a *binder agreement* (not to be confused with an insurance binder), which a broker may try to force on you. Often described as an "agreement to agree," this is a document by which, in some states, a buyer and seller com- mit themselves to a specific price, with the idea of negotiating from there on all remaining issues.

A broker who says signing a binder agreement doesn't com- mit you to anything is uninformed or lying. If that were true, why would he want you to sign the thing? One possible con- sequence of signing a binder agreement is that even if the deal falls through, the broker may be entitled to his commission.

8. *Altering standard form contracts.* Everything in a real estate deal is negotiable. The fact that the standard form contract sup- plied by somebody's lawyer or broker includes certain terms already in print doesn't mean you can't change them or strike them out. Neither does the fact that the form includes only a limited number of blank spaces mean you can't add new pro- visions on another piece of paper.

9. *Discovering closing costs.* If you're the prospective buyer of a house, be aware of the myriad hidden closing costs that will have a tendency to accrue to you upon the signing of the final papers. Under the federal Real Estate Settlement Procedures Act (RESPA), you're entitled to receive at least one day in advance of the closing a "Settlement Statement" (or HUD-1 form) listing

those closing costs that are associated with the loan. Get and review this document as soon as possible. Also, insist that the seller and closing agent identify in advance any costs they're expecting you to pay. The longer you wait, the harder it becomes to allocate these costs to someone else.

A Word on Title Insurance

As a discriminating person, you don't want just any kind of title to your new house. You want *clear* title, or *good and marketable* title, or *nondefective* title, which is to say you want the place with no claims against it that will adversely affect your interest.

How do you find out about such claims? Someone has to perform a *title search*, which involves going to the city or county clerk's office and checking the real estate records going back to Christopher Columbus. If the title search reveals certain types of claims or encumbrances, and the seller can't or won't promptly remove them, you're presumably entitled under the contract of sale to back out of the deal, or perhaps to require a reduction in price.

Be aware that title searches invariably reveal minor encumbrances that a seller can't be expected to do anything about. If nothing else, there will be *utility easements*, that is, legal rights-of-way for telephone and electric lines and for the people who install and maintain them. Sidewalk and sewer easements are also common. These shouldn't bother you, but anything else warrants concern.

Suppose one neighbor possesses a legal right to use a path across your land to reach some portion of his land. "Well, I'm not worried about his occasionally strolling across my turf," you say. But what if his son, home from college, takes to driving his unmuffled motorcycle along that path every night after midnight? You're not being unreasonable in standing firm on this type of thing.

Never buy real estate without having someone perform a title search. (This "someone" won't be you. The process is complicated and arcane, even by the standards of the law. Whoever performs it—possibly but not necessarily a lawyer—usually has special training.) It can cost anywhere from $75 to $800.

If the title search turns up no major encumbrances, is that it? Can you proceed to the closing without concern for the state of the title?

You can. But what if the person who performed the search screwed up? What if he simply overlooked something?

The way you protect against this is by purchasing title insurance. Since the lender will almost definitely require you to buy a title insurance policy naming *it* as the beneficiary, the question is, should you buy *another* title insurance policy for yourself?

I recommend taking the cautious route here, unless your lawyer can give you good reasons why caution isn't necessary. The chances of trouble are small, but the stakes are gigantic, and you'll probably sleep better knowing you're protected.

Title insurance typically costs $4.00 or $5.00 per $1,000 of the purchase price of the house—or about $500 for a $100,000 house. This is in addition to the cost of the search itself.

In some states an alternative to buying standard title insurance is paying a lawyer to "certify" the validity of the title, based on his own search or that of someone else. This way, if the title ever proves defective, you can go after the lawyer for negligence. If you choose this option, there's something to be said for using a young practitioner, to maximize the chances that he'll be around for as long as you own the house.

LANDLORD-TENANT LAW

If you are going to have a landlord you had better have a rich land-lord . . . you will find that every man is the worse for being poor.
                                                        GEORGE BERNARD SHAW
                                                              (1856–1950)

I lived in an efficiency once. The sink flushed.   MARTIN J. YUDKOWITZ
                                                              (1954–   )

You'd think a signed lease would govern the relations between a given landlord and tenant. If there is one, it probably purports to do so.

But statutory and judge-made law override private contracts, which is what leases are. To illustrate, your state may have a statute which provides that regardless of the terms of your lease, your landlord can't terminate your monthly tenancy on less than thirty days' notice. Hence, in trying to figure out where you stand vis-à-vis your landlord or tenant, you have to look at both statutory and judge-made law, on the one hand, and private or contractual law (the lease), on the other.

How do you determine statutory and judge-made law? The only alternative to researching it yourself—a lot easier said than done—is to consult a lawyer—a lot *cheaper* said than done.

Regarding the expense of consulting a lawyer, however, note two points. First, merely consulting a lawyer about your rights is entirely different from retaining one to wage full-scale war for you in court. If all you're after is information—you want to know, for example, if you may legally repair your leaky faucet and then deduct the cost from your rent—you should be able to get the answer from an experienced real estate lawyer in fifteen minutes. The cost shouldn't exceed thirty dollars.

Second, if the problem in question is common to a number of units in the same apartment building—a broken central-heating unit, for example—perhaps you could get the other tenants to go in with you on the cost of a lawyer.

If your co-tenants aren't interested, or you have no co-tenants, don't despair just because you can't afford a lawyer on your own. Call or stop by a public legal aid bureau, or check with the legal aid bureau at a nearby law school. (Many schools have such programs, and typically they take on a number of landlord-tenant cases.) Unless you're really poor, none of these programs is likely to take you on as an actual client, but you can probably beg or cajole the desired information out of someone.

Finally, try calling the landlord-tenant court. Whoever you get there may be able to steer you to some organization that's geared to assisting people in your situation. Be resourceful; the information is out there.

*   *   *

So diverse and unsettled are the various landlord-tenant laws around the country—on many issues the states are split right down the middle—that comparatively few generalizations are possible. Rather than attempting a comprehensive survey of the laws of all the states, the following discussion seeks to give you an idea, through specific examples, of the kinds of laws that have been enacted in this area, as well as practices that could get you into trouble—or keep you out of it.

1. *Repair and deduct.* As a tenant, you may be permitted, despite the terms of your lease, to repair defective conditions in your apartment and then deduct the cost of the repairs from your rent. Usually you can do this only for conditions that are seriously defective—a stained rug isn't enough; it was your cat, anyway—and usually you can deduct no more than one month's rent.

2. *Housing codes.* Countless communities around the country have housing codes. The typical housing code requires landlords to maintain heat and hot water, keep their premises safe and sanitary, and generally be decent landlords. Often the code establishes some local authority to whom tenants can complain about code violations, and in most states landlords aren't permitted to evict or otherwise retaliate against tenants who complain. If your landlord ever tries to evict you for nonpayment of rent, you may have a defense based on his failure to correct a housing code violation—*if* (a) you've had a housing inspector come by to confirm the existence of the violation, and (b) your landlord was aware of the existence of the violation. The moral: *Make* your landlord aware of it.

3. *Warranty of habitability.* The laws of many states say every residential lease carries an implied *warranty of habitability.* If your landlord breaches this warranty—by failing to provide heat or hot water, for example—you may be legally entitled to reduce your rent to the fair market value of the premises. (Mentioning this warranty in a letter to your landlord might be a good idea, just to show him he's dealing with a savvy tenant.)

4. *Last-minute payment of overdue rent.* If your landlord has obtained a court order directing the police to evict you for nonpayment of rent, it may be that you're legally entitled to avoid this catastrophe at the last minute by offering the amount due—

in cash (or possibly a certified check)—to the officers who've come to throw you and your furniture out on the street. You should do anything possible to avoid such eviction, because furniture on the street has a remarkable tendency to get rained on or take up residence in someone else's house.

5. *Rent-acceleration clauses.* Suppose you've missed one rental payment, and a clause in your yearly lease provides that upon any such default your obligations under the lease are accelerated, rendering you liable *now* for all the rent due under the lease for the rest of the year. In this situation, before turning over your life's savings to your landlord (or skipping town), check the law. The courts in many states view such clauses as "unconscionable" and refuse to enforce them.

6. *Waiver.* A tenant who observes some defect in his apartment but fails to complain about it for a prolonged period may be held to have "waived," or given up, his right to require the landlord to repair it. Similarly, a landlord who accepts rent from a tenant before acting on a prior breach of the lease may be held to have waived his right to terminate the lease. The moral: Whether you're a landlord or tenant, assert your rights quickly, if you're going to assert them at all.

7. *Notice of termination.* If yours is a *periodic tenancy*—month-to-month, say—generally your landlord may neither evict you nor raise your rent without giving you notice equal to at least one rental period—in this instance, one month. For year-to-year tenancies, many communities have laws or regulations establishing specific notice periods, such as three months.

8. *Apartment security.* Generally a landlord is required to take reasonable measures to keep his properties safe and secure. This means providing locks on apartment doors, bars on the windows of ground-floor units, and anything else a jury might consider appropriate in light of all the circumstances. It also means performing a background check on any employee who'll have access to tenant premises. If the janitor that you (the landlord) hire turns out to be a thrice-convicted child molester, and he assaults someone, and you never bothered to check his references, you're in big trouble.

9. *Rent control.* Rent-control laws now exist in California, Connecticut, Massachusetts, New York, New Jersey, and Wash-

ington, D.C. Basically these laws limit how much certain land-lords—those who own at least four rental units, for example—can raise their rents—7 percent, for example—each year. (Land-lords who make "capital investments" in their properties or who can show special "hardship" might be allowed to exceed the limits.)

As a landlord, be aware that if you cheat on the rent-control laws, your tenants may be able to sue you for overcharges, some-times multiplied by three. Also, overcharges may give them a defense if you should sue to evict them for nonpayment of rent. As a tenant, be aware of whether and how these laws apply to you. Take the time to calculate whether they've been complied with when your landlord raises raises your rent.

10. *Landlords' permits and certificates.* Many states require a landlord to go on a virtual scavenger hunt for stamps, seals, permits, certificates, verifications, and Mickey Mantle baseball cards before going into business. Depending on the state, a landlord's failure to obtain all the required items might result in a fine or even nullification of all rent increases imposed over a number of years. If you're about to become a landlord, hire a lawyer to identify absolutely every requirement under the law.

11. *Landlords' self-help.* If you're a landlord with a tenant overdue on his rent, your options aren't necessarily limited to suing for eviction. In some states you're permitted to walk in and take over the delinquent tenant's premises—*if* you can do so peaceably. Definitely consult a lawyer before resorting to any such measure; you don't want to find yourself in jail for the crime of breaking and entering.

12. *Subleases.* As a tenant, you may be legally permitted to sublet your apartment, even if your lease says you can't. Be aware that if you do sublet it, in accordance with the lease or otherwise, you'll probably remain personally responsible for the rent. So protect yourself: Require your subtenant to send his rental payments to you, for example, so you can forward them to the landlord personally. One way or another, make sure the payments are getting where they're supposed to be getting, and getting there on time.

13. *Security deposits.* Before signing a lease that requires a

security deposit, make sure the lease calls it a *security* deposit and clearly provides for its return when the lease expires. Otherwise, the landlord may attempt to treat it as a sort of signing bonus and keep it. Landlords and tenants alike should note that in some states security deposits *have* to be placed in interest-bearing accounts.

14. *Condominium conversion.* If you receive a notice saying your apartment building is "going condo," don't go berserk, wailing that you can't afford to buy the place but have nowhere else to go. It may be that you have a legal right to stick around as a renter indefinitely. Your first step should be to find out the law. Then go berserk.

15. *Notice.* As a tenant, you should give your landlord advance notice of virtually anything you plan to do that's out of the ordinary—withholding rent, terminating your lease, whatever. Why? In lots of circumstances notice is legally required, and that's that. Also, if you're terminating your lease prematurely, you want to maximize your landlord's chances of finding a new tenant—and thereby minimize your potential liability. Finally, if you should find yourself confronting your landlord in front of a judge, you want to be able to show that you've acted fairly and reasonably at all times. (This suggestion regarding notice applies equally if you're a landlord, and for the same reasons.)

16. *Landlord-tenant courts.* In most sizable communities there exists a landlord-tenant court, or housing court, or some such thing. In 1984, New York's landlord-tenant court received 361,356 petitions. Clearly, a lot of people consider it worthwhile.

Landlord-tenant courts are notorious for making you sit around all day waiting for your case to be called. Also, because they operate under severe time pressures, they dispense what could be called a rough form of justice. Compared to most courts, however, they're cheap and quick. And they're usually informal enough that you have a decent chance of prevailing in one without a lawyer. Before resorting to brute force to avenge the offenses of your landlord or tenant, give the landlord-tenant court a chance.

5. Setting Up a Business

Did you ever expect a corporation to have a conscience, when it has no soul to be damned, and no body to be kicked?
                                    EDWARD, FIRST BARON THURLOW
                                                          (1731–1806)

Corporation, n. An ingenious device for obtaining individual profit without individual responsibility.   **AMBROSE BIERCE**
                                                          (1842–1914)

A partnership, like a marriage, involves constant bickering as to who will be on top.   **MARTIN J. YUDKOWITZ**
                                                          (1954–   )

Do you ever get fed up with working for somebody else? Do you ever spend half the day (the *work*day) fantasizing about telling your boss he's a gravy-sucking pig and then going into business for yourself? Suppose one day, weary of fantasies, you decide to act on your impulses.

Now you're an entrepreneur. Right away you have several critical choices to make, some obvious, some not so obvious.

First, you have to choose between the two basic options for conducting any business in the world: alone, or with others. (That's one of the obvious ones.) Do you need someone else to supply a certain kind of expertise? Could you bear working shoulder to shoulder every day with the one person you know who has that expertise—your brother-in-law Marvin, who always slaps you too hard on the back and calls you "Amigo"?

If you've decided to work alone, you now have to choose between two more options: whether to conduct your business as (1) a corporation, or (2) a sole proprietorship, that is, an individual—yourself. If, on the other hand, you've decided to work with others, you again have to choose between two more options: whether to conduct your business as (1) a corporation, or (2) a partnership.

In either situation, then, the basic question is: To incorporate or not to incorporate?

You can't avoid this question. If you don't answer it for yourself, the law will answer it for you. Specifically, if you decide to work alone and don't bother to incorporate, the law will *deem* you to be acting as a sole proprietor. Similarly, if you decide to work with others and don't bother to incorporate, the law will *deem* you and the others to be acting as partners. (This last point assumes the others are co-owners of the business—rather than, on the one hand, salaried employees, or, on the other hand, friendly folks who just stopped by to help out.)

As this suggests, a corporation, like a baby, doesn't come into existence on its own. You have to take deliberate, well-established steps to create one.

The first part of this chapter discusses the special characteristics of corporations. The significance of these characteristics, particularly as they differ from those of sole proprietorships and partnerships, is discussed in the second and third parts, respectively. The fourth part discusses the nuts and bolts of setting up and operating each of these three types of business entities. Finally, the fifth part discusses three hybrid entities—the *S Corporation*, the *statutory close corporation*, and the *limited partnership*—whose characteristics place them somewhere between corporations and partnerships.

CORPORATIONS

Lawyers say a corporation is a "legal fiction." Lawyers say lots of things, but this one is valid. You can't see, touch, or hang a corporation. It exists only in theory, by permission of each state. This permission is signified by a *certificate of incorporation*, a piece of paper signed and stamped by some bureaucrat in the office of the local secretary of state.

The structure of a corporation generally depends on its size. A giant corporation resembles a pyramid. At its base are its comparatively numerous owners, the stockholders. At its peak are its officers, usually consisting of at least a president, vice-president, secretary, and treasurer. In between are its directors. Power theoretically flows from the bottom up: The stockholders elect the directors; the directors select, set company policy for, and look over the shoulders of the officers; and the officers make things happen. Although the power to manage the day-to-day operations of the business lies with the president, the really big cheese is the chairman of the board of directors.

This structure differs, to say the least, from that of a one-stockholder corporation. This one stockholder may constitute the entire "board" of directors of the corporation and wear the hat of every officer as well. Even if he should allow someone else to serve as an officer or director, his ownership of all of the company's stock ensures his complete control.

Often there's little tangible evidence that a business is operating *as a corporation*. The indicators may consist of no more than a certificate of incorporation, which virtually no one sees; shares of stock, which few people other than the stockholders see; and the word *Incorporated* or *Corporation* (more commonly, *Inc.* or *Corp.*) on the company letterhead, business cards, and advertising materials, which ideally *everyone* sees.

Legally, a corporation is semihuman: It has its own name, it has its own bank account, it can sign contracts (through its agents), it can sue and be sued, it can (and will) be taxed—all as if it were a flesh-and-blood creature with a birth certificate, Social Security number, and Visa card.

CORPORATIONS VERSUS SOLE PROPRIETORSHIPS

Suppose you're a millionaire. You don't need to work for a living. Your impression of work, based on watching the rest of us do it, is that it's *work*; if it weren't, they'd call it something else.

The closest thing to work you really enjoy is cooking, and you happen to be good at it. When you throw a party, people rave about your cakes, pastries, and white chocolate mousse. Hence the idea of setting up a baking and catering business. Your veal cutlets with wine sauce—just one of "Larry Durkin's Secret Sauces"—would make Stouffer's Salisbury steak look like Alpo dog food (and Alpo look like the mystery meat at Arby's).

Your normal instinct would be to plunge headlong into this project. All you'd need to do, as you see it, is buy several large ovens, hire three or four teenagers to perform the manual labor (at subminimum wages), and peddle what you produce to your wealthy friends for their parties.

In a rare display of caution, you ask the family lawyer if he has any advice. He says, in no uncertain terms, that you should incorporate. Why?

Often, especially with small businesses, there's no clear answer as to the best mode in which to operate—which leads us to the sixth of White's Irregular Rules, the first for this chapter:

> When in doubt, don't incorporate.

But consider five distinguishing features of corporations that, considered together, favor incorporating rather than operating as a sole proprietorship in your particular case. (In "Partnerships," below, these five features, plus a sixth, are used to compare corporations to partnerships.)

Limited Liability

What are the chances that someone would bother suing, or could come up with plausible grounds for suing, a caterer? In the usual case, not much. Conceivably a customer would go so far as to withhold payment if you served spoiled melon balls or meat that showed bruises from where the jockey had been hitting it, but that's about it.

Your catering case isn't the usual catering case, however. You're filthy rich, and people sniff out excuses for suing the filthy rich the way bloodhounds sniff out felons. If a sliver of broken glass makes its way into one of your apple tarts, or a bottle cap winds up in one of your carrot cakes, you may face a million-dollar lawsuit for broken dentures and alleged pain, suffering, humiliation, psychiatric care, and remedial trips to the Bahamas.

"That's ridiculous," you say.

"Of course it is," your lawyer replies. "But you have too much to lose. It's just not worth the risk."

If you operate your business as a sole proprietorship, "Larry Durkin Enterprises," someone claiming to have been injured by one of your desserts can go after not only your business assets but also your *personal* assets: your jewelry, your Mercedes, your stock portfolio, possibly even family assets in which you hold an interest.

If, on the other hand, you operate your business as a corporation, "Larry Durkin, *Inc.*," the same claimant can go after only the *corporation's* assets: its ovens, its utensils, its leftover cooking ingredients, the cute aprons you make those teenagers wear. (Another asset any plaintiff can and undoubtedly will go after is the corporation's liability insurance, which you'd better stock up on for just such contingencies, lest a judge decide the only fair thing to do is allow the plaintiff to go after you personally. More on "piercing the corporate veil" below.)

Tax Considerations

In the eyes of the Internal Revenue Service, your sole proprietorship, Larry Durkin Enterprises, has no independent existence. It is synonymous with you, and profits and losses from its activities are treated as accruing to you personally. In contrast, your corporation, Larry Durkin, Inc., does have independent existence for tax purposes, and profits and losses from its activities are treated as accruing not to you, but to it. In this regard, a corporation approximates a separate human being, with one key difference: *Corporations and human beings are taxed at different rates.*

Under the Tax Reform Act of 1986, a human being's maximum *marginal* income-tax rate, that is, the rate at which a human being's *last* dollar is taxed, is 28 percent. Three qualifications: (1) This 28 percent rate doesn't commence until 1988. For one year, 1987, the maximum marginal rate is 38.5 percent. (2) This 28 percent rate doesn't kick in until your income reaches a certain level. Below that level, the rate is 15 percent. (3) Because Congress wanted only lower-income people to get the benefit of the 15 percent rate, it imposed an additional, or *recapture,* tax of 5 percent on income within a certain high range. Within this range, the actual marginal rate is 33 percent.

Now, because any profits generated by Larry Durkin Enterprises are treated as accruing to you in your capacity as a human being, those profits are taxed at identical, human-being rates.

The maximum marginal income-tax rate applicable to a corporation is higher: 34 percent (a 5 percent recapture tax similar to that described above raises the marginal rate to 39 percent within a certain high range). Thus, at the maximum marginal levels, you'd presumably prefer to make money as Larry Durkin Enterprises rather than as Larry Durkin, Inc.

Don't jump to conclusions, however. Once upon a time the difference between the maximum corporate and individual rates was 24 percent—an amount that could well be determinative. (The higher rate, 70 percent, applied to individuals, and the lower rate, 46 percent, applied to corporations—the reverse of the situation today.) But the difference under the new law—6 percent—just isn't all that much.

Moreover, that fact that you may have incorporated your business doesn't necessarily mean its earnings will be taxed at corporate rates. If you should have your corporation distribute its earnings to you (in the form of dividends or salary), those earnings would be taxed at *your* rates, namely, the rates applicable to individuals, rather than the rates applicable to corporations.

Are tax considerations worth thinking about here at all? Tax considerations are *always* worth thinking about, if for no other reason than that Congress tinkers in this area constantly, and you need to know if it has done anything lately that affects you. Besides, there are two additional factors you should take into account.

First, the option of having your corporation distribute its earnings to you might prove to be of minimal significance, because you might choose not to exercise that option, instead you would let the corporation sit on its earnings indefinitely. Why would you ever do this?

Perhaps your long-range goal is to let the company grow through retention of earnings, so you can leave it in an enhanced form to your children. Or perhaps you want to postpone receiving any of its earnings until a year in which you incur offsetting personal losses—which raises the significant point that corporate losses, unlike corporate gains, can't be passed on to you for your personal benefit. (Contrast this with the rule for partnerships, discussed below.)

Note that the IRS will tolerate accumulation of corporate earnings only up to a point. It thinks a corporation should either use its earnings or pay them out, and it will impose an *accumulated earnings tax* to penalize a corporation that hoards money beyond its "reasonable needs." What needs are "reasonable"? Under current IRS guidelines a corporation can accumulate up to $250,000 without fear of imposition of the accumulated earnings tax—a sum that may or may not be big enough to do you any good. Check with a tax lawyer or accountant if you think you might have cause for concern along these lines.

A second factor you should take into account is that incorporating allows a company to provide its employees with certain tax-free fringe benefits that you, Larry Durkin, could take advantage of in your capacity as a company employee (who also happens to be the company's sole stockholder). These benefits, which aren't available to the self-employed, include various retirement perks, some kinds of insurance, and other important but tedious things most people hate to deal with. The law respecting these matters is so complex that you shouldn't let them influence your decision on whether to incorporate without first consulting a lawyer.

I said above that the IRS thinks a corporation should either use its earnings or pay·them out. There are two basic forms in which a corporation can pay out its earnings: (1) dividends, or (2) salary. Either is better than neither, but is one better than the other for you, or for your corporation? This carries us to the critical matter of "double taxation" of corporate earnings.

Suppose Larry Durkin, Inc., is a big success in its first year, earning $250,000. The IRS will take a cut of this money (at the corporate rates discussed above) directly from the corporation. Suppose next that the corporation distributes the remains of its earnings to you personally in the form of dividends. The IRS will take a further cut of this money (at the individual rates discussed above) from you. This is *double taxation*: two separate hits on the same funds.

Consider the tax consequences if, alternatively, the corporation pays its earnings to you in the form of *salary*, for your work as president, sales manager, and all the other positions you hold. (The result would be the same if it paid you the money in the form of rent or interest.) To you there's no difference; whether you get the money as dividends or as salary, you're taxed on it at your individual rate, and the amount you owe Uncle Sam is the same.

From the corporation's standpoint, however, there's a huge difference. Any earnings it pays you in the form of salary can be deducted as an ordinary and necessary business expense, reducing its profits commensurately. If the corporation "zeroes out," that is, unloads *all* its earnings in the form of salary, it will have no profits to be taxed—and the problem of double taxation is licked. This doesn't mean the corporation itself will have more money left over than if it had distributed its earnings in the form of dividends, but—and this is the main point—it will have avoided the corporate tax altogether, thereby conserving money for *you*.

One caveat (a big one): The salaries corporations pay their employees have to be *reasonable*. The IRS doesn't like corporations to escape taxation on their profits by unloading huge sums of money on employees and calling these sums "salaries." There's flexibility here, but recall the fifth of White's Irregular Rules (in Chapter 3, "Taxes"):

Don't be a hog.

Keep your salary within shouting distance of the salaries of your peers in similar companies.

What's the bottom line on taxation as a factor in deciding whether to incorporate or do business as a sole proprietor? If you anticipate losses for the first year or two—the experience of most young businesses—you should probably act as a sole proprietor so you can take personal advantage of those losses, offsetting them against your gains from other sources. (Again, corporate *losses*, unlike corporate *gains*, can't be passed on for your personal benefit.)

If, on the other hand, you anticipate gains from your business early on, you need to calulate the probable extent of those gains and how they might affect your overall personal tax picture. This suggests making one of your first business expenditures the fee for consulting a good accountant.

Keep in mind that there's no now-or-never rule with respect to incorporating. This option, like Odysseus's Penelope, will wait around for you indefinitely.

Indefinite Duration

The humblest, most unpretentious corporation in existence can lay claim to potentially eternal life. More often than not, a company's *articles of incorporation* (its governing rules, discussed below) provide that it shall "survive in perpetuity." (Many states' corporation laws provide that a corporation's life shall be perpetual unless its articles of incorporation provide otherwise.)

Despite this supernatural longevity there are few reported cases of a corporation running amok, rampaging through the countryside and terrorizing livestock. A corporation can be dissolved at any time, in compliance with the laws of the state in which it was established. If you're worried, you can limit Larry Durkin, Inc.'s, life at the outset to fifty years, or one year—as long or short a period as you like. And you can expand or reduce this period at any time.

Such flexibility isn't enjoyed by sole proprietorships. Although Larry Durkin Enterprises, like Larry Durkin, Inc., can be dissolved at any time, it can't be prolonged indefinitely. When you go, it goes.

What happens to Larry Durkin, *Inc.*, when you, the only one who knows the secret recipes, give up the ghost? In all likelihood, your corporation will do the same, just as if it were a sole proprietorship. But because it's a corporation, it doesn't *have* to do this. When you die, someone—your daughter, say—will inherit your stock in Larry Durkin, Inc. And it's in this stock, rather than in you or any other human organism, that the life of the corporation resides.

The fact that a corporation's life and ownership inhere in and are represented by *stock*, capable of being passed from person to person like a relay baton in a race through time, ties in directly with the two remaining corporate features discussed below: transferability and access to capital through issuance of stock.

Transferability

Larry Durkin Enterprises, sole proprietorship, is itself incapable of being sold or otherwise transferred. Since its legal existence is inextricably bound up in you, a human being, the most you could sell or give anyone are its *assets*. In contrast, Larry Durkin, Inc., whose ownership inheres in its stock, is entirely capable of being sold or given away through transfer of that stock.

Transferring assets versus transferring stock—this apparently minor legal point has three practical ramifications that, if you ever find yourself selling or buying a business, you should understand:

1. *Convenience.* If you own 100 percent of the stock of Larry Durkin, Inc., all you have to do to transfer the entire business to someone (subject to restrictions in your lease, say, or other key contracts) is hand him the signed stock certificates. It's simple.

If you own 100 percent of the assets of Larry Durkin Enterprises, on the other hand, the transfer may be more challenging. Suppose the assets of Larry Durkin Enterprises consist of four kitchens, twenty-seven ovens, two warehouses, nine delivery vans, and a partridge in a pear tree. Transferring the entire business would require delivery of title to each separate item.

Although this comparative inconvenience shouldn't by itself govern your decision about how you'll set up your business, you might take it into account if other factors balance out.

2. *Access to contracts.* If you're operating your business as a corporation, you'll sign all its contracts not as an individual— "Larry Durkin"—but as an officer of the corporation:

> Larry Durkin, Inc.
> By: Larry Durkin, President

You should sign all corporate contracts in precisely this form, not only because it shows you're familiar with standard corporate practices, but also because doing otherwise could subject you to personal liability on the contract.

So what? Someone buying your *corporation* receives with it all existing contracts. The corporation being the party named in the contracts, the contracts go with it, not with you.

In contrast, someone buying your *sole proprietorship* receives no more than its physical assets. Since *you* are the party named in the contracts, the contracts go with you, not with the business.

If your long-range plan is to sell your business, you need to consider at some stage whether incorporating would enable you to lock up those critical contracts—your lease, say—without which the company might be impossible to unload. No one wants a giant oven sitting on blocks in his garage.

Note that even if the business you're selling is a corporation, you could still find yourself personally on the hook for its contracts. Landlords, suppliers, and others often require (wisely) some *individual* to *personally guarantee* the contracts of a small, comparatively untested corporation.

3. *Liabilities.* Suppose that just as you're about to acquire a company operated as a sole proprietorship, a woman files a $250,000 lawsuit, alleging that one of the company's delivery trucks gave her a pair of unsightly tire marks on her face. Do you back out of the deal?

Not at all. The woman can't be suing the company itself, because it has no legal existence of its own. She is, and must be, suing the *owner* of the business.

If the business were incorporated, on the other hand, you

might indeed want to back out. Corporations can be sued in their own names. When you buy one you get not only its contracts (as described above) and its assets, but also its *previously acquired liabilities*.

If you want to buy a given corporation despite such a lawsuit, you should consider buying just its *assets*. Businesspeople do this all the time, in effect mimicking the purchase of a sole proprietorship. Although this option entails giving up automatic access to the company's contracts, you may be able to arrange for the contracts to be assigned to you when you take over the company's assets.

Access to Capital Through Issuance of Stock

Suppose you're not fabulously wealthy. In fact, the current health craze having killed the market for your company's pastries, you're broke. You're trying to shift into yogurt, tofu, and lawn clippings, but the transition is proving expensive. You've mortgaged your house, broken into your son's piggy bank, and sold your dog for medical research. Still, you're short about $20,000 of what it would cost to restock your plant with the proper machinery.

If you're a sole proprietor, you have two options for coming up with the money: hope to find it on the street, or borrow it.

If you're the owner of a corporation, you have both of these options, plus a third: sell shares of the corporation's stock.

As a practical matter, the fact that your corporation has stock to sell doesn't mean anyone will buy it. Two equivalent businesses, one organized as a sole proprietorship and the other as a corporation, will likely confront similar problems in acquiring outside cash.

Still, these two basic approaches to raising capital—selling stock versus borrowing—differ in significant respects. For one thing, borrowed funds usually carry both a fixed rate of return and a fixed schedule for repayment, whereas only *preferred* (as opposed to *common*) stock carries a fixed rate of return, and stock usually carries no scheduled repayment obligation at all.

A more significant difference is that while the most likely

source of borrowed funds is a bank, the most likely purchasers of stock (at least if the company is too small to "go public") are wealthy individuals or venture- ("vulture") capital companies. Although a bank may impose certain operating restrictions on your company (a limit on further borrowing, for example) and require regular inspections of your records, purchasers of your company's stock are likely to demand a substantially more active, hands-on—from your perspective, meddlesome—role.

Even if these purchasers don't assume they know more about running your business than you do, selling even one share of your corporation's stock will dramatically inhibit your independent style of doing business, forcing you to hold regular stockholders' meetings, conduct formal stockholder votes, and generally respect the ownership interests of someone other than yourself. (More on required corporate procedures below.) Moreover, in selling stock it's ridiculously easy to run afoul of federal and state securities laws—a mean can of worms.

The bottom line is, if yours is a small, freewheeling company, selling stock isn't something you want to do if you can help it.

CORPORATIONS VERSUS PARTNERSHIPS

You're thinking about setting up a business. You don't want to do it alone, however. You want someone else around to handle the inevitable piles of scut work.

The one person you could stand working with on a daily basis, your cousin Arnold, is game. Arnold *likes* scut work. But Arnold insists on being a principal of the business—either a stockholder, if the business is incorporated, or a partner, if it's not. You decide you can live with that.

Your plan is to set up a chain of premium laundries, the Häagen-Dazs of laundries. It will charge top prices, but it will cater to the Aflu-American—the man who can't afford to discover just as he reaches the embassy ball that last week's gazpacho still adorns the lapels of his dinner jacket, the woman who can't afford to discover just as she enters the Oval Office that her blouse has fewer buttons than sleeves.

You propose to call your laundry "O'Malley's Cleaners" (notwithstanding that your name is Fred Schwarz). The only open question is whether to put *Inc.* at the end of the company name.

You consult a lawyer, who, after reflecting a while, suggests that you operate as a partnership. Why?

It's not clear. There's no manifestly correct answer here, so perhaps he applied the "when-in-doubt . . ." rule and decided against incorporating. A different answer wouldn't have rendered him guilty of malpractice. In any event, his analysis presumably went something like the discussion below.

To be able to weigh for yourself the advantages and disadvantages of operating as a partnership, the first thing you need to understand is, what *is* a partnership? The commonly accepted legal definition is: a *voluntary* association of two or more persons carrying on a *business* as *co-owners for profit*.

Each of the emphasized terms in this definition counts:

• The association has to be *voluntary*. Arnold can't sell his place in the partnership to his cousin Manfred without your permission, lest you find yourself in business with Manfred against your will. No one can become a member of a partnership without the agreement of all the existing partners.

• You and Arnold have to be involved together in the operation of a *business*. Mere joint ownership of something—say, a building, from which you split the rents—isn't enough.

• You and Arnold have to be *co-owners*. If Arnold signs on as a hired hand, no amount of responsibility or pay can transform his essentially subordinate, employee's role into that of a partner.

• Your association with Arnold has to be *for profit*. Be aware, however, that sharing in a company's profits doesn't by itself make one a partner. Suppose Manfred lets your company rent space in one of his buildings, in return for a share of the company's profits. Manfred still isn't a co-owner of the business; he has no control over it. If his rent consisted (as it does for most landlords) of a fixed sum per rental period, there would be no basis whatsoever for viewing him as a partner; the fact that his rent varies with the profitability of the business cracks open the door on the issue, but it's not enough in and of itself.

The real test of partnership is one of intent—did the current partners *mean* Manfred to be a partner?—as well as the extent of his control, if any, over the business.

Consider with respect to O'Malley's Cleaners the five distinguishing features of a corporation discussed above.

Limited Liability

If you decide to operate O'Malley's Cleaners as a partnership, you'll face the same potentially unlimited personal liability you'd face if operating it as a sole proprietorship. That you aren't working alone affords you no personal shield, only someone with whom to split the liability.

Perhaps you're not worried about liability for your own screwups. But a critical legal point to keep in mind regarding partnerships is, *every partner is liable for the screwups of every other partner.* Thus, *you* could find yourself personally liable for *Arnold's* blunders, possibly even his frauds. This is a key distinction between partnerships and corporations: Although no stockholder could cause another stockholder to lose a nickel more than his original investment, one partner could create potentially unlimited personal liability for every other partner.

The bottom line? If you think a laundry poses few really serious risks of liability, or you're just a gambler, you might choose to operate O'Malley's Cleaners as a partnership. If you're worried about lost or damaged garments, injuries from delivery trucks, or maimings of your employees by malfunctioning equipment, you might choose to operate it as a corporation.

Tax Considerations

One of the most attractive features of a partnership is that in the eyes of the Internal Revenue Service its profits and losses accrue not to the partnership itself, but to its individual members. Thus, if the partnership of O'Malley's Cleaners finds itself in the red, you and Arnold can claim its losses on your personal tax returns—a benefit not available to corporate stockholders.

Similarly, if the partnership of O'Malley's Cleaners finds itself in the black, its profits will be treated as income flowing directly to you and Arnold, rather than flowing first to the partnership and *then* to you and Arnold. As a result, you and Arnold will be spared the double taxation you would suffer if you received the same money in the form of *dividends* from O'Malley's Cleaners, *Inc.*

To stay out of trouble with the IRS, remember that the profits of a partnership, like those of a sole proprietorship, are taxed in the year they're earned, regardless of whether they're actually distributed in that year or instead left under the mattress of the Murphy bed you keep in your office. Remember, too, that *un*like a sole proprietorship, a partnership must file an annual tax return—purely for informational purposes—with the IRS.

Under current IRS rules, while the losses as well as profits of a partnership accrue to its members in their personal capacities, the losses do so only within limits. Unlike simpler subjects such as Einstein's theory of relativity, IRS rules limiting the deductibility of partnership losses will never be capable of reduction to a child's-play formula like $E = mc^2$. If you want to take a shot at mastering these rules, they're set forth in IRS Publication 541, "Tax Information on Partnerships." My advice, at least for the first year of your partnership's operation, is that you simply keep in mind that not all partnership losses are deductible on your personal tax return, and get an accountant or a tax lawyer to show you how the limits apply in your situation.

To what extent should these limits affect your decision on whether to operate your business as a partnership or a corporation? Very little. In a better world, you could deduct all your business losses, but even in this world, you can deduct *most* of them. The limits are limited, so to speak.

The bottom line? If your business is going to lose money, tax considerations probably favor operating it as a partnership so you can take advantage of the losses on your individual tax return. Even if your business is going to make money, tax considerations might favor operating it as a partnership if your personal tax bracket is low enough.

Indefinite Duration

What happens to the partnership of O'Malley's Cleaners if you or Arnold dies? The basic legal rule is, the death (or withdrawal) of any partner triggers the automatic dissolution of a partnership (although the partnership isn't completely "gone" until the "winding up" of its affairs is completed). It's generally possible to override this rule, however.

To obtain indefinite duration for a partnership you need two things. First, you need an appropriate provision in your partnership agreement, such as "This partnership shall survive the death of any partner." Equivalent provisions undoubtedly appear in the partnership agreements of the giant law and accounting firms around the country, which lose members to the Grim Reaper every year without the slightest loss of continuity; indeed, often no one but the janitor notices.

Second, you need at least one living partner. (Actually two, or the entity would become a sole proprietorship, but I'm assuming the surviving partner would move quickly to replace the most recently departed one.) If every member of a partnership were to die, no agreement for its indefinite duration would suffice to keep it alive, because who would be around to admit new members?

Contrast a partnership in this regard with a corporation, whose capacity for indefinite duration is more absolute. Even the simultaneous death of literally every stockholder would have no greater effect than shifting every share (by the laws of inheritance) into someone else's hands.

What's the practical significance of the differing survival capacities of corporations and partnerships? Not much, because a simple contractual provision can ensure a partnership's indefinite duration in every situation except the death of literally every partner. Still, you should understand the difference, if just to make sure you don't forget that contractual provision.

Transferability

Suppose you decide to incorporate your laundry, O'Malley's Cleaners, Inc. You get 51 percent of the stock, and Arnold gets

49 percent. Then one day Arnold dies. His will leaves everything, including his stock, to his brother Sammy, whose single-digit IQ places him, in your estimation, one step above a professional hockey player and one step below a toaster oven. Now you're in business with Sammy, meaning you have to notify him of stockholder meetings, let him vote his shares, and generally accord him all the rights legally guaranteed to stockholders. You thank God for your extra 2 percent, which assures you of control.

Suppose, on the other hand, you decide to organize your laundry as a partnership, with you and Arnold as its partners. Once again, Arnold dies. His will, which again leaves everything to Sammy, includes the following provision: "Sammy shall take my place as a partner in O'Malley's Cleaners." You shudder. If this provision is valid, you could find yourself not only in business with Sammy, but personally liable for his countless screwups.

Fortunately for you, the law has encountered plenty of Sammys over the centuries. Hence the basic legal rule (incorporated into the very definition of a partnership as a *voluntary* association) that no one can make someone else a member of a partnership without the consent of all the existing partners.

This rule, like most rules pertaining to partnerships, can be overridden by your partnership agreement—which underscores the importance of knowing your state's partnership law backward and forward when formulating your partnership agreement. It would be unusual for a partnership agreement to authorize the introduction of someone into the partnership without the consent of all the existing partners, but it could be done.

Assuming your partnership agreement doesn't override the otherwise applicable law and allow Arnold to bequeath (or give, sell, or otherwise transfer) to Sammy his right to *be a partner* in O'Malley's Cleaners, is there anything at all connected with the company that Arnold can transfer to Sammy? Again, it's a matter of contract—what does your partnership agreement say?

If your agreement is silent, the law will, as usual, cheerfully supply a rule, in this case the rule being that a partner may transfer to an outsider only one of his rights as a partner, namely, his right to a share of partnership profits and *surplus* (basically,

the excess of assets over liabilities, upon dissolution of the partnership).

Which of a partner's rights does the law say he may *not*
transfer to an outsider, absent a contrary provision in the partnership agreement? In other words, once a partner has transferred his right to a share of partnership profits and surplus,
what's left over? First, and of primary importance, his right to
participate in the management of the partnership. Second, his
rights in specific partnership property. (The latter rights are extremely limited. A partner has *no* rights in specific partnership
property except to use it in the business of the partnership.)

Perhaps a more important question for a partner than what
he can transfer to someone else is what he can take with him
from the partnership when he leaves—not necessarily for another world, like Arnold, but just for another city, or another
job. (He may not be able to take anything if he leaves in violation
of some term in the partnership agreement. In that situation the
question shifts from what he can take from the partnership to
what the partnership can take from him—in court.)

Once again, it depends on what your partnership agreement
says. If your agreement is silent, the rule on what you can take
with you is the same as for what you can transfer to an outsider,
namely, your right to a share of partnership profits and surplus.
Once you're out of the partnership, you have no right to participate in its management and no rights in specific partnership
property.

Note that your partnership agreement isn't required to be
generous. So long as there's no fraud, duress, or the like, it can
provide that a departing member gets nothing whatsoever. Under
such a survivor-take-all arrangement, the capital contributions
and undistributed earnings that might otherwise be subject to
the claims of departing partners will accumulate over time for
the benefit of whichever partner's heart continues to beat the
longest.

The discussion above focuses on the rights of the departing partner—the extent to which he may transfer his interest in the
partnership to someone else, and the related question of what

he may take from the partnership when he leaves, besides a gold watch. Now consider what, if anything, a partner may transfer to someone else while still in the partnership.

Once again, it's a matter of contract.

Presumably neither you nor any other partner cares what Arnold does with his own money, so it's unlikely that you've included in your partnership agreement anything that would preclude Arnold from signing over to Sammy his right to a share of the partnership's profits (along with, perhaps, his right to a share of the partnership's assets in the event of dissolution).

What *can't* Arnold give Sammy? In the absence of some contrary agreement, the law precludes Arnold from transferring (at least without the permission of all the partners) either of the two basic rights that make up the remainder of his partnership interest, namely, his right to participate in the management of the partnership, and second, his rights in specific partnership property.

Contrast the limited transferability of partnership interests with the easy transferability of corporate stock. In the absence of contractual restrictions, you can sell, give, or bequeath your stock to anyone you like. You can put it in the name of your cat.

Terminating your status as a corporate stockholder is simple and nondisruptive. If you sell your stock or die and leave it to someone, the corporation will proceed heartlessly onward, your shares passing to your heirs or perhaps being picked up by the other stockholders under a *right of first refusal*.

As portrayed thus far, because partnership interests are largely incapable of transfer without the permission of the other partners, it's theoretically much easier to recoup your investment in a corporation than in a partnership. But reality often conflicts with theory.

Suppose you want to sell your one-third or one-tenth portion of the stock of O'Malley's Cleaners, Inc.—who'll buy it? Assuming the remaining stockholders are longtime golfing buddies or members of the same chapter of the Junior League, what outsider wouldn't feel concern about whether his voice in the corporation's governance would be heard? And this concern would hardly be the product of paranoia: It's not at all uncommon for stockholders of small corporations to adopt stock-transfer restrictions to exclude strangers—in no way an unsavory practice. The result is that their stock is no more transferable than an interest in a partnership.

To be sure, you might find a purchaser for your shares among the remaining stockholders, but then you're at their mercy as to price—and no better off than a departing partner seeking to sell his partnership interest to the other members of the partnership. Although all of you might be able to agree in advance that the remaining stockholders or perhaps the corporation itself will buy a departing stockholder's shares at a specified price, or a price to be determined by appraisal or in accordance with some formula, there's no guarantee that such price will reflect the true value of your investment. This is especially so if the main benefit of holding stock in a corporation lies not in receiving its paltry dividends but in being one of its stockholder/officers to whom its earnings are funneled in the form of generous salaries.

What about transferring not just a single partner's interest in a partnership, but the interests of all the partners—in other words, the entire partnership business? Consider the three factors discussed above in comparing the transferability of a corporation with that of a sole proprietorship:

1. *Convenience.* Transferring the business of a partnership, like transferring that of a sole proprietorship, involves shifting individual assets rather than a unitary business. The reverse is true for a corporation, whose component parts remain united regardless of what you do with its stock. Because it's less convenient to transfer individual assets—land, equipment, money—than to sign over certificates representing corporate stock, you'd do well to conduct your business as a corporation rather than a partnership if maximizing convenience of transfer is your primary goal (which it should rarely be).

2. *Access to contracts.* Suppose O'Malley's Cleaners signs a lease for office space. The signature line for the tenant on this contract names either O'Malley's Cleaners or perhaps its individual partners, you and Arnold. Either way, it doesn't name something capable of being sold. (If it names a steam iron, delivery truck, or some other inanimate object, someone is being flimflammed.)

Given that this contract names *individuals* rather than a transferable entity such as a corporation, and given that any contract and its obligations go where its named (signing) parties go, this contract doesn't go with your partnership's assets upon their sale to a new owner; it goes with *you*. Unless you can obtain the landlord's permission to assign the lease to the prospective buyer, you're stuck with it. And assuming the prospective buyer will need the lease to continue the business, he may back out of the deal.

3. *Liabilities*. If someone driving a delivery truck for the partnership of O'Malley's Cleaners runs over the sheriff's elderly mother, you and Arnold, as the driver's employers, become personally liable for her injuries (assuming—an important legal point—that the driver was acting within the scope of his employment and not just joyriding). Moreover, as partners, you and Arnold *remain* personally liable for her injuries, whether you sell, give away, or deep-six your delivery trucks, steam irons, and other assets of the business.

How does this bear on whether to incorporate or operate as a partnership? If your business is likely to generate a lot of liabilities and your primary concern is ease of transfer, it's arguable that you should operate as a partnership, because transferring the business of a partnership doesn't entail transferring its accumulated liabilities. On the other hand, even if you operate as a corporation, a buyer could avoid getting the business's liabilities simply by buying the corporation's *assets*, rather than its stock. It all comes down to the terms of the deal.

Access to Capital

A corporation, as already mentioned, has three options for raising capital: (1) hope to find it on the street, (2) borrow it, or (3) sell stock.

A partnership also has three options for raising capital. It has the first two options just mentioned, and also a third unique to itself: admitting another partner who'll contribute new capital.

Suppose your small corporation decides to raise capital by selling stock. Ideally the current stockholders will buy the newly issued shares. If they don't, your corporation will have to sell them to an "outsider."

Even if this new stockholder owns only 1 percent of the outstanding shares, he constitutes one more person guaranteed the rights of any stockholder under your founding documents and state corporation statute. At a minimum he possesses the right to receive notice of and attend all regular and special meetings of stockholders; to participate in the election of directors; to vote on major corporate actions, such as mergers; and to bring lawsuits against the management if he thinks it's somehow harming his interests or those of the corporation as a whole. In other words, he has it within his power to make a major nuisance of himself.

Now suppose your *partnership* decides to raise capital by admitting a new partner. This approach, too, suffers from a substantial downside: Afterward you have a new partner—an even greater potential nuisance than a new stockholder.

One more partner means one more person entitled to participate actively in the management of the business; one more person capable of binding the partnership with respect to outside parties; one more person capable of incurring massive liability for which every member of the partnership is personally liable; one more person entitled to review your records and—especially galling—*comment* on your work.

Is the bottom line that if you anticipate needing new capital, you're better off conducting your business as a corporation? Possibly. But again, the fact that you have stock to sell doesn't mean anyone will buy it, just as the fact that you're willing to take on a new partner doesn't mean anyone will apply for the position. In reality, businesses of a similar size are likely to confront similar problems raising capital, regardless of how they're legally structured.

Centralized Management Authority

Suppose ten of your college classmates with time to kill and money to burn ask to go in on O'Malley's Cleaners with you and Arnold. They figure that given the increasing populations of oldsters and yuppies in the world, commercial laundries could be the wave of the future—the one group lacking the strength and energy to clean their own clothes, the other lacking the time and humility.

You're delighted at the thought of enlisting your friends' talent, energy, and money. You're *not* delighted at the thought of sharing with them the control and day-to-day management of the business. For you this is more than a Monopoly game, more even than a livelihood; it's a way to win the approval of your parents.

Organizing O'Malley's Cleaners as a partnership will diffuse your control and day-to-day management authority, rendering it a commercial democracy. To be sure, your partnership agreement can restrict your friends' voting rights on major policy decisions. But it can't abolish those rights altogether. And even partners with restricted voting rights remain capable of contractually binding the partnership with respect to outsiders,* not to mention running over the sheriff's elderly mother or otherwise incurring unlimited personal liability for everyone.

In contrast, organizing O'Malley's Cleaners as a corporation will centralize your management authority to a high degree. If a partnership is a democracy, a corporation is a monarchy, or at least an oligarchy. While the authority of a corporation's chief executive officer is subject to the oversight of the board of directors and, ultimately, the wishes of the stockholders, his control over the daily management of the corporation typically goes unchallenged. Moreover, in a small corporation like O'Malley's Cleaners, Inc., he'll presumably *be* one of the major stockholders, and possibly the chairman of the board of directors as well.

Centralization of power is by no means always in your best interest. What if Arnold has all the money, and you have none? In this case, if power is to be centralized in anyone, "anyone" will presumably be Arnold, even though he wouldn't know a steam iron from a leaf blower. Unlike the five previously discussed corporate features, which in varying degrees would *always* be nice to have, centralized authority can be good or bad,

---

*They can do this through their *apparent authority,* a concept based on the rule that if a partner, or even a former partner, *appears* to possess the authority to bind the partnership, and an outsider reasonably relies on that appearance in signing a contract with him, the partnership is legally bound.

depending on your circumstances. In any event, it suggests no necessary answer to the question of the best form in which to operate your business. ·

SETTING UP AND OPERATING YOUR COMPANY

A Sole Proprietorship

SETTING IT UP

There you are, ready to kick your new business into gear. You've decided to go it alone, and since you don't see any present need to incorporate, you're left with operating as a sole proprietorship. The only remaining question is, how to set it up?

Don't move an inch. It's already set up, or rather, it doesn't need setting up.

This isn't to say you don't need an architect's license if you plan to design buildings, or a vendor's permit if you plan to run a sidewalk bagel stand. But it *is* to say you don't need permission from the state authorities to operate a sole proprietorship.

A word of caution with respect to your name: If you choose to *do business* (see the discussion of setting up a corporation, below) under any name other than your own, you may be required to file an *assumed name* certificate (also called a *fictitious business name* or *doing business as* certificate) with the local authorities, usually a county clerk. If you do business in another state, you'll have to file some sort of certificate no matter what name you use.

OPERATING IT

The primary legal matter you need to remember with regard to operating your sole proprietorship is, recognize the profits (or, God forbid, losses) from it on your personal tax return, *whether or not* you actually use any of those profits for personal purposes.

Also, given the unlimited personal liability you risk by doing business as a sole proprietor, you'd be wise to stock up on liability insurance, as well as (if you're married) put your home in a *tenancy by the entirety* (see Chapter 10, "Wills") to protect it from your individual creditors.

A Partnership

SETTING IT UP

You're still a hot young entrepreneur, but now it's not just you—it's you and four friends. You want to work together as partners. Logistical preparations having been completed, all that remains is to set up the partnership itself.

It's tempting to tell you again not to move an inch. Setting up a partnership, like setting up a sole proprietorship, doesn't actually require you to do anything, at least not anything formal. All that's legally necessary is that you and your friends *act*—and *intend* to act—like partners.

So, do what you were planning to do anyway: Pool your money, start running your business, and—this is key—print up some stationery, business cards, or sales receipts that identify you collectively as a partnership—"Schwarz, O'Malley & Associates, A Partnership." (As with sole proprietorships, if you do business under a name other than your own, or under *any* name in another state, you'll probably have to file certain identifying materials with the local authorities.)

The point of identifying yourselves as a partnership is that someone who makes loans to your business or otherwise puts himself at risk has a legitimate interest in knowing the form in which you operate your business. That way he knows whether your personal resources stand behind its commitments (as of course they do if the business is operated as a partnership—and don't if it's operated as a corporation).

Although no formal steps are required to create a partnership, it's best to put something in writing. It would be enough, for example, to label a piece of paper "Partnership Agreement," and on it write, "We hereby agree that as of this day we shall constitute the partnership of Schwarz, O'Malley & Associates."

This piece of paper doesn't by itself render you and your buddies partners; you still have to act as such. This document's primary function vis-à-vis the outside world is to evidence everyone's *intent* to join the partnership, precluding anyone from later saying, "I don't know what the others may have been thinking, Your Honor, but *I* certainly never intended to become a partner with those boobs."

As long as you have paper and typewriter out, you might as well attempt to identify problems that could someday cause fights within the partnership, and then set forth for each problem some means of resolution more humane than last-person-standing-gets-all. In the absence of an agreement, oral or (better) written, the state partnership statute will determine the rights and relations of the partners. Hence, if you aren't happy with the statutory arrangement, it's crucial to reach some meeting of the minds.

While the types of problems that need to be addressed will depend in part on the terms of the local partnership law, certain issues should always be addressed:

• How much will each partner be required to contribute to the partnership capital? Will cash alone be acceptable?

• How will profits be divided? On the basis of capital contributed, hours worked, or, God forbid, merit?

• How will the partnership be governed? What matters will require the vote of every member?

• How will conflicts among partners be resolved?

• What will be the rights of a partner who dies or voluntarily withdraws?

• On what basis will new partners be admitted?

• How long will the partnership last? What events will trigger its earlier dissolution? How will partnership assets be divided upon dissolution?

The easiest way to get a partnership agreement is of course to have a lawyer prepare one for you. Although preparing your own is certainly possible, the vital importance of knowing your state's partnership law makes doing so a risky proposition.

A legal clinic should be able to give you a workable if somewhat standardized partnership agreement for around $500. A lawyer in a sizable firm might charge two or three times that, possibly more if you're trying to do something fancy.

OPERATING IT

You should note four points regarding the operation of a partnership:

1. *Outgoing partners.* Suppose one of your partners—Milton—departs. You should do more than wave good-bye. Specifically, you should give notice of Milton's departure to every outsider with whom he used to transact business on behalf of the partnership. Why?

Under the doctrine of *apparent authority,* at any time before an outsider learns Milton is no longer with you, that person is legally entitled to assume Milton is still a partner, and hence still has authority to charge things to the partnership, borrow money on its behalf, and otherwise get it into trouble. The rationale here is that businesspeople can't be expected to research the current roster of your partnership every time they transact business with someone whom they have reasonable cause to believe is acting on behalf of your firm.

By the same token, if you're Milton, consider giving your own notice of departure to outsiders with whom you used to deal. At any time before they learn you're no longer a member of the partnership, they're legally entitled to assume your personal assets still stand behind it, and some day you might find to your amazement that one of them has sued you to collect on partnership obligations incurred *after* you left.

2. *Categories of partnership income.* In preparing your personal tax return, don't confuse the three types of income you could receive from your partnership.

First, there's old-fashioned salary or wages, any fixed compensation awarded to you in your capacity as an employee, rather than a member, of the partnership.

Second, there's income to the partnership, whether made up of interest, dividends, capital gains, professional fees, or whatever. Your share of all such income must be reported on your personal tax return for the year in which it comes in, regardless of whether it makes its way into your own wallet.

Third, there are nontaxable distributions that lawyers refer to as *return of capital*. This requires a bit of explaining. If partnership income isn't distributed in a given year, two things happen: first, you're taxed on it anyway (your share of it); and second, your *capital account* in the partnership (consisting initially of money or property that you kicked in upon becoming a partner) rises in an amount equal to your share of the income, as if you had contributed new money.

In the following year, one of two things happens: Either the money sitting in the partnership coffers still isn't distributed, so that your capital account remains at the higher level, or the money *is* distributed, reaching you as a nontaxable return of capital. That it's nontaxable makes sense, either because you've paid taxes on it already, or because you're merely getting back what you paid in.

3. *Allocating profits and losses.* What if Arnold works substantially longer hours in the service of O'Malley's Cleaners than you do? What if you bring in twice as much business as Arnold does? The answer is, the two of you can duke it out over the allocation of profits and losses, reaching any conclusion you like.

The IRS doesn't have to accept your conclusion, however. It assumes, allowing room to be persuaded otherwise, that the allocation of a partnership's profits and losses will reflect the relative level of each partner's capital account; and it assumes that the relative level of each partner's capital account will reflect, in turn, the relative level of each partner's initial and subsequent capital contributions. Although you and Arnold are permitted to adjust your capital accounts—and, thereby, your allocation of profits and losses—to reflect factors *besides* your capital contributions (factors such as hours worked and business brought in), the IRS really doesn't trust you, and it won't accept your adjustments unless you can show a substantial economic reason for them other than avoiding taxes.

It's worth emphasizing here how maddeningly, ulcer-producingly, get-down-on-your-knees-and-promise-never-to-skip-church-again *hard* it is to determine the proper tax treatment of partnership profits and losses, and the wisdom of hiring a tax lawyer or accountant to help you through it.

Unless yours is just a two-person partnership that divides

everything straight down the middle (and, moreover, never suffers losses), you might discover too late how easy it is to overlook an obscure but controlling regulation—or, just as easy, to screw up in applying a regulation you didn't overlook at all but erroneously assumed to mean what it says.

4. *Dissolution.* Dissolution of your partnership can be triggered by any event—bankruptcy, for example, or the departure of one of its members—specified in either the local partnership law or your partnership agreement. The partnership doesn't simply vanish upon the occurrence of such an event, however. Rather, *winding up* commences—which refers to the often time-consuming process of disposing of the partnership's assets, collecting on its claims, paying its creditors, distributing its surplus, and otherwise bringing it to a tidy end.

While these chores are being taken care of, the business activities of the partnership may well continue, although to a limited and presumably decreasing extent. Only upon the conclusion of the winding-up process does the partnership *terminate;* that is, only then is it really gone.

It's important to distinguish between dissolution and termination, and to remember that at any time before your partnership actually terminates, it's still in existence. Hence, it's still possible that your soon-to-be-former partners could saddle you with personal liability.

Once dissolution occurs, make sure you do whatever is necessary under the local partnership law to complete the winding-up process as quickly as possible. Only then will you be completely in the clear.

A Corporation

SETTING IT UP

Whether you're working alone or with others, you always have to take affirmative steps to set up a corporation. The particulars of these steps vary from state to state, but in general they can be reduced to three:

1. *Selecting a state in which to incorporate.* Although you're permitted to incorporate in any state in the Union, generally you

should go with the state in which you'll be doing most of your business (presumably your home state), and not just because you owe it a favor since you'll be taking advantage of its roads, restrooms, and genial climate.

First, if you incorporate in some remote state, your company could get sued there. How would you feel about having to fly back and forth across the country to defend yourself before a jury of people who think anyone with an accent like yours molests children? Second, your company might have to pay franchise and other taxes in that state, as well as in the state where it's doing most of its business. Third, since you'll obviously be carrying on extensive activities in your home state, you'll have to take whatever steps are necessary to *qualify* (as discussed below) to do business there. (Note that you don't necessarily escape these burdens by operating as a sole proprietorship, say, rather than as a corporation. An individual is as vulnerable to geographically burdensome litigation and dual taxation as a corporation. Also, an individual doing business in a remote state usually must inform the local tax authorities of his presence—a process similar to *qualifying* a corporation.)

If your corporation will unavoidably be doing business in a number of states, you should consult a lawyer about the best place to incorporate. A commonly recommended possibility is, believe it or not, Delaware, whose rules are as clear, flexible, and generally hospitable to corporations as any you'll find. To cite two of twenty or more possible examples, Delaware permits a corporation to operate with only one director, whereas some states require at least three, and Delaware allows directors to act by teleconference or written consent, whereas some states require directors to hold meetings at which a quorum is physically present.

In order for your corporation to do business in any state other than the one in which it's incorporated, the former commonly referred to as a "foreign state," it has to *qualify* to do business there. A corporation can conduct some activities in a foreign state without having to qualify, but it's not clear how many activities, or what kind. Mailing advertisements? Holding directors' meetings? Maintaining a bank account or telephone listing? Each state has its own rules. If you're uncertain about whether you have to qualify somewhere, consult a lawyer, the person in charge of foreign corporations in the local secretary of state's office, or, at the very least, a booklet titled "What Constitutes Doing Business," which you can get free from the CT Corporation System, one of the "corporate-services companies" described below.

Invariably a nuisance, qualification in a foreign state typically entails filing documents, paying a fee, and finding someone in the foreign state to serve (for another fee) as your corporation's *registered agent* to receive summonses, subpoenas, tax notices, and other materials the authorities want to be sure will reach you.

2. *Preparing and filing the articles of incorporation.* Once you've decided where to incorporate, your next step is to file a document—variously called the *articles of incorporation* (or *articles*), *certificate of incorporation*, or *charter*—with the local secretary of state. You'll have to pay a fee ranging from $20 to approximately $300, depending on the state.

The required contents of the articles vary slightly from state to state. Many local secretaries of state supply blank forms showing the minimum necessary information. You can get the same or similar forms from any of the corporate-service companies around the country, the larger of which have offices in all or most of the states and offer information, forms, and services that can be extremely useful for both new and existing corporations. (Three of the nation's largest corporate-service companies are: CT Corporation System, 1633 Broadway, New York, NY 10019, 800/223-7567; Prentice-Hall Corporation System, Inc., 136 Madison Avenue, New York, NY 10016, 800/223-1727; and United States Corporation Company, 70 Pine Street, New York, NY 10270, 212/952-0400. The person with whom you speak at any of these companies may decline to provide the forms or information you want unless you identify yourself as a lawyer.)

Normally your articles will constitute a short document, perhaps two or three pages, containing the following:

• *The name of the corporation.* You or one of the corporate-service companies should call the local secretary of state or other appropriate authorities to confirm that the name you want isn't the same as or confusingly similar to a name already in use. If the name is available, you can usually reserve it for a month or two.

• *The name and address of the corporation's registered agent.* You can be your own registered agent in the state where you live. In other states you can get one of the corporate-service companies to act as your registered agent for a small fee.

• *The purposes for which the corporation is being formed.* In Delaware and many other states, it's sufficient to say, "Any act permitted under the laws of this state."

• *The capital structure of the corporation.* You have to identify all classes of stock and the number of shares authorized for each class. A few states require you to specify a minimum capital contribution, such as $1,000.

• *The names and addresses of the corporation's incorporator(s) and initial director(s).* Your incorporator can usually be anyone, including you, your lawyer, or your lawyer's janitor. His authority typically extends no farther than signing and filing your articles, along with the required fee. Thereafter, the initial directors named in the articles take over, and the incorporator departs the stage forever.

• *The duration of the corporation.* The usual approach is to say its duration shall be "perpetual." This doesn't prevent you from dissolving it at any time.

• *Any special powers you want to give, or restrictions you want to impose upon, the corporation's officers and directors.* You could give them, for example, explicit permission to transact business with the corporation—a touchy matter, given the potential for conflicts of interest. You could also explicitly authorize (or prohibit) their indemnification for any personal liability they might incur while acting on behalf of the corporation.

Once you've filed your articles, some bureaucrat in the local secretary of state's office will review them. If they're approved, the secretary of state will issue a certificate of incorporation, at which time your corporation will be deemed officially in existence.

3. *Holding the organizational meeting.* To say your corporation is in existence after the filing of the articles is hardly to say your work is over, any more than God's work was over after the first

day. You need, among other things, officers and directors to get the corporation into trouble, just as God needed Woman and Man to do the same for the world.

The first meeting of the corporate directors should be held as soon as conveniently possible after the approval of your articles. If your state doesn't require initial directors to be named in the articles, there has to be a preliminary meeting of the incorporators to elect the directors, after which the incorporators resign. If, as is usually the case, there's only one incorporator, he can simply sign a statement appointing the initial directors and then resign.

The directors' first order of business is to adopt *bylaws*, which constitute a sort of operating manual for the corporation. If you're like most directors and officers you'll treat them the same way you treat the operating manual that came with your car, glancing through them once and then forgetting about them until something goes wrong. That would be a mistake.

Often quite detailed, bylaws address such matters as:

• The place, date, and hour of directors' and stockholders' meetings;

• The powers, salaries, and terms of office of each of the officers, including who has authority to sign checks, deeds, contracts, and other legal items on behalf of the corporation; and

• The procedures for amending the bylaws, for executing and transferring shares of stock, and for giving directors and stockholders official notice of meetings.

The relation of bylaws to articles of incorporation is analogous to that of laws passed by Congress to the United States Constitution: In each case the latter represents the supreme law of the land. Whereas articles are usually short, like the Ten Commandments (and ignored at similar risk), bylaws are usually long. And whereas articles are hard to amend (requiring both a directors' resolution and a formal vote of the stockholders), bylaws can usually be amended by a simple majority vote of the directors.

Next on the directors' organizational agenda is electing the president, vice-president, secretary, treasurer, and any other officers the bylaws say the corporation should have. Then the directors must approve the form of the corporate stock certificate, adopt a corporate seal, authorize the treasurer to open a bank account, and, as required by some banks, authorize the bank to pay out corporate funds pursuant to checks signed by specified officers. Finally, the directors approve the issuance of the corporation's stock—usually for cash, sometimes for property.

How do directors actually go about taking all these actions? By a series of written *organizational resolutions*. For example:

Upon motion duly made, seconded, and unanimously carried, it is HEREBY

RESOLVED, that the following persons having been duly nominated to serve as officers of the Corporation, such persons are elected to assume the duties and responsibilities, as set forth in the Bylaws, of the offices indicated beside their respective names:

William Nelson ....President
J. Jeffrey Walker ....Vice-President
Henry Williams, Jr. ....Secretary/Treasurer

And it is

FURTHER RESOLVED, that the corporate seal, an impression of which is affixed in the margin hereof, be, and the same shall be, adopted as the official corporate seal of the Corporation.

What language is that?

Good question. But that's how resolutions invariably look. If you study them long enough you'll find they do parse.

Who drafts the bylaws and organizational resolutions? (Whoever does this should also prepare minutes of the organizational meeting, stating who attended, what was done, how everyone voted, and so on.) Theoretically such work falls to the corporate secretary (although technically the corporation doesn't have a secretary until bylaws are adopted). A more realistic answer, at least for a small corporation, is that such work falls to the person most capable of doing it.

What if you and the other corporate principals speak nothing but English? The same corporate-service companies that supply model articles of incorporation also supply model bylaws, organizational resolutions, and minutes. These documents aren't likely to be of the highest quality, however. Your best bet, if you can afford it, is to have a lawyer prepare your incorporation documents. A legal clinic or small firm will charge around $600 for the work; a large firm, around $2,000, although possibly a good bit less if what you want is straightforward.

Two minor logistical points: Where do you obtain the corporation's stock certificates? And what's the story on corporate seals?

In most cities there are corporation-supply companies (check the yellow pages under "Corporation Supplies") that for under fifty dollars will print and deliver a set of eagle-emblazoned stock certificates bearing your corporation's name.

As for corporate seals, you'll receive along with your stock certificates a hand-held device that you squeeze like a stapler to emboss your corporation's name and birthday (which together constitute your corporate seal) onto a piece of paper. The mark occupies a space about the size of a fifty-cent piece.

Today the corporate seal serves no real purpose, but it lends an air of gravity to corporate affairs, and the stamp device makes a good pacifier for senior executives.

OPERATING IT

Operating a corporation involves a lot of rigamarole. Sometimes the major legal issue isn't *what* you do, but *how* you do it. To help you preserve your corporate status, and with it your limited liability, I offer three rules:

Rule One: Read your articles and bylaws—not only at the corporation's inception but again in connection with board meetings, stockholder meetings, and other major corporate events. Keep a special lookout for (a) every act you can't do without a vote by the directors and/or the stockholders, and (b) every explicit limit on the authority of any officer. With regard to the former, pay attention to which votes must be preceded by formal notice of the subject to be voted upon. With regard to the latter, note who is and who isn't authorized to execute checks and contracts on behalf of the corporation.

Rule Two: Whatever your governing documents require you to do, *do it*. Give the notice, hold the meeting, take the vote.

Rule Three: Cover your tracks—with paper. Suppose one of your corporate employees injures someone, who then sues you for $1 million. Your corporation's assets, including liability insurance up to the limit of coverage, amount to only $300,000.

In court the plaintiff's lawyer is likely to attempt to "pierce the corporate veil," arguing that your corporate status is a sham and that therefore you should be *personally* liable for the plaintiff's injuries. Whether this argument will prevail is unclear. Noncompliance with corporate formalities, although not dispositive, will certainly weigh against you with regard to the validity of your corporate status, and hence your entitlement to limited liability.

Note that it's not enough to have sent all the requisite notices, held all the requisite meetings, taken all the requisite votes. You need *proof—copies* of your notices, *minutes* of your meetings, *records* of your votes.

What about your articles, bylaws, and organizational resolutions—don't they show you're playing by the rules of the corporate game? They help, but their value depends partly on timing: If the injury occurred one day after your organizational meeting, your founding documents are all you could be expected to have. On the other hand, if the injury occurred four years later and you can't produce a single document from the interim, you're in trouble.

Keep in mind that the surest way to keep your corporate veil from being pierced is to maintain adequate insurance or other assets—adequate *capitalization*—to cover your potential liabilities. That way no one will ever *want* to pierce your corporate veil. Undercapitalization is perhaps the single greatest indicator of a sham corporation, and in conjunction with that, noncompliance with corporate formalities can be fatal.

If you're ever asked to serve as a corporate director, keep in mind that this is no longer, if it ever was, a purely honorary position. Directors are expected to observe two duties: (1) loyalty and (2) care or diligence.

The duty of loyalty is essentially a prohibition against self-dealing. Conversely, it's a requirement that you put the interests of the corporation ahead of your own. Suppose that in the course of serving as a director of a communications corporation you learn of an opportunity to acquire a nearby radio station at a fantastic price. Do you pounce on the deal, or do you first disclose its availability to the disinterested directors of your corporation, in effect giving the corporation a right of first refusal?

The answer imposed by the duty of loyalty is clear: Take the high road. Disclose everything.

The duty of care is commonly defined as a duty to use such care as an ordinarily prudent person would use in similar circumstances. Does this mean that as a director you have to show up at the corporation's offices every day? Not at all. But neither should you take a nine-month sabbatical just as the company's creditors discover they can play basketball with its checks.

The much-debated *business judgment rule* affords directors considerable protection for honest, good-faith mistakes—to err is human, and all that. But understand that directors are expected to direct, not just hold office and collect fees. The same is true for corporate officers, although the lower you go in the corporate hierarchy, the lower the requirement of absolute selflessness toward the corporation.

The question you have to ask yourself is, do the pay, prestige, travel, business contacts, and other benefits of being a corporate director or officer offset the time commitments, potential liability, and potentially forgone opportunities that the position entails?

Not an easy call.

S CORPORATIONS, CLOSE CORPORATIONS, LIMITED PARTNERSHIPS

You're starting a business, and you're trying to decide whether to set it up as a sole proprietorship, partnership, or corporation. (Good! Thinking early on about the best form in which to operate is precisely what you ought to be doing.) Because you'll be work-

ing with two friends, you know you can rule out a sole proprietorship. As you survey the remaining options, however, you
become distressed: Each has some significant flaw.

Your first impulse is to incorporate: You like the idea of
having *Inc.* on your letterhead, and limited liability would be
nice. But you anticipate losses in the company's first year or two,
and you'd like to be able to take advantage of those losses on
your personal tax return.

Okay, you think, forget about the losses. Maybe they won't
come to pass anyway. But there's still the problem of all those
notices, meetings, votes, and resolutions. You and your friends
are laid back. You loathe such rigamarole.

Moreover, all of you want guaranteed positions as officers
of the company, with guaranteed salaries, as well as some guaranteed measure of personal control over the company's activities, possibly even personal vetoes. Putting those kinds of measures
into effect in the corporate context would likely require restrictive
agreements among the directors, whose discretion is supposed
to remain unfettered.

Maybe a partnership is the way to go after all, you think.
That way we could take personal advantage of any losses the
business incurs. We could operate with none of the procedural
hassles imposed on corporations, and we could give each partner
veto powers or other forms of guaranteed personal control over
the company's activities. But then, you recall, you've lost the
one thing your friends would be most reluctant to give up: limited liability.

Precisely this kind of pained analysis has led to the creation
in recent decades of three hybrid business entities that combine
the features of corporations and partnerships in different ways.
These entities are popular among businesspeople, and not nearly
as complex as they sound.

S Corporations

An S corporation is organized like a corporation under state
law, but taxed like a partnership by the IRS. In other words, it's
a standard corporation (with limited liability, transferability, and
so on), but (1) its stockholders may take personal tax advantage

of its losses, and (2) it doesn't present the usual corporate problem of double taxation.

While an S corporation must, like any standard corporation, be set up in accordance with the laws of a chosen state, the tax status of an S corporation is a matter of federal law. Hence the rules for becoming and staying an S corporation are the same everywhere.

The option of becoming an S corporation—or "electing partnership taxation"—is available only to a corporation that has (1) no more than thirty-five stockholders, (2) only one class of stock, and (3) has no stockholders who are corporations or partnerships. (In addition, it must be organized in the United States, have no nonresident aliens among its stockholders, have no active subsidiaries, and not be one of four types of institutions, such as a bank or an insurance company.) To become an S corporation, a corporation's stockholders must unanimously consent.

The process of obtaining S corporation status is simple: If your corporation qualifies, you file IRS Form 2553, "Election by a Small Business Corporation."

Note that an S corporation is taxed similarly but *not identically* to a partnership. A number of special provisions (set forth in IRS Publication 589, "Tax Information on S Corporations") apply. If you haven't mastered partnership taxation, which is no less challenging than Chinese arithmetic, the additional or varying requirements pertaining to S corporations are well worth leaving to a tax expert.

Statutory Close Corporations

The term *close corporation* (or *closely held corporation*) is generic for any corporation whose stock is held by a small number of persons—say, fifteen or twenty. A *"statutory* close corporation" (my own coinage) is a corporation that meets certain criteria, and elects such status, under the "close corporation" provisions of a state's corporation law.

A statutory close corporation is a standard corporation (with limited liability, transferability, and so on) that's permitted to operate in roughly the same manner as a partnership. In particular, it may ignore most corporate formalities, and its stock-holders may exercise various powers and privileges not usually permitted to stockholders of standard corporations. (Contrast a statutory close corporation, which is permitted to *operate* like a partnership, with an S corporation, which is *taxed* like a part-nership.)

A number of states, including Delaware, have statutes au-thorizing close corporations. While these statutes differ in their specifics (unlike the law of S corporations, which is uniform across the country), they share the goal of freeing small corpo-rations from the procedural constraints their stockholders too often curse and ignore.

Close corporation statutes authorize the management of a corporation by its stockholders—in contrast to the usual require-ment of management by directors. Delaware's law, typical in this respect, provides that if stockholders of a close corporation are in fact managing it—and such management must be ex-pressly authorized by its articles of incorporation—those stock-holders shall *be* the corporation's directors. This eliminates an entire tier from the usual tripartite corporate pyramid, and with it much of the procedural fuss commonly associated with op-erating a corporation. (Note that if you're a stockholder acting as a director, you're subject to the same duties of loyalty and care as a director.)

Delaware's law says that if the stockholders of a close cor-poration do decide to elect directors, a stockholder agreement restricting their discretion isn't necessarily invalid, as it would be in the case of a standard corporation. It also says that a cor-poration's charter may grant each stockholder an option to have the corporation dissolved at will, thus allowing even small-per-centage stockholders potent veto power over corporate conduct.

As with S corporations, not just any Tom, Dick, & Harry, Inc., has the option of becoming a statutory close corporation. Certain states permit a corporation to become a statutory close corporation only if it has no more than a certain number of stockholders. The statutory maximum is usually between ten and thirty-five.

Also, the articles of incorporation must state that (1) all the corporation's stock is subject to some kind of transfer restriction—for example, one that says no stockholder may sell his shares without first offering them to the existing stockholders— and (2) the corporation will not make any "public offering" of stock within the meaning of the Securities Act of 1933. Regarding the latter point, securities law ranks with tax law in terms of complexity, so you should consult a lawyer for guidance about what constitutes a public offering. (As a rule of thumb, keep the number of people receiving the stock as low as possible, and make sure they're personal acquaintances of one of the founders of the company. Try to pick people who are rich and financially knowledgeable, the kind of people you'd want for in-laws.)

From a technical standpoint, becoming a statutory close corporation is easy. The process is generally the same as for a standard corporation, except that your corporate charter must (1) designate the corporation as a close corporation, and (2) make explicit reference to the eligibility restrictions listed above.

From a practical standpoint, becoming a statutory close corporation can be hard. One reason is that few lawyers have a working familiarity with the relevant laws. Close corporation statutes are of recent vintage, and from the very beginning every lawyer who stumbled upon one in the course of his research asked himself, "Should I send my client down this uncharted path, when he can reach virtually the same destination via a well-traveled highway?"

Also, some courts have recognized the special needs of closely held corporations under the "regular" state corporation law. Hence a lawyer may well feel that his client is safe in incorporating under the regular law and letting the courts make the appropriate adjustments.

Limited Partnerships

A limited partnership is called such because some of its partners—*limited partners*—have limited liability, just like corporate stockholders. The other partners—*general partners*—are personally liable for all the debts and obligations of the business, just like members of a regular (or "general") partnership.

The general partners run the show. They alone enjoy full rights of participation in the management of the partnership.

Both types of partners are taxed as if they were members of a general partnership, with profits and losses accruing to them in their personal capacities.

What's the point of this odd arrangement? To induce people blessed with money to join people blessed with skill—a frank recognition by the law that the two are rarely the same.

If the inducement to those with money consists of limited liability, which is enjoyed by the humblest corporate stockholder, how does this arrangement differ from a corporation?

With respect to its formation, it differs very little. You draw up a certificate (similar to articles of incorporation) in accordance with the limited-partnership law of a given state, and then file this certificate, along with a fee and perhaps a copy of your limited-partnership agreement, with the prescribed local authorities.

Beware! Limited partnership interests constitute *securities,* the sale of which can get you into big trouble if you fail to comply strictly with federal and state securities laws. *Definitely* consult a lawyer before selling any such interests.

The primary difference between a limited partnership and a corporation is that investors in a limited partnership are taxed not as stockholders but as partners—no small benefit, depending on your individual needs.

General partners also enjoy two other benefits they wouldn't have as managers of a corporation. First, they get to operate as regular partners vis-à-vis each other and the outside world, sharing executive responsibility and so on. They get to do this without interference from the limited partners, except for certain limited veto powers over extraordinary acts, such as admitting new general partners or giving away partnership property. (Note that you can be both a limited and a general partner in the same limited partnership.)

Second, they typically receive hefty fees for organizing and managing the partnership, directing its investments, and any other services they can think of to charge to it. Although these fees may be well deserved for the talent and entrepreneurship required to put one of these deals together, you should examine them closely and take them into account in deciding whether to invest in a limited partnership.

Don't let the idea of limited liability lull you into thinking a limited partner can do anything he wants without putting himself and his assets at risk. A limited partner can lose his limited liability through active participation in company management—negotiating with lenders, glad-handing clients, and the like. The thinking behind this rule is that creditors and other outsiders should be permitted to assume that someone who *acts* like a general partner *is* a general partner, and hence is personally on the line for the partnership's obligations.

This consideration shouldn't affect your investment decision greatly, if at all, because limited liability couldn't be easier to protect: Simply stay at home, read a book, and don't take part in the affairs of the business.

There are other, more significant considerations, such as whether the business is likely to experience losses, and whether you're likely to be in a position to take personal tax advantage of those losses. If it is, and you are, investing as a limited partner may be a good idea for you. On the other hand, if it isn't, or you aren't, you may be better off investing as a stockholder.

One other benefit of being a limited partner that could conceivably cause you to prefer that status is the right to monitor and supervise (although not to participate in) the management of the partnership business. Specifically, a limited partner typically enjoys the right to inspect the partnership's books and records as often as he likes. In contrast, a stockholder's rights along these lines are circumscribed. Many statutes limit a stockholder's right of inspection to "proper purposes," for example. Other statutes explicitly limit the frequency of stockholder inspections, and a few deny the right of inspection altogether to anyone holding less than a specified percentage of the corporation's stock.

If you're like most people, you have neither the time to inspect a company's records, the knowledge to understand what you'd find if you had the time to find it, nor a strong desire to inspect such records in the first place.

The bottom line is, although the liberal rights of inspection you'd enjoy as a limited partner might *become* important at some stage in the life of your investment, they shouldn't *be* important at the outset. If they are, you presumably don't trust the general partners. And in that case, why are you giving them your money?

6. Bankruptcy and Debtor-Creditor Law

Creditors' Remedies (Short of Bankruptcy) •

Debtors' Remedies (Short of Bankruptcy) •

Bankruptcy •

It has been long my deliberate judgement that all bankrupts, of whatsoever denomination, civil or religious, ought to be hanged.   CHARLES LAMB
(1775–1834)

I've got all the money I'll ever need if I die by four o'clock.
HENNY YOUNGMAN (1906–   )

Normalcy is when you run out of money. Insolvency is when you run out of excuses. Bankruptcy is when you run out of town.
MARTIN J. YUDKOWITZ (1954–   )

Let's hope you never need the information in this chapter. It's no fun to go broke. The only thing worse is having people who owe *you* money go broke. Still, who among us has never spent time on the financial edge?

A layoff, an illness, an unexpected but sizable expense of any sort—how much would it really take to start the snowball rolling? It begins tamely enough, with minor bills accumulating unpaid. Then interest obligations mount, and for each bill you pay, a new and bigger one mysteriously takes its place. Your bank account runs low, and one day a statement arrives showing a negative balance. Default notices begin appearing in your mail, initially just a few, then several every day; their tone gets nasty.

Your newspaper stops coming, and early one morning a man shows up to remove your telephone. Things are way out of control . . .

Knowledge of bankruptcy law could prove valuable for anyone. Like knowledge of divorce law, it's not something you actually hope to be able to use, but statistics suggest that a tremendous number of people will in fact be in a position to use it sooner or later.

Regrettably, this area of the law is extremely complicated. Not as intellectually challenging as tax law, say, but crammed with specific, narrowly drawn rules and deadlines that not even William Buckley could figure out simply on the basis of what's logical.

This area is messy, too. Like a pizza with everything on it. For one thing, while the law of bankruptcy, formally speaking, is federal law, the answers to a number of questions in federal cases turn on state law, which of course varies depending on the state. Also, the relationship of bankruptcy judges to other federal judges is awkward and uncertain. I don't mean on a personal level—that's their own business, as long as they're consenting adults—but in terms of the authority of the former. The Bankruptcy Code refers to bankruptcy courts as *units* of the federal district courts, and nobody knows what that means. Finally, the Bankruptcy Code contains provisions with the same subparagraph number in two separate sections: Section 523(a)(9) and Section 523(a)(9); Section 362(b)(9) and Section 362(b)(9)—a small matter in itself, but revealing.

I mention all this complication and messiness to put you on guard. Whether you hire a lawyer to handle your debtor-creditor problems, as I strongly recommend, or attempt to handle them yourself, you need to be alert to the sheer difficulty of interpreting and applying the law in this area.

The first two parts of this chapter address state debtor-creditor law, the first part dealing with the concerns of creditors, and the second part dealing with the concerns of debtors. The third part addresses federal debtor-creditor law, that is, the law of bankruptcy.

A word on terminology. While both lawyers and laypeople

casually use the term *bankrupt* to describe anyone whose finances seem to have gone belly-up, in the law that term refers to a particular type of proceeding under the federal Bankruptcy Code—specifically, a *liquidation* proceeding under Chapter 7 of the Code. (Actually, a person seeking relief under Chapter 7 is no longer called a *bankrupt* but simply a *debtor*.) This chapter sometimes uses the nontechnical term *insolvency proceedings* to refer to both federal "bankruptcy" and also belly-up proceedings under state law.

CREDITORS' REMEDIES (SHORT OF BANKRUPTCY)

Suppose you've lent someone money—what's your number-one concern? It is, of course, that he pay you back, preferably at the agreed-upon time. The easiest way to get money from a debtor is to have him give it to you. But suppose he can't, or won't. If he owes you at least $5,000 unsecured by collateral, you can send him into bankruptcy.

Is this a good idea?

Not if it isn't absolutely necessary. Bankruptcy is strong medicine. It's costly (for you as well as him) and, in all likelihood, extremely time-consuming; the simplest cases run several months, and many run several years. If a judge thinks your case shouldn't have been brought, he can dismiss it and make you pay the debtor's costs and legal fees, plus compensatory damages. If he thinks your case not only shouldn't have been brought, but was brought in "bad faith" (in other words, you were trying to be a jerk), he can award the debtor "punitive damages," which are often disastrously large.

Nonjudicial Remedies

Before resorting to the courts in any manner, why not try old-fashioned dunning letters—first cordial, then hostile, finally downright bloodthirsty? If the debtor doesn't respond, you could try phone calls and personal visits. You could even try communicating with the debtor's employer.

Note that there are legal limits on such measures. Reasonable communications to the debtor's employer are generally acceptable, on the dubious theory that an employer has a legitimate interest in his employee's debts, but don't call the employer repeatedly. Don't call the debtor in the middle of the night, and don't call his neighbors at all. Don't publish the debtor's name and the amount of his debts in the local newspaper, and don't post a notice of his delinquencies on telephone poles in his neighborhood, along with the "Lost Kitty—Answers to 'Ralph' " notices. There are no fixed standards in this area, but keep in mind that juries are usually comprised of poor people who've had more than their share of trouble with creditors.

A particularly aggressive means of getting your money back is to help yourself to some of the debtor's property. You can't do this in just any situation, to say the least. Suppose someone borrowing money from you puts up a specific piece of property—a car, say—as collateral for your loan and, by clear agreement, grants you a "security interest" in it. (More on security interests below.) Then he defaults on his repayment obligations. In these circumstances, some states would permit you to take possession of the car without going through the courts, *if* you could do so without breaching the peace.

A point from the debtor's side. If one of your creditors hires a professional debt collector, usually a former mud wrestler, you're protected in a number of ways by the federal Fair Debt Collection Practices Act. Although a debt collector can legally contact persons other than you, he can do so solely for the purpose of locating you, and he can't volunteer to anyone other than you that he is what he is (a debt collector); he can admit this only if expressly asked. A debt collector can't contact you at times or places "which should be known to be inconvenient." And—a bit of law that can be a godsend—you can force a debt collector to get off your back altogether by informing him *in writing* either that (1) you have a lawyer (whom he must thereafter deal with, if he wants to deal with anyone), (2) you refuse to pay, or (3) you want him to cease communicating with you. It's as simple as that.

Judicial Remedies

You've tried everything mentioned above, and the debtor still won't yield a penny. *Now* it's time to resort to the courts. Judicial remedies fall into two categories: those you obtain *before* a judge has rendered a final judgment in your favor, and those you obtain *after* that point.

1. *Prejudgment judicial remedies.* From what you know of the law, you understand that in order to get what's yours you'll have to file a *complaint* (describing how the debtor came to owe you money), await a trial date, suffer through the presentation of evidence for however many days or weeks it takes, and then await a judgment in your favor. But meanwhile the debtor continues to pour buckets of your money down the drain. At this very moment he's trying to sell the cows that he put up as collateral for your loan. Is there nothing you can do to protect your interests now?

There are several measures you can take pending a final judgment. Except in really drastic circumstances, the debtor is constitutionally entitled to come into court and oppose these measures, but if you can persuade the judge the collateral is really at risk, you can get those cows out of the debtor's hands and into those of the local sheriff. The prisoners who have to share a cell with them won't love you for it, but that's their problem.

The two most common prejudgment remedies are *attachment* and *garnishment.* To attach someone's property is to persuade a court to order the local sheriff to take custody of the property (to *levy* on it) and hold it safely pending a judicial ruling on your claim against the debtor. Usually you have to file a complaint, an affidavit swearing to the facts supporting your position, and a bond to cover the debtor's damages in case you fail to win a judgment.

While attachment goes against property in the hands of the *debtor*, garnishment goes against property in the hands of an *outsider*—the *garnishee*—who owes something to the debtor. Thus, if you garnish the debtor's employer (an employer-garnishee), you get the court to order the employer to hold some or all wages owed the debtor, pending judgment on your claim. Similarly, if you garnish the debtor's bank (a bank-garnishee), you get the court to order it to refuse to pay out some or all of the funds it's holding in the debtor's accounts.

Fortunately for debtors, neither attachment nor garnishment is available just for the asking. Typically a creditor has to show statutorily specified grounds for such a remedy—that the debtor has left the state, for example, or that he's trying to dispose of the collateral in an effort to defraud his creditors. If you're the debtor, stay cool; don't give your creditors anything to use against you in court.

If you're the creditor, note that these remedies have definite drawbacks. They force you to incur substantial legal fees, as well as the cost of a bond to protect the debtor in case you lose in the underlying collection action. Also, they might force the debtor into bankruptcy, which could render your chances of recovering your money more doubtful than ever.

A third prejudgment remedy, a harsh one that courts are notably reluctant to grant, is *receivership*. This involves persuading a court to appoint a responsible neutral person, a *receiver*, to take charge of specified property of the debtor and look after it—oil it, fertilize it, refrigerate it, feed it, whatever it needs. A receivership is most useful when the property in question—an office building, say, or a retail business—requires active management, such as collecting rents or disposing of inventory, tasks that the debtor may have shown he isn't up to performing.

2. *Postjudgment judicial remedies.* The obvious step between a prejudgment and a postjudgment remedy is . . . obtaining a judgment. That is, you have to litigate the matter to a conclusion or, if the debtor doesn't mount an opposition, demand a *default judgment.* (Default judgments are how most collection actions are in fact resolved.)

Now you're a *judgment creditor*, that is, you have a court's formal proclamation that you're entitled to a specific sum of money from the debtor (who is now a *judgment debtor*). Unfortunately, just as you can't eat money, you can't spend a judgment. How to turn your judgment into property or cash?

First, garnishment and receivership are available here, as well as in the prejudgment context. The most straightforward postjudgment remedy, however, is *execution*—not of the debtor, although by now that's more than tempting, but of your judgment. To execute on a particular piece of property, you needn't bother with a judge; in most jurisdictions you can go instead to a court clerk or the like and show him a copy of your judgment. This clerk will issue, without discussion (not that clerks are innately taciturn; they just don't have the authority to deny your request), an order directing the local sheriff to seize the property, sell it, and, after deducting the costs of the sale, turn the proceeds over to you. (Execution on real estate bears the familiar name *foreclosure*.)

A point from the debtor's side. If the bank holding your mortgage forecloses, do you have to sit by at the sale and watch some smirking hustler pick it up for one-third of its actual value, just because the real estate market is in the dumps? In most cases, no. To ensure that a debtor's property isn't sold at an unreasonably low price, many states require that it be appraised before the sale and that the sale bring a certain percentage of its determined value. Other states guarantee debtors the right to repurchase their property if they can somehow come up with the necessary money within a specified period.

FRAUDULENT CONVEYANCES

The person who owes you money isn't someone you'd want dating one of your children. It's bad enough that he's a borrower rather than a lender (you never subscribed to the admonition against being either), and worse that he hasn't made timely payment on his debts. But now, as you try to collect on those debts, the no-count four-flusher has started transferring his most valuable assets to friends, neighbors, and relatives—invariably for a pittance, and invariably with the understanding that he'll continue to have the use of them. Can he get away with this?

No. Such a transfer is considered a *fraudulent conveyance*, because (1) the debtor is making the transfer for less than fair value, and (2) it's rendering him insolvent.

If you're a debtor, think real hard before resorting to a fraudulent conveyance to protect your property. In addition to the fact that you may be committing a crime, a creditor can usually go to court and have such a conveyance nullified. Perhaps most galling from your perspective, if someone to whom you've made a fraudulent conveyance decides he wants to keep your property, you can't get it back. A judge will tell you to get lost, citing the venerable if anal maxim, "Let no person come into court with unclean hands."

EXEMPT PROPERTY

Every state has enacted laws exempting certain types of property from the reach of creditors. Among the critical items you're typically permitted to retain are your rifle, your mule, and several bags of grain. States that consider nourishment for the soul as important as nourishment for the body allow you to keep the family Bible. More modern jurisdictions let you keep a car if its value doesn't exceed, say, $1,500. (Presumably you also get to keep the blocks on which such a car would sit in your front lawn.)

All of the above is true. It's also illustrative of the striking antiquatedness of most states' exempt-property laws. To be sure, many states exempt additional categories of property, such as your life insurance, some or all of your wages, and your personal property worth up to several thousand dollars. And federal law protects your Social Security and veterans benefits. Still, all these things together are hardly sufficient to assure that you won't become a ward of the state.

Note that some exemptions, such as those for your clothes and Bible, are "absolute": You get them without actually doing anything. Other exemptions are yours only if you take certain steps—for example, declaring to the proper authorities, "I hereby claim the four thousand dollar personal property exemption. The items to which I want it to apply are: my tuba, my stuffed owl . . ." Check with a lawyer to make sure you don't overlook anything along these lines.

More meaningful protection for debtors arguably lies in *homestead exemption laws*, which have been enacted in many states to protect debtors' houses. These laws frequently carry such requirements as that the debtor have a family and that he and his family live in the house he seeks to protect.

Don't assume that just because you meet such requirements

your creditors can't touch your house, no matter how great its value and how extensive your debts. In most states the protection afforded by the homestead exemption is modest, covering only $5,000 or $10,000, say, of the value of the house (beyond whatever you owe on the mortgage). Even in rare states like Florida, where the dollar amount of the homestead exemption is unlimited, certain types of claims—for example, taxes, alimony, and child support—can generally be enforced against your house.

Note that homestead laws do nothing for apartment dwellers and other renters, which most prospective wards of the state are. However, many states grant such people a substitute exemption for other types of property, often in an amount equal to the homestead exemption.

Priorities Between Creditors

The state-law collection devices described above are available to any creditor. No matter who you are, if someone owes you money, you can attach his car, garnish his wages, execute on his stamp collection—in short, take any step allowed in the state in question. But assume you take one of these steps—what about his other creditors?

Who cares, right? You and your claim stand at the front of the line.

JUDICIAL LIENS

The technical explanation for your superior ranking here is that your attachment, garnishment, or execution on the property in question gives you a *lien* on it—more specifically, since these remedies have to be obtained through the courts, a *"judicial* lien" on it. This puts you in the enviable position of being a *lien creditor*, or, to be precise, a *"judicial* lien creditor." All other creditors are mere *"general* creditors."

But what if more than one creditor establishes a judicial lien on the same property? This could happen. Then it's not a matter of judicial-lien-creditor-versus-general-creditor, but judicial-lien-creditor-versus-another-judicial-lien-creditor.

Ranking judicial lien creditors against each other presents a "priority" question. Under state law (which is where we are until we get to bankruptcy law), priority among judicial lien creditors is governed by a "first-in-time, first-in-line" principle: Thus, if you attach or otherwise establish a lien on a debtor's prize pig, and you do it before anyone else, you'll get the best cut of pork, or at least your claim will have first call on the proceeds of the squealer's sale.

Other Sources of Priority Between Creditors

The option of obtaining a judicial lien through attachment or any of the remedies discussed above is available to literally any creditor. No matter how tacky your table manners or dubious your lineage, you can get into that club. Three other types of liens aren't available to just anyone, however, and any of these three types of liens gives you priority not only over general creditors but also over creditors whose priority is based solely on an attachment, a garnishment, or some other mere judicial lien.

1. *Consensual liens.* A consensual lien is one that the debtor *consents* to give the creditor, and that the creditor *consents* to accept, before the loan is made. A consensual lien on real estate bears the familiar name *mortgage*—what most people give a bank in exchange for money to buy a house. A consensual lien on *personal* property (meaning anything other than real estate—for example, your tractor, your sofa, your lint brush) is called a *security interest*.

To get the maximum priority out of a security interest, you have to complete or "perfect" it. Why? Because an *un*perfected security interest is junior or subordinate to a judicial lien on the same property.

The mechanics of perfecting a security interest depend on the rules of the state in which you're operating, and also on the nature of the collateral. If the collateral consists of stocks and bonds, for example, perfecting your security interest in them probably requires taking possession of them. You say to the borrower, "Hand them over."

If the collateral consists of four large cows, on the other

hand, perfecting your security interest in them probably requires filing a *financing statement*, a simple document bearing the names and addresses of the parties, along with a brief description of the collateral: "Four bovines, considerable in bulk but equable of disposition, answering to . . ."—with someone such as the clerk of the county in which the beasts reside.

2. *Statutory liens.* A number of liens superior in priority to judicial liens arise from state (and sometimes federal) statutes. There's nothing you can do to create one of these liens; either you meet the statutory criteria, or you don't.

Perhaps the most common statutory liens are mechanics' and "materialmen's" liens on buildings and other property, which secure payment for labor performed or materials furnished to repair or improve the property.

3. *Federal government liens.* The federal government didn't get to be the federal government by pussyfooting around with competing creditors. Certain federal laws give Uncle Sam priority over all other creditors in state-law insolvency proceedings, although with potentially significant exceptions. Whether the rules established by these laws affect your chances of collecting against a debtor with some kind of debt to Uncle Sam is a critical legal question. You're playing financial roulette if you attempt to collect against such a debtor without first coming up with an answer, ideally by consulting a lawyer.

DEBTORS' REMEDIES (SHORT OF BANKRUPTCY)

Debtors aren't without their own remedies or options under state law. They don't have many, and the ones they have aren't great, but you might take them over lumbago.

A debtor's two basic remedies in the event of a financial squeeze are: (1) an "assignment for the benefit of creditors," and (2) a "composition" or "extension." (Other remedies, such as a "slow-pay" motion, that is, a request to a court that you be allowed to pay your debts on an extended schedule, may also be available in your state.) These remedies are often described as "debtor-initiated," although that's like calling someone's delivery of his wallet to a mugger "victim-initiated."

Assignments for the Benefit of Creditors

The idea here is simple: You give or *assign* all or substantially all your assets to another person, the *assignee* or *trustee*, who then sells them and distributes the proceeds to your creditors.

An assignment for the benefit of creditors, like an actual bankruptcy proceeding, puts your assets beyond the reach of most of your creditors, the point in both contexts being to permit the trustee to deal with your assets without interference. However, an assignment for the benefit of creditors doesn't afford you the primary benefit of actual bankruptcy, namely, complete forgiveness or "discharge" of your obligations. In the assignment context, creditors whose claims aren't fully satisfied by the trustee's distribution could *choose* to let you off the hook for the rest of your obligations, but they don't have to.

Why might they ever do that? Because they figure your only alternative to an assignment for the benefit of creditors is formal bankruptcy, which takes longer and costs more. Hence, they might prefer an assignment simply to maximize their return.

Compositions and Extensions

A *composition* is a contract between a debtor and two or more of his creditors, under which the creditors agree to accept less than full payment of what they're owed. An *extension* is a contract between a debtor and two or more of his creditors, under which the creditors agree to stretch out the time in which the debtor has to pay. (A single contract can be both a composition and an extension.)

What's in either of these arrangements for the participating creditors? Their mutual concessions render the debtor better able to pay at least something to all of them.

From a debtor's perspective, how does a composition or extension stack up against bankruptcy? Quite well. Among other things, it offers all the benefits of bankruptcy, with less of the stigma. There's less stigma because—I acknowledge the circularity—the debtor hasn't actually "gone bankrupt." Another advantage is that if someone has guaranteed one of the debtor's obligations, a composition protects the guarantor as well as the debtor from further pursuit by the debtor's creditors. In contrast, a proceeding under Chapter 7 or Chapter 11 of the Bankruptcy Code leaves a guarantor completely vulnerable.

The bottom line: If you can get all your creditors to sign a composition, do it—in a heartbeat, before they change their minds.

BANKRUPTCY

Perhaps the very thought of filing for bankruptcy brings you close to losing your last meal. How mortifying, you think. And having to stand by and watch my creditors divvy up all my worldly possessions.

And yet things seem to be closing in on you. Over time, as your subconscious bends to accommodate necessity, the idea of bankruptcy takes on a semblance of tolerability. "Thousands of people do it every year," you say to yourself. (True enough. In 1985, 341,189 people filed for personal relief under the Bankruptcy Code.) "Maybe it wouldn't be so bad. Like divorce, which has become chic."

Think again. You were right the first time. Bankruptcy *is* humiliating. Your creditors *do* divvy up all your worldly possessions (at least in a Chapter 7 proceeding, the most common type under the Bankruptcy Code). Moreover, your credit rating is shot for a decade—the period that federal law allows credit investigators to continue mentioning your bankruptcy in their reports. Finally, while an employer can't legally discriminate against you simply because of a bankruptcy, what are the chances that he won't take it into account in evaluating you vis-à-vis your peers?

All these considerations carry us to the seventh of White's Irregular Rules, and the only one in this chapter:

Bankruptcy should be your *last* resort.

You have two basic options under bankruptcy law. First, you can throw in the towel completely, beseech the mercy of the court, and try for an entirely fresh start—free of assets, free of debts. (Mostly free of each, anyway.)

Second, you can ask for more limited help, conceding that you've got yourself into trouble, but insisting that with significant concessions from your creditors you could make a go of it—insisting, in other words, that you're capable of rehabilitation.

The first option, going entirely belly-up, is available under Chapter 7 of the Bankruptcy Code, titled "Liquidation." It's to such cases that the term *bankruptcy* is usually applied. The second option, rehabilitation, is available under Chapter 13, titled "Adjustment of the Debts of an Individual with Regular Income."*

Chapter 7—"Liquidation"

The basic idea of Chapter 7 is that you turn over your nonexempt assets to a trustee, who in turn sells them and distributes the proceeds to your creditors. In most cases this won't cover the full amount of your creditors' claims, but hey, things are hard all over. The point from your perspective is, you're off the hook. You've obtained a release or *discharge* of your debts.

Does every debtor who files under Chapter 7 receive a discharge of his debts? No! Bankruptcy discharges *some* debts of *some* debtors—a crucial point to keep in mind if you're contemplating this option.

Note a related point. If you file for bankruptcy and don't receive a discharge, it's not as if you've done no worse than

---

*Chapter 11, titled "Reorganization," offers an option similar to that of Chapter 13 but is intended primarily for businesses. In certain cases an individual can file under Chapter 11 as an individual; indeed, that would be your only alternative to Chapter 7 if your debts were large enough, because Chapter 13 is available only to debtors with unsecured debts of under $100,000 and secured debts of under $350,000. The discussion below, however, focuses on Chapter 13 to the exclusion of Chapter 11. If your debts exceed the figures just mentioned, you need more help than any one book can offer.

waste a little time and perhaps a little money. When you walk away, you'll walk away with your pockets empty, but you'll still be on the hook for the unpaid portions of your debts! This is like forcing down your mother's brussels sprouts, only to get sick before dessert.

There are several sets of circumstances in which you might fail to receive a discharge of your debts. This is the first of several lists you'll encounter in this section. The second list consists of exceptions to the first list. There should be a list of the lists. I include several lists in this section rather than, say, twenty pages of *Hamlet*, because lists are what bankruptcy law consists of. The harder you find it to keep track of these lists, the greater your understanding of the value of hiring a professional to guide you through this field.

The circumstances in which you might fail to receive a discharge include:

1. If you're filing not as an individual, but as a partnership or corporation.

2. If you're guilty of some form of dishonesty or lack of cooperation, such as making a fraudulent conveyance or failing to maintain adequate financial records. The latter point merits special attention. If your finances start swirling down the tubes, you may be tempted to let your accounting and recordkeeping do the same. Be aware that this could cost you the option of obtaining a discharge of your debts.

3. If you've received a discharge under Chapter 7, 11, or 13 within the past six years (except that an earlier discharge under Chapter 13 doesn't have this preclusive effect if you obtained it by paying off at least 70 percent of all unsecured claims).

Now, suppose it's clear that you're entitled to a discharge. Does that mean you'll walk away from the bankruptcy court owing not so much as a nickel to anybody in the world? No. Here comes the above-mentioned list of exceptions to discharge, that is, claims that individual creditors may legally continue to pursue, notwithstanding that you're in bankruptcy and headed for a general discharge:

1. Claims for certain taxes.

2. Claims for money or property obtained through fraud or any other form of dishonesty. Banks and finance companies frequently invoke this exception, because so many desperate loan applicants manage to overvalue their assets or overlook a number of existing debts.

3. Claims of a creditor who didn't participate in the bankruptcy proceeding because he never heard about it.

4. Claims for fines and penalties owed to governmental entities. These include your student loan obligations, unless, among other things, you filed your bankruptcy petition over five years after your loan repayment period began. The justification for this rule appears to be that a five-year delay ensures a lack of premeditation, students being psychologically incapable of looking further than a semester or two down the road.

THE COMMENCEMENT OF A CHAPTER 7 CASE

Every case under the Bankruptcy Act starts with the filing of a petition. A case under Chapter 7 can be either voluntary, in which case the petition is filed by you, or involuntary, in which case the petition is filed by your creditors. The current price of admission is $60.

You can't file a voluntary petition every other week. Suppose you filed one last month, but it was dismissed yesterday. If the reason for the dismissal was that you failed to obey orders of the bankruptcy judge or personally requested dismissal, you have to wait 180 days before you can file again.

Regarding dismissal, you don't have an absolute right to it in a Chapter 7 case, not even a voluntary one. Bankruptcy isn't like a movie, which you can walk out of if you don't like what you see. The decision rests with the judge.

Only a minority of cases are involuntary, partly because many creditors don't know how much trouble their debtors have got themselves into, but also because creditors probably calculate that they'll come out better in the long run if they keep a debtor afloat.

THE TRUSTEE

The next step in a Chapter 7 case is the appointment by the bankruptcy judge of an *interim trustee* to take possession or control of all your property. This occurs immediately after the issuance of the judge's "order for relief," which sets the case in motion—or even earlier, if the judge is persuaded it's necessary to protect your property. This same trustee serves throughout the proceeding unless creditors holding at least 20 percent of the unsecured claims elect a new one.

Who'll be the trustee in your case? Generally he'll be someone randomly selected from a standing panel of trustees—possibly a lawyer, although that's not mandatory. The trustee's tasks in a Chapter 7 case include collecting your assets (including property you unloaded shortly before the case began), selling your assets, distributing the proceeds of your assets to your creditors, resisting excessive claims by your creditors, and, sometimes, opposing discharge of your debts.

The trustee's fee is paid out of your estate, based on a percentage of the value of the property he handles—3 percent for property worth more than $3,000. He can earn additional fees by appointing himself to serve as the lawyer for the trustee, that is, for himself. (If you're still thinking clearly, this should strike you as odd.)

YOUR ESTATE

Your *bankruptcy estate* consists of all your (nonexempt) property—tangible and intangible, real and personal, in your hands and in the hands of others—as of the time of commencement of the case. Your estate doesn't include property you acquire *after* the commencement of the case, with exceptions for such things as property you receive by inheritance or as the beneficiary of a life insurance policy, if you receive such within 180 days of the commencement of the case.

EXEMPT PROPERTY

In federal bankruptcy proceedings, as in state-law collection actions, certain property is considered exempt, or protected, from the collection process; the trustee leaves it alone, and the creditors get no part of it.

Typical of the way bankruptcy law is structured, it's not enough that there are exemptions; there must also be exceptions to the exemptions. Specifically, creditors are permitted to go after even exempt property if their claims are of certain types, such as claims for taxes, claims for child support and alimony, or claims based on certain types of security interests in property *other* than certain household items, work tools, and health aids. (These last three items could be said to constitute exceptions to the exceptions to the exemptions.)

THE AUTOMATIC STAY

While the bankruptcy case is pending, what are your creditors doing to enforce their claims against you? Nothing, if they're doing what they're supposed to be doing (or, rather, *not* doing what they're *not* supposed to be doing). The filing of any form of bankruptcy petition automatically calls a halt to—or *stays*—every form of collection activity, from deep-breathing phone calls to the obtaining and perfecting of liens.

Are there exceptions to the application of the stay? Of course. Among the collection activities not stayed are efforts to collect child support and alimony and efforts to collect from third parties, such as guarantors of your debts. Thus, if your mother cosigned your application for a car loan, the lender could still go after her. The swine.

INVALIDATION OF PREBANKRUPTCY TRANSFERS

Suppose all your assets in the world consist of $10,000 in cash and $40,000 in property. Your debts total $100,000. There's no question that you're headed for bankruptcy, but there's plenty of question—in your mind, at least—as to who's going to end up with your $50,000 of assets. *You* aren't going to end up with them; that's clear. But isn't there some way you could see that they get to your mother?

"Why not make a gift of them to your mother before filing your bankruptcy petition?" a resourceful friend suggests. "Or sell them to her for a nominal price, such as one apple pie."

Your friend isn't the first to have conceived such schemes. Hence the reams of statutory and judge-made law dealing with the power of bankruptcy trustees to invalidate—or *avoid*—various types of prebankruptcy transfers.

What's the effect of a trustee's invalidation of a given transfer? It results in recovery of the property from the recipient, for the benefit of the estate. This is a key area of bankruptcy law, because often a flurry of transactions takes place immediately prior to the filing of a bankruptcy petition. Indeed, it's often to bring such transactions to a halt that involuntary bankruptcy petitions are filed.

The major categories of transfers that a trustee is empowered to invalidate include:

1. *Preferences.* A preference is just what it sounds like, a transfer that "prefers" one creditor over another. A transfer constitutes a preference if: (a) it occurs within ninety days of the filing of the bankruptcy petition (or within one year if the transfer is to an *insider,* such as a relative); (b) you're insolvent when you make the transfer; (c) you make it for the benefit of a creditor; (d) its purpose is to repay an *antecedent debt,* that is, a debt you already owe; and (e) it has the effect of increasing what that creditor would otherwise have received under Chapter 7. (In the statute, there now follow various exceptions to this definition, such as payments to the local utility company for your monthly electric bill and other transfers in the ordinary course of business.)

2. *Fraudulent conveyances.* Bankruptcy law, like state debtor-creditor law, doesn't like fraudulent conveyances. Note that gifts constitute fraudulent conveyances if made by someone who isn't solvent—a hard rule for bankrupts around Christmas and Hanukkah.

3. *Landlords' statutory liens.* Suppose you've fallen behind in your rent payments. If some state statute grants your landlord an automatic lien on your property for unpaid rent, a trustee can invalidate that lien.

WHO GETS WHAT—SECURED AND UNSECURED CLAIMS

Various things in life are well established as better than other things. Two heads are better than one; a bird in the hand is better than two in the bush; to light a single candle is better than to curse the darkness; to have loved and lost is better than never to have loved at all; and you're a better man than I am, Gunga Din.

Similarly, a secured claim is better than an unsecured claim—a principle to live by. This is because secured claims must be paid off before unsecured claims.

A *secured claim* is one backed up by some form of collateral—for example, one for which the creditor (the *secured creditor*) has a lien on specific property of the bankrupt (assuming the lien isn't a preference or some other form of avoidable transfer). Not surprisingly, an *unsecured claim* is one *not* backed up by some form of collateral.

How is a secured creditor satisfied under Chapter 7? He gets one of two things: the collateral supporting his claim, or the cash value of the collateral. (If the value of the collateral is less than the value of the claim, he's treated as if he had two claims, a secured one and an unsecured one.)

How is an *un*secured creditor satisfied under Chapter 7? In theory, unsecured creditors get whatever remains after: (a) the debtor has received his exempt property; (b) all secured creditors have been satisfied; and (c) all administrative expenses (such as the trustee's fee and the trustee's lawyer's fee) have been paid. In *reality*, unsecured creditors get nothing. There just never seems to be anything left after the secured creditors have come and gone.

Chapter 13—"Adjustment of the Debts of an Individual with Regular Income"

The idea of Chapter 13 is to give you a chance to pay off your debts. Unlike Chapter 7, which wipes out your debts in one fell swoop by liquidating all your worldly possessions and turning the proceeds over to your creditors, Chapter 13 lets you hang on to your worldly possessions and attempt to satisfy your obligations out of current income—usually paying on a revised schedule, often with some reduction in the amount owed—in accordance with a detailed, court-approved plan.

Which is preferable from your point of view, Chapter 7 or Chapter 13? That depends on your individual circumstances, but Chapter 13 does offer several clear advantages. First, you get to retain your possessions while paying off your debts—no small benefit, *if* you have possessions you want to retain. Second, a discharge under Chapter 13 is broader than a discharge under Chapter 7, that is, it has significantly fewer exceptions. Third, and perhaps most important, a Chapter 13 proceeding isn't generally viewed as "bankruptcy," and hence doesn't carry the same stigma—with creditors, employers, the public, possibly yourself.

The chief disadvantage of Chapter 13 is that you do have to pay off the bulk of your debts—which is obviously worse than *not* having to pay off the bulk of your debts. Another disadvantage of Chapter 13 is that until you've completed the payments required under your plan, you live under certain financial restrictions that may make you feel like you're on parole. For example, you can't dispose of any property, real or personal, without permission of the court.

What do you want out of a Chapter 13 proceeding? The same thing you want out of a Chapter 7 proceeding: discharge of your debts. Which debts are discharged under Chapter 13? All of them covered by your plan (which is usually all of them), except for (1) claims for alimony and child support, and (2) claims for obligations that stretch beyond the duration of your plan (for example, a seven-year loan for the purchase of a boat).

You receive your discharge under Chapter 13 upon completion of the payments required by your plan. In some circumstances, the bankruptcy judge can grant you a "hardship" discharge—when, for example, a serious illness prevents you from making good on the terms of your plan.

COMMENCEMENT OF A CHAPTER 13 CASE

A Chapter 13 proceeding, like a Chapter 7 proceeding, begins with the filing of a petition, accompanied by a "plan."

Again, the price of admission is $60. You can file under Chapter
13 only if you meet three criteria: (1) you're acting as an individual, rather than as a corporation or partnership (but a sole
proprietorship is okay); (2) you have a "regular income," that
is, one sufficiently stable to enable you to comply with a reasonable Chapter 13 plan; and (3) your unsecured debts are less
than $100,000, and your secured debts less than $350,000.

The same frequent-filing limitation that applies under Chapter 7 also applies here: a 180-day wait if your earlier case was
dismissed either for failure to obey court orders or at your request following a creditor's motion for relief from the automatic stay.

All filings under Chapter 13 are voluntary; your creditors
can't force you into it, as they can under Chapter 7. Because
creditors, especially unsecured creditors, are likely to come out
better under Chapter 13 than under Chapter 7, they're often well
advised to attempt to persuade you to opt for the former, either
by financial concessions or by appeals to your love of your family
and pets.

A filing under Chapter 13, like a filing under Chapter 7,
automatically stays all creditor collection efforts. The one difference is that under Chapter 13, creditors have to stay away not
only from you, but also from most of your co-debtors.

YOUR PLAN

A Chapter 13 *plan* consists in essence of a list of your creditors and a declaration as to how much and when you propose
to pay them. Normally a Chapter 13 plan lasts no longer than
three years, but a court can extend the limit to five.

Certain provisions are mandatory for Chapter 13 plans, the
most important being that you'll either pay off all your creditors
in full, or turn over to them all your "disposable income" for
the duration of your plan. *Disposable income* means income in
addition to whatever you and your family need for bread and
water.

Regarding secured creditors, unless they agree otherwise,
your plan must either surrender to them the actual collateral

securing their claims or pay them the collateral's cash value. Regarding unsecured creditors, your plan may pay them less than the full amount of their claims, but it can't pay them less than they would have received if you had filed under Chapter 7 instead of 13.

A trustee gets into the act under Chapter 13, but with somewhat different responsibilities than under Chapter 7. His role here may consist of little more than receiving money from you and then sending it back out to your creditors. This role could expand if he has to invalidate a preference, a fraudulent conveyance, or some other improper transfer. Similarly, if you fail to make a payment—even one payment—required by your plan, he's required to seek dismissal of your case or conversion to Chapter 7.

AFTER YOU FILE

Filing your petition and plan starts things happening on a number of fronts. First, notice goes out from the court to your creditors, informing them that you've filed under Chapter 13, providing them with a copy or summary of your plan, and indicating the date and time of the usual postfiling meeting of creditors—typically a month or two down the road. It also tells them how much time they have to file their claims against you, usually ninety days from the creditors' meeting.

The purpose of the creditors' meeting, which is attended by you, your lawyer, and the trustee, but not the bankruptcy judge, is to permit your creditors to question you directly under oath. This meeting also gives your lawyer a final opportunity to confer with your creditors, negotiate the terms of your plan, and just plain beg.

After the creditors' meeting comes the *confirmation hearing*, at which the judge listens to and considers anyone's objections to your plan. The final decision is his alone. Bankruptcy lawyers refer to a judge's confirmation of a plan over the objections of creditors as a "cram down"—a rare instance of vigor in legal terminology. The judge's confirmation order puts the plan formally into effect.

FUNDING THE PLAN

Under Chapter 13, your money doesn't go directly to your creditors; it goes first to the trustee, and *then* to your creditors. In most cases, you don't even make your own payments to the trustee; the norm is for the court to issue a payroll deduction order to your employer, who then directs a specified portion of your wages or salary to the trustee.

Upon the filing of your Chapter 13 petition, every nickel of your income from then until the time your plan is confirmed becomes at least theoretically available for the funding of your plan. Only upon confirmation by the court is the amount that the trustee can claim for such funding reduced to the amount specified in your plan. (Note that within thirty days from the filing of your petition and plan you're required to commence making the payments specified in your plan. In other words, things happen quickly under Chapter 13.)

The Role of Lawyers

Three questions confront anyone contemplating filing for relief under Chapter 7 or Chapter 13:

1. *Do you need a lawyer?* Note first that you're not legally required to have a lawyer in a bankruptcy case. The issue is whether it's *wise* to have one.

As suggested above, this area is so complex and just plain messy that consulting a lawyer before filing anything would be eminently prudent. This is especially true at the outset of your financial troubles, when you're deciding whether to file at all. Remember that your primary goal isn't just to get through bankruptcy as painlessly as possible; it's to stay out of it altogether. A lawyer who helps you do that will be sparing you not only the misery of bankruptcy, but also the additional cost of keeping him around any longer than necessary.

Suppose you've made up your mind, with or without advice from a lawyer, to file under one of the bankruptcy chapters. Can you get by on your own from here?

It depends. Are you financially sophisticated? How complex

are your problems? What kinds of issues are likely to be raised by your creditors?

Regardless of your answers to these questions, this much is clear: Although you might be able to pull it off on your own under Chapter 7, it's foolhardy to attempt to do so under Chapter 13.

Chapter 7 can be comparatively easy. You file your petition, turn over your assets to the trustee, and promise not to screw up again. No doubt this comparative ease goes far to explain why many bankruptcy lawyers reflexively steer clients toward Chapter 7, rather than Chapter 13. (Today a lawyer is legally *required* to tell you about both chapters. If he doesn't mention *non*bankruptcy alternatives as well, however, get a new lawyer.)

Chapter 13 involves more—notably your plan. First, and most technically difficult, there's the task of formulating it. This requires not only a detailed review of every aspect of your finances, but also potentially lengthy negotiation with each of your creditors. Then there's the creditors' meeting, followed by the confirmation hearing before the judge. Finally, once your plan is confirmed, there's the job of *living* with it—and with its enforcer, the trustee—for up to five years.

Perhaps you're still determined to go it alone. You'd sooner sleep on a park bench for the rest of your life than hire a lawyer, or you feel that you're so close to having to do that anyway (sleep on a park bench) that hiring a lawyer couldn't possibly be cost-justified.

Good news: You don't have to work from scratch. Standard blank forms are available for a Chapter 7 or Chapter 13 petition, as well as for a Chapter 13 plan. (Check the yellow pages under "Legal Forms," or call Brennan Printing Company, 613 North 6th Street, Kansas City, KS 66101, 800/255-4548.) The full package of about twelve forms and schedules costs around fifteen dollars. Just fill in the blanks and take them to the courthouse with your fee. Clerks there will grimace when they discover you're acting *pro se*—on your own—but ignore their churlishness. They work for you—John Q. Public.

For information on any part of the process, be resourceful. Call the bankruptcy court. Call the local bar referral service (ask for the name of someone willing to provide *pro bono*—free—advice). Call the legal aid clinic at a nearby law school; the students there may or may not know what they're doing, but their faculty advisers will.

2. *How much does a bankruptcy lawyer charge?* Lawyers at the giant bulk-process legal clinics charge around $500 for a standard case under Chapter 7, and around $700 for a standard case under Chapter 13. Lawyers at standard firms charge more, but usually only a few hundred dollars more, because bankruptcy judges ride close herd on legal fees.

When a lawyer (or someone at his office) quotes you a fee, pin him down on what type of case he's talking about. Only with considerable persistence was I able to get receptionists at various offices of Hyatt Legal Services to concede that the comparatively low fee they were quoting me was solely for a Chapter 7 filing. Presumably they would have informed me of the higher fee for a Chapter 13 filing only when I arrived for an appointment.

3. *If you're broke, how are you supposed to pay a lawyer?* The usual practice under Chapter 13 is to pay your lawyer through your plan, that is, to include his fee as one more debt to be paid in installments via the trustee. The usual practice under Chapter 7, since no plan ever comes into existence, is to pay your lawyer up front. Bankruptcy lawyers often insist on this, because clients with zero assets can be slow to pay.

Under either chapter, how you plan to pay your lawyer's fee is required to be fully disclosed in your petition, and it's subject to the approval of the judge. If the fee doesn't exceed an amount recognized as reasonable in your locality—$750, say—the judge will probably approve it without ado. If it does exceed that amount, the judge will probably hold a hearing on it and require an explanation.

7. Intellectual Property

Copyright •

Trademarks •

One of the greatest pains to human nature is the pain of a new idea.

WALTER BAGEHOT

(1826–1877)

$E = mc^3$

MARTIN J. YUDKOWITZ

(1954–   )

COPYRIGHT

New ideas really can be painful. Especially coming up with one. Name two ideas that you'd be prepared to go on national television and claim as your own.

That's why the law surely protects original ideas, ensuring that any benefits to be had from one go to its originator. Right?

Wrong. Suppose your name is Saul Steinberg. You're an artist. Occasionally your work appears in *The New Yorker*. One day you begin fiddling around with a sketch that strikes you as cute: It shows the streets and buildings of New York City looming in the foreground, with tiny doodles in the background representing the world beyond the Hudson River. The idea—the joke—is that this is the typical Manhattanite's perspective on the world.

You show this to the people at *The New Yorker*. They agree it's cute, and several weeks later they run it on the cover. It looks good. No big deal, though; your work always looks good.

Then the world goes berserk. The phones at the magazine switchboard begin ringing off the hook. Letters and telegrams pour in. People everywhere *adore* your drawing, and they're raving about you. Reporters want to know what inspired the drawing. What will you draw next? What do you think about the Middle East situation?

Soon the *New Yorker* people want to make a poster out of your painting. You say, "Why not?" Eight printings and almost 70,000 copies later, you've made your mark on the world. And your mother wanted you to be a lawyer.

One morning you find yourself in the elevator with a colleague who says, "Saul, I saw your *Bostonian's Perspective* poster. Great idea. There's bound to be a market for those everywhere." Someone else in the elevator chimes in, "Yeah, I saw your poster of *The Harvard View of the World*. You're going to make a million, guy."

This is irritating. You don't know what they're talking about, but you do know you're in it for the art, not the money. You scoot down to the nearest poster store, only to have your worst fears confirmed: Retailers are selling imitations of your now-classic drawing.

Parodies! Nowhere do they mention your name or *The New Yorker*, and no one with the intelligence of a one-speed blender would confuse the "artwork" with yours. But the *idea* is the same: a colorful, loosely drawn rendering of a city or campus, with an exaggerated portion given over to the primary locale and a minimal portion conceded to the world beyond. Can this be legal?

Yes.

Mr. Steinberg's story (related here with a few embellishments) illustrates a key principle in the area of "intellectual property": *Ideas* aren't protected. Only *expressions* of ideas are protected. Why? The law figures it's bad for society to grant anyone a monopoly on an idea. Besides, if an idea isn't reduced to expression, how is a judge to determine where one person's idea ends and another person's begins?

To continue with our *New Yorker* story, Mr. Steinberg is distressed as he learns from the magazine's legal office that his idea isn't protected. "But," the chief counsel tells him, "there's good news and bad news. The bad news is, people are not only parodying your Manhattan poster, but counterfeiting it—selling thousands of exact duplicates. The good news is, *that's* illegal."

What's the difference? Again, ideas themselves aren't protected, but expressions of ideas are. To illustrate, still in a visual medium, if you take a beautiful photograph of the Grand Canyon and sell it for use on greeting cards, no one else may legally use your photo for any purpose. On the other hand, someone *could* take advantage of your *idea*, making a greeting card or poster out of his own photo of the Grand Canyon.

To shift to the literary domain, the fact that you've written a wonderful story about romance in the South during the Civil War doesn't give you a monopoly on the general *idea* of romance in the South during the Civil War. On the other hand, if someone borrows verbatim passages from your book—you're particularly proud of your descriptions of the characters Scarlett and Rhett— he's copying your *expression* of an idea. And that's protected.

To apply some jargon, a lawyer would say you hold the "copyright" to the *expression* of that story idea. Or that photo idea, or that poster idea. (You get the idea.)

As for "characters" like Scarlett and Rhett, to what extent are they protected under copyright law? To what extent do such characters constitute expressions of ideas?

Suppose you want to manufacture and sell dolls, miniature male and female figures bearing the names Scarlett and Rhett and dressed in antebellum clothes identical to those worn by Vivien Leigh and Clark Gable in the movie *Gone With the Wind*. You probably can't do it.

Copying, to be illegal, needn't be in the same medium. So ruled a federal court in a 1924 case involving alleged infringement of a character from the cartoon strip *Barney Google*. The infringed character was Mr. Google's swaybacked, weather-beaten horse, Spark Plug. The infringing item was a toy horse, identical in appearance to the cartoon horse and also called Spark Plug. Differences of size or material, the court said, don't preclude a finding of infringement.

In 1934, the same court reached essentially the same result in a case involving the cartoon character Betty Boop, a comely blond woman later popularized in movies. The defendant in that case had produced a Betty Boop doll, and the court ruled that a three-dimensional copy is fully capable of infringing the copyright of a two-dimensional picture or drawing.

Such *visually* represented characters are generally easier to protect than *verbally* represented characters, the former being so clearly identifiable, and hence so clearly constituting expressions of ideas. How much debate can there be, for example, as to whether a stuffed animal duplicates the cartoon dog Snoopy or the cartoon cat Garfield?

Where's the line between an idea and the expression of that idea? God only knows.

Suppose you're trying to develop a television series, but all you know so far is that it'll be a police story. That alone is clearly no more than an idea. How about a police story set in the precinct headquarters of a tough urban neighborhood? It's still too abstract to constitute the expression of an idea. How about such a story based on the lives of a reformed-alcoholic captain named Furillo, a foxy but abrasive public defender named Davenport, and a growling, dog-breathed detective named Belker, among others? Now you're into *expression*.

There's a continuum—from unprotected ideas, to possibly protected story lines, to definitely protected dialogue and other detail. The more detail you include, the farther you get from mere ideas, and the closer you get to expression. The question is, how close can one story (or picture or song) come to another without ripping it off?

Again, there's no clear line, although a judge or jury would have to draw one if someone tried to rip off—"infringe the copyright of," a lawyer would say—material from "Hill Street Blues," the tremendously popular television series in which these characters appear. The test of whether an imitator has gone beyond copying the idea and has borrowed the expression must be, according to one court, "the response of the ordinary reasonable person."

Determining the parameters of someone's copyright in a show (or picture or song) is often far from easy. Is singer Billy Joel ripping off James Brown or the Four Seasons with his imitations of their sound and style in his *Innocent Man* album? People who hear songs from that album over the radio may think they're actually hearing James Brown or the Four Seasons.

This brings us to the eighth of White's Irregular Rules, and the first for this chapter:

Always add something of your own.

Note that the rule can't be stated as simply as "Don't rip people off." There are only so many ideas in existence, and they're all based to some extent on each other. Thus, you can't help copying other people's ideas somewhat—ripping them off. We all do it.

How much of your own must you add? There's no clear answer. All you can do is consider what an "ordinary reasonable person" would think. Billy Joel added lots of his own to the material of James Brown, the Four Seasons, and the others he modeled his songs after in *Innocent Man*. Consider the music-and-dance shows *Fame*, *A Chorus Line*, and *All That Jazz*: While all three have substantial elements in common, each contains additional, distinguishing elements that eliminate (or ought to eliminate) copyright problems vis-à-vis the other two.

Novelty versus Originality

If you have to add something of your own, the question becomes, add what? Not something new; the law doesn't require *novelty*. What it requires is *originality*.

Is this classic lawyer's bushwa—a distinction without a difference? Sort of. But consider the idea bandied about among statisticians that if you put a monkey alone in a room with a typewriter for thousands of years, it would, by the laws of chance, not only render the room unsuitable for company, but also compose *Hamlet*. Just banging away randomly on the Olivetti.

Now, if a monkey could produce *Hamlet* in a few millennia, who's to say *you* couldn't produce *Tender Is the Night* in a century? Or *Love Story* in a decade? Or *Elvis Is Dead, and I Don't Feel So Good Myself* (by Atlantan Lewis Grizzard) in a week? The point is that it's *conceivable* that two people working independently in remote places could come up with the same copyrightable book (or picture or song).

To be sure, some things are less likely than others. Try convincing a judge you had never even heard of Herman Wouk's *Caine Mutiny* when you wrote your own identical story. But if this somehow happened, you and Mr. Wouk would *both* have copyright in the work.

"So what," you ask, "since we agree that as a practical matter no one will ever just stumble into writing *The Caine Mutiny*?" Maybe not, but people write similar television scripts all the time. Not identical, but close enough to raise copyright-infringement questions if it could be proven that the author of one script had read the other in advance. This is why television networks are loath to read or even open unsolicited manuscripts.

If novelty were the test, copyright would be a race to the publication wire, with every later version barred by the first. But with originality as the test—also called the "sweat" test, granting copyright to any artist who has put enough of his own sweat into the creation—multiple copyrights for similar works are possible.

Intent to Infringe

No doubt you're glad these issues are being addressed from the perspective of an artist whose copyright has been infringed. Because that's the only way these issues could ever become important in your life, right?

One day, as you and a friend are strolling to lunch, your friend says, "What's that tune you're whistling?" "I don't know," you reply. "Just something I made up." "It's nice," your friend says. "Get Burt Bacharach to play it and you could retire in

luxury." On the way back you observe that both you and your
friend are humming that tune.

At home that night you pull out some crinkled, yellowing
blank score paper left over from your tuba days in college and
scribble out the tune. It *is* nice, you think. I'll bet this is how
Mozart got started.

The next day you mail a copy of the tune to your old college
roommate, a music agent in New York. You enclose a note asking
how much you could get for it.

Three days later your roommate calls. "I'm no lawyer," he
says, "but I think the most you could get for it is"—he pauses—
"seven years at hard labor, with time off for good behavior.
Manilow's people don't like copyright infringers."

You're stunned. You could have *sworn* you made up that
tune. Your roommate is still giggling when you hang up.

An impossible scenario? Tell that to George Harrison. In
1976 a New York court ruled that the former Beatle's song "My
Sweet Lord" plagiarized "He's So Fine" by the Chiffons. Nobody
said George did it deliberately. The court generously commented
that "his subconscious knew . . . a song his conscious mind did
not remember."

The point is that you don't have to steal material *intentionally*
to infringe someone's copyright. Access is the key. In 1984 a
court ruled that the Bee Gees' hit song "How Deep Is Your
Love," which did so much for the movie *Saturday Night Fever*,
didn't infringe composer Ronald Selle's earlier song "Let It End."
The court held that there was no "reasonable possibility" that
any of the Bee Gees had had access to Selle's comparatively
obscure song.

Putting the Work on Paper

You're an aspiring comedian. Your best friend is a funny
guy who writes for David Letterman, and you and your friend
spend a lot of time trying out new material on each other. A
week before your important gig at New York's Comic Strip, you
ask your friend to check out your new routine, a ten-minute bit
on life at a Catholic high school, with jokes about how you grew

up thinking "original sin" meant making up a new one every day.

Your friend loves the routine. He asks for a copy of the script so he can review it for you again at home. "Script?" you say. "It's nowhere but in my brain."

The next night you turn on the Letterman show, just in time to hear David say, "You know, I spent a few years at a Catholic high school. I thought 'original sin' meant making up a new one every day." And then, word for word, he moves through your entire routine. You throw up and call your lawyer. Copyright infringement?

Not if you never wrote down your routine. The federal copyright statute protects only artistic material that's "fixed in any tangible medium of expression." A hand-written draft would suffice, or a videotape of the routine. It would be enough if you recited the whole thing into someone's answering machine.

The Letterman story is fictional. But the requirement that your song, story, comedy routine, or other artistic product be captured on paper, tape, or your bathroom wall is real. If you swim in the shark-infested waters of novelists, screenwriters, television producers, and others constantly hungry for material, it's especially real.

Suppose you've spent a number of years developing an extraordinary wild-west persona. You appear in rodeos, parades, and horse shows as a mustachioed, derringer-toting cowboy who dresses in black. You carry a card that features a chess knight and reads, "Have Gun Will Travel—Wire Paladin." One day you discover that CBS television has turned a virtually identical character into a tremendously successful television series, "Have Gun Will Travel." You point out that the series is obviously based on a character created by you. CBS tells you to get lost.

According to Victor DeCosta, the plaintiff in a 1967 lawsuit, this is exactly what happened. DeCosta's suit failed, however. Although the court based its ruling on technicalities of the law as it was then written, the suit would fail again today. Why? A creation can be original, and it can be sufficiently detailed to constitute expression, but if it hasn't been reduced to writing or some other tangible form, it isn't protected.

State Law Remedies

Perhaps the results in the fictional Letterman case and the true Paladin case don't sit well with you. "Why," you ask, "must the material have been reduced to tangible form to be protected?" The answer involves evidence or proof; if you never wrote the song or story down, why should a court believe you developed it first? Furthermore, doesn't the fact that you never wrote it down suggest that you never really took it beyond an abstract stage, that for you it was just a vague idea and hence *shouldn't* enjoy copyright protection?

"No, dammit," you say. "I come up with piles of original, concrete material that sit in my head for a long time before going down on paper. If the law won't protect those gems, there's a hole in the law."

And so there is, at least in the *federal* law in this area. But where the federal law leaves off, various state doctrines pick up, filling in the holes. Most states where you'd want to live have laws that cover areas known as "misappropriation," "unfair competition," and "passing off," not to mention old-fashioned "fraud."

Suppose you're broke. To make some quick cash, you agree to let a circus shoot you out of a cannon. The publicity goes out, unprecedented crowds show up to watch, and it occurs to you as you climb down the barrel that if you survive, you'll make a minor fortune.

You do survive. Moreover, it wasn't so bad, although your knees hurt a little, and the smell at the bottom of the barrel has you suspicious as to what those mischievous elephant trainers have been up to.

Then the television people show up. "Beat it," you tell them. "Who'd pay to see me in person after watching me on the evening news?"

Can you stop them from broadcasting your performance, or at least penalize them if they do?

Yes. And the U.S. Supreme Court will back you up, as in 1977 it backed up "Hugo the Great" Zacchini, whose fifteen-second Human Cannonball act was broadcast without his permission by a television station in Burton, Ohio. The Court said that while Zacchini's act didn't qualify for protection under the federal copyright statute, since it hadn't been reduced to a tangible form, it did qualify for protection under state law. Specifically, his obvious economic interest in the display of his act gave him a "right of publicity" analogous to the audiovisual rights of an author whose book someone wants to make into a movie.

The Human Cannonball case is true, and it illustrates a significant point: While the federal copyright statute is the primary source of protection for "intellectual property," there are numerous other ways you can protect your work from unscrupulous or unthinking people. Similarly, there are numerous other ways people can protect their work from an unscrupulous or unthinking you.

TITLES

Not every quirky hole in federal copyright protection is filled by state law. Suppose you work in the car-manufacturing industry. People always kid you about your funny Italian name, but you keep your nose to the grindstone. Later, as head of a major company in the industry, you rescue it from one of the largest potential bankruptcies in history, in the process becoming a national hero. You write a book (or rather, a sharp fellow named William Novak writes a book based on conversations with you), which is to be released as your official autobiography.

The last question you and Novak ponder before your book goes to press in 1984 is, what to call it? The obvious title is your name, Iacocca. Two years earlier, however, a fellow named David Abodaher put out a biography of you using that very title. His book never went anywhere, but the darn thing has the title you want.

"Relax," your publisher's lawyer tells you. "You want *Iacocca*, you got *Iacocca*. Book titles can't be copyrighted."

"We don't want to go overboard," he says. "We can't use an identical cover design, with the same colors, type, and layout. People would confuse our book with Abodaher's, and vice versa. Then he could nail us under some state law pertaining to fraud, passing off, or unfair competition. But the title itself is fair game."

You're delighted to hear this. You're also delighted when your book becomes one of the best-selling hardbacks of all time. (Not coincidentally, Abodaher's book, a paperback, became a national best-seller at the same time.)

This story, in its essentials, is true, as is the legal point that titles aren't subject to copyright protection. To be sure, because of the state laws mentioned above, if you use another book's title you'd better make sure your own book's cover design is substantially different and that your own, presumably different name (as author) is prominently featured. If possible, you should come up with an altogether different title.

What Can Be Copyrighted

There's no clear limit on what you can copyright. The copyright statute carries a nonexclusive list, including literary works, musical works, dramatic works, pictorial and sculptural works, pantomimes and other choreographic works, motion pictures and other audiovisual works, and sound recordings.

What *can't* you copyright? Ideas (as opposed to *expressions* of ideas), as discussed. The statute also excludes "processes," "systems," "principles" and "discoveries"—which are just different ways of saying "ideas."

The other big category outside the scope of copyright protection consists of "utilitarian" objects, that is, things that are useful. Why? The law doesn't want to give you a monopoly on a particular form of lamp, shoehorn, or paper clip. (If you come up with something *really* useful, you may be entitled to a *patent*, that is, a seventeen-year legal monopoly on a "product" or "process" that meets the statutory requirements of being "new," "nonobvious," and "useful.")

The idea/expression and utilitarian/nonutilitarian dichotomies overlap. Consider several examples:

• A lamp (useful) is not copyrightable, but an artistic lampstand (in effect, a sculpture) may be.

• A towel or bedsheet (useful) is not copyrightable, but an artistic pattern or design on the fabric may be.

• A house (useful) is not copyrightable, but a house's architectural blueprint (as the written expression of an idea) is.

These issues lie at the heart of the dispute between sculptor Nancy Holt, who in 1980 produced the iron, birdcagelike gazebo that now sits in a park in Washington, D.C., and Josie Orr, the wife of the governor of Indiana. Ms. Orr saw Ms. Holt's work in Washington and asked her to donate it to the state of Indiana. Ms. Holt refused. Ms. Orr then commissioned a similar *but not identical* gazebo, which was produced in 1981 and now sits on the lawn of the governor's residence in Indiana.

Does a specially designed and crafted gazebo such as that produced by Ms. Holt contain elements of artistic originality? Clearly. Is it also useful? Arguably. Did Ms. Orr copy Ms. Holt's work? The answer appears to be yes, because the two gazebos differ only in minor, ornamental details and in some of their materials. But how a judge would decide such a case one can only speculate.

SOME COPYRIGHT SPECIFICS

Obtaining copyright. Suppose you've come up with the detailed expression of an idea. The expression is original, and you've reduced it to some tangible form. Now, how do you *get* copyright? Don't move: You already have it. You don't have to register your work, or publish it, or anything.

How long can you keep it? The statutory rule is life-plus-fifty: Copyright is yours until you die, and then fifty more years after that. (Your heirs get the benefits once you're gone.) There are special rules for "joint works," "works for hire," and anonymous and pseudonymous works.

Forfeiting copyright. Suppose you've just completed a screenplay. In order to generate interest among the right people, you mail a copy to every address in the Beverly Hills phone book. Nice work—you've just lost your copyright. You've *published* it, and you've done so without *notice* to the outside world—which causes a forfeiture of your rights.

You can cure this disastrous error by (1) registering the work with the Copyright Office within five years (more on registration below), *and* (2) making good faith efforts to affix notice to all remaining copies. But these remedial measures won't help against an infringer who can show that in the interim he acted innocently in reliance on the lack of notice.

What notice? Where? How? On the front page or just inside the dust cover—neon letters would not be inappropriate; you *want* people to see this—place three things: (1) your name; (2) the year of the work's publication (the statutory definition of *publication* is complex; for simplicity, use the year in which you first showed it to anyone other than your family and friends); and (3) the word *Copyright* or the letter *C* in a circle: ©. (If the work is a phonorecord or other sound recording, rather than a "visually perceptible" work, place on it the letter *P* in a circle: ℗.) I recommend the following format:

Copyright 1986 Daniel R. White

Registration. There are two questions here:

1. *How do you register?* Simply donate two copies of your work (one copy if it hasn't been "published"), plus ten dollars, to the Register of Copyrights (Copyright Office, Library of Congress, Washington, DC, 20559, 202/287-9100), along with an application form that you can get for a phone call. (There are different forms for literary, musical, and other types of works, so make sure you get the right one.) You can easily do this without a lawyer.

2. *Why register?* Although registering a work isn't legally required (you *are* required to deposit two copies of any published work with the Copyright Office), it's so easy that you might well ask why *not* do it (except that ten dollars is ten dollars). The benefit of registering a work, given that you have the copyright whether you register it or not, is that it's a prerequisite to *enforcing* your copyright in court.

You can register your work even after you discover an infringement, but there are two money-related reasons for registering on time, which in the case of a published work means within three months of first publication, and in the case of an unpublished work means any time before the infringement occurs. If you register late, you can't recover from an infringer:

• The money you'll have to pay your lawyer to sue; or

• *Statutory damages,* which refers to money that a judge is statutorily authorized to give you ("as the court considers just"), even when you can't *prove* the extent of your losses.

Proving it's yours. Suppose you've written a movie or play. You're savvy enough to understand that Redford can't star in it if he hasn't heard of it. But once you've unveiled it in the carnivorous world of the entertainment industry, what's to prevent some other writer from claiming it (inadvertently, of course) as his own?

Putting a copyright notice on it is a good first step. But what if another writer puts *his* copyright notice on it, and wonder of wonders, his notice predates yours?

One solution would be to give a copy of your work to a lawyer, asking him to mark the date of receipt and then place it in safekeeping, with a written vow to let no one touch it except in the event of litigation. This would work.

A cheaper alternative would be to place a copy of your treasure in storage with the Writers Guild of America, East, Inc. (Room 1230, 555 West 57th Street, New York, NY 10019, 212/ 245-6180), or with its affiliate, Writers Guild of America, West, Inc. (8955 Beverly Boulevard, Los Angeles, CA 90048-2456, 213/ 550-1000). They're in the business of holding (they call it "registering") writers' manuscripts, marked with a date of deposit to establish priority. They won't look at you funny when you walk in and explain what you want. Neither will they look at your work, or even open your envelope. That's just the kind of people they are.

The registration fee for nonmembers of the Guild ranges from ten dollars to fifty dollars, depending on the size of your work. Registration lasts ten years (five years with the West Coast affiliate) and is renewable. You can handle the whole procedure by mail.

Fair use. Recall Saul Steinberg's *Manhattanite's Perspective* poster. In late 1984 *The Wall Street Journal* ran a front-page article discussing copyright problems Steinberg encountered with this work. Accompanying the article, also on the front page, was an approximately two-inch by three-inch black-and-white copy of the poster (along with "© Saul Steinberg" underneath).

Why didn't Steinberg sue the *Journal* for copying his work? (He spoke with *Journal* editors in connection with the article but never expressly granted them permission to include a copy of the poster.)

The most likely answer, in two words: *fair use.* A central principle of copyright law is that one has a right to make fair use of even protected creations for certain purposes, such as teaching, research, criticism, parody, or *news reporting.*

How much use is *fair* use? The copyright law sets forth a nonexclusive list of factors a judge must consider in deciding whether a given use is fair:

• The purpose of the use (news reporting is a highly favored use);

• The "amount and substantiality of the portion used" (the less you take, the safer you are);

• The nature of the copyrighted work (a "form" book invites large-scale copying, for example; a book of poems does not); and

• The effect of the use on the potential market for the copyrighted work.

The last of these factors is especially important. Suppose you're a dress manufacturer named Abraham Zapruder. (You know this story has to be true.) You live in Dallas, Texas. With your home-movie camera, you happen to capture the assassination of President Kennedy. You sell the pictures to *Life* for $150,000. Four years later Random House publishes—without payment to you or *Life*—a book containing copies of frames from your film. Copyright infringement?

In Zapruder's 1968 lawsuit, a federal court in New York held that such a film could definitely be a subject of copyright. But the court concluded that Random House's use of the pictures was a "fair use," and hence no payment or permission was required. The court emphasized that the Kennedy assassination was a uniquely newsworthy event and that publication of the book had had no effect on the market for Zapruder's film.

In 1985 the Supreme Court ruled that *The Nation* magazine's unauthorized publication of 300 to 400 words verbatim from Gerald Ford's memoirs did *not* constitute a fair use of the former president's copyrighted material. *Time* magazine had subsequently canceled its contract to publish portions of Ford's memoirs—which the Court cited as clear evidence of the adverse effect on the market for Ford's work.

Other fair-use cases arguably present less significant social issues. Consider *Mad Magazine*'s parody of some twenty-five popular songs in a 1964 issue titled "More Trash from Mad—A Sickening Collection of Humor and Satire from Past Issues." The judge in that case cited *Don Quixote* and *Gulliver's Travels*, concluding,

> [W]here, as here, it is clear that the parody has neither the intent nor the effect of fulfilling the demand for the original, and where the parodist does not appropriate a greater amount of the original work than is necessary to "recall or conjure up" the object of his satire, a finding of infringement would be improper.

In what situations does a parody "fulfill the demand for the original"? When is a parodist using "more than is necessary" to get the joke across? There are no clear answers. For your own purposes you'd do well to make sure you're in no way trading on a work you're parodying. This takes us full circle in the law of copyright, because here, as at the beginning of this chapter, the rule is: Always add something of your own.

Consider one last aspect of fair use that becomes increasingly important with the constant proliferation of office technology: photocopying. A limited amount of photocopying is permissible for scholarly purposes, including teaching, research, and library and archive use, and also for standard fair-use purposes, including criticism and news reporting. The rules here aren't crystal clear, but it's safe to say that photocopying a *portion* of a work is better than photocopying an *entire* work, and photocopying a work that is nowhere available for purchase is better than photocopying a work that you could purchase thirty copies of at the corner bookstore.

I submit that everyone reading this book has broken the law in this area more than once. How often have you photocopied a magazine or newspaper article, even though you could have purchased a copy of the original without extreme inconvenience or expense? How often, when you were in school, did you photocopy a portion of someone else's book in order to avoid having to buy the entire volume?

I've committed scores of such violations myself. But a law of cosmic retribution seems to be at work. I continue to receive comments from people who say they've read *photocopied* portions of my articles or books.

What Kind of Lawyer?

Copyright law is out of the legal mainstream. Most lawyers never studied one page on it in law school. To find someone knowledgeable in the field, be resourceful: Consult fellow artists. Call someone on the board of a local museum, or even the president of your city's bar association.

If you live in any of approximately fifty cities around the country, there's good news: You may be able to obtain free or semifree advice (and certainly a referral) from one of the various "volunteer lawyers for the arts" (or similarly named) programs around the country. VLAs vary in size, structure, and the nature of what they offer, but the idea is that a number of lawyers are so interested in meeting people who don't wear pinstripes that they're willing to give artists a break on legal fees.

To get free help from a VLA you have to be poor. The New York City VLA requires you to prove your gross income is under $10,000 per year (which in New York is definitely poor). To find out if your city has a VLA, check the phone book, or call the local bar referral service or even the local arts council. As a last resort, call the New York City VLA, the granddaddy of them all, at (212) 977-9270. Note that many of these programs help out only with arts-related problems, so you'll have to take your tax and divorce problems elsewhere.

TRADEMARKS

I would to God that thou and I knew where a
commodity of good names were to be bought.   WILLIAM SHAKESPEARE
(1564–1616),
Henry IV, Part I I.ii.92

What's in a name? Plenty.

Suppose you're considering opening a fast-food franchise, a McDonald's. The problem is, the McDonald's people charge a lot of money for the right to use their name. Is it worth it?

It ought to be. In 1984 McDonald's spent over a quarter-*billion* dollars on television advertisements alone. Try opening a food stand under your own name: "Ralph's Hamburgers." Maybe people will come in, maybe they won't.

But suppose your name is Ralph *McDonald*. Couldn't you open a fast-food restaurant under your own name? Or suppose your name is Susan Gschwendtner. Couldn't you recruit your neighbor—*his* name is Ralph McDonald—to serve as a partner, lending his surname to the operation?

People have tried this kind of thing. When Walter Taylor began marketing wines under his name, the Taylor Wine Company (no relation) sued him and won. The court told Walter he could place his signature on wine labels and advertisements, but he couldn't use his surname alone as a trademark ("Taylor Wines"), and even his signature would have to be accompanied by a conspicuous disclaimer of any connection with the original Taylor Wine Company.

Do all cowboy hats look the same to you? That, apparently, was what Stephen Stetson was hoping when he began marketing hats under his own name, to the irritation of the John B. Stetson Company, the original producer of the famous Stetson-brand cowboy hats. As in the Taylor Wine case, the court said Stephen would have to take substantial measures to eliminate confusion among prospective purchasers—it wasn't enough to put a tiny notice in an obscure place on the sweatbands—and prohibited Stephen from using his name at all except in a conspicuous "notice of differentiation."

The point is that courts are aware of the commercial value of a name and will do whatever is necessary to prevent you from trading on someone else's.

What if, by accident or design, you go into business using a name that's already being used by some small company in another state, a Mom-and-Pop operation that's unlikely to discover what you're doing, couldn't afford to sue you if it did, and in any event has no plans to expand into your area and therefore doesn't *care* what you're doing?

If you're correct that no one is going to sue you, you can of course do anything you want. If the Mom-and-Pop people do sue, you might get away with using their name anyway, if you can convince a court that (1) the market in which you operate doesn't overlap with theirs, (2) you were the first user of the disputed trademark in your geographic market, and (3) you began using the trademark unaware that they were using it first.

As for the last of these points, note that if the Mom-and-Pop people have registered their trademark with the Patent and Trademark Office (PTO) in Washington, D.C., a court will say you should have known about their prior use, no matter where you live. Once they've registered, everyone in the country is deemed to be on notice of their use.

This suggests a basic rule in the law of trademarks: Don't use somebody else's. Dream up your own. Admittedly, that's easier said than done. Over 500,000 trademarks are currently registered with the PTO, and that number is growing fast; in 1985, 71,167 new trademarks were registered. There's no telling, moreover, how many *un*registered trademarks are now in use.

An entire body of law has arisen around the protection of *trademarks*, the term used to refer to the names, marks, labels, logos, and other devices that producers of anything put on their goods to identify and distinguish them in the marketplace.

The purpose of trademarks isn't to structure or package goods; just the opposite. Here, as in the copyright area, courts don't want you monopolizing things that are "utilitarian." The purpose of trademarks is to indicate to consumers the *source* of goods they're buying (or to indicate the existence of a common, if unknown, source of a number of goods), thus enabling them to buy the highest quality goods they can afford. (In practice, trademarks may do no more than enable you to spend 50 percent extra for ties and underwear bearing the name of somebody you don't know.)

A trademark can be just about anything:

- A word: *Rolex, Gucci,* or *Calvin Klein.*
- A symbol: the Playboy bunny logo.
- A design or configuration: a distinctively shaped bottle for wine or perfume.
- An ornament: the flying lady that appears on Rolls-Royce radiators, or the alligator that appears on preppies' Izod shirts.
- A slogan: "Have it your way" for Burger King, or "It's a good time for the great taste" for McDonald's.
- A color.

That a *color* can be a trademark was established as recently as 1985, in a case involving a manufacturer of home insulation material. For almost thirty years this manufacturer had colored its product . . . pink. The court reasoned that if a company has established a link in the public mind between its product and some color—in other words, the color serves the traditional trademark function of indicating to consumers the source of the particular product—the company can obtain trademark protection for that color so long as its competitors aren't thereby seriously disadvantaged. Here, the court observed, there appeared to be no utilitarian reason for using pink on home insulation (as there might be for using, say, gray on sunglasses), so competitors weren't being denied something essential for their own goods.

Selecting a Trademark

Your fundamental goal in selecting a trademark should be to find one sufficiently distinctive to qualify for registration with the Patent and Trademark Office. This is true even if you have no present plans to register your trademark, for two reasons: First, when your company gets big and you want to take it national, you may well change your mind about registration.

Second, the distinctiveness that renders a trademark registrable with the PTO makes for a good trademark generally.

Before considering how and why to register your trademark, consider how to go about *selecting* one. Assume you want your trademark to be a word, rather than a symbol, design, or any of the other possible types of trademarks. (Note that your trademark may be the same as the name of your company—*Coca-Cola*, for example, is both the name of the company and the trademark of its chief product—but it doesn't have to be.)

The world of words can be divided into four categories, which for trademark purposes rank from terrible to great: generic, descriptive, suggestive, and arbitrary or fanciful.

An example of a generic term is *refrigerator*. Anyone can call his refrigerator a refrigerator. Nouns like *shoe, chair,* and *yo-yo* are the same; they *define* the product. You can't prevent others from using those words to describe their products, because they *need* those words to get the point across. (Try describing a yo-yo without using the word *yo-yo*.) Because your goal is to come up with a word that no one else will be allowed to use, generic terms are bad.

Examples of descriptive terms are *sturdy, compact, smooth, fuel-efficient*—basic adjectives. A slightly subtler example is *Frigidaire* as a trademark for refrigerators. (Get it? *Frigid air?*) Descriptive terms aren't absolutely essential for the marketing of particular products, but courts are nevertheless reluctant to give any individual a monopoly on one of them. And a monopoly—exclusive control—is what you want.

A suggestive term gets its point across indirectly, through association. *Penguin* is an example of a suggestive trademark for refrigerators—it *suggests* ice, freezing temperatures, and polar conditions. Consider *Genentech*, the name of a prominent genetic engineering company. Its combination of the first part of each of two words, *genetic* and *technology*, suggests modern, sophisticated, high-tech, gene-related products and processes—which fits. Yet the sequence of letters required to spell it doesn't appear in any dictionary. Hence it's arguably not even a word, but a mere sound. This is good!

In and of themselves, arbitrary or fanciful terms tell you nothing whatsoever about the product or company with which they're associated. Two easy examples: *Kodak* and *Xerox*. But for heavy advertising over the years, we would view them now as nonwords. They have no independent existence. Nobody needs them to describe a product. That's what makes them *great* trademarks.

Another great trademark. Häagen-Dazs, which is both arbitrary—the now fabulously wealthy creator of Häagen-Dazs "superpremium" ice cream contrived the term while studying a map of Scandinavia—*and* suggestive—it suggests, as it was intended to, European origins and style, even though the container, which carries a map of Scandinavia, states that the ice cream is made in New Jersey.

You can play games in this area. Take *apple*—people need the word to describe those things that keep the doctor away. But they don't need it to describe computers; in this context, *apple* is arbitrary. It neither defines, describes, nor even suggests computers. This is why it has been a good trademark for the producers of Apple Computers.

Note that I say "good," rather than "great." Through advertising, the Apple Computer people have succeeded in conferring upon an ordinary word what lawyers call *secondary meaning*; that is, because of their labors, the otherwise generic word *apple* now has two meanings: It signifies not only red things on trees (its primary meaning), but also a certain source of computers (its secondary meaning). It's precisely because of this secondary meaning that the Apple Computer people are entitled to prevent anyone else from marketing computers under the name *Apple*. They have trademark rights to the term, that is, exclusive control over it, *within the computer field*.

What if someone wants to use *Apple* to market, say, footballs? Apple is so basic a term—when referring to the red thing that fell on Sir Isaac Newton, it's "generic"—that courts would normally be disinclined to give anyone a *complete* monopoly on it. Still, the Apple Computer people might prevail even against someone proposing to use *Apple* in connection with footballs, if, having invested heavy sums in endowing that term not only with secondary meaning but also with generally positive associations in the public mind, they could show either (1) they were contemplating their own expansion into the football market; (2)

the use of *Apple* in connection with footballs might tarnish their valuable trademark; or (3) the use of *Apple* in connection with footballs might cause confusion among members of the public.

How about *Xerox* footballs? Photocopiers aren't much closer to footballs than computers are, so if it's okay to use *Apple* on footballs, it's also okay to use *Xerox* on them, right?

Wrong. It's entirely different. *Xerox* is a far "stronger" trademark than *Apple*. In the abstract, to be sure, the word *Xerox* has nothing to do with footballs. But most people would assume there must be some relation between the people who make Xerox photocopiers and those who make Xerox footballs. A judge would say that *Xerox* was an arbitrary trademark from the very beginning, that its originators developed it through vast expenditures of time and money, and therefore that its use by anyone else for *anything* would *dilute* it.

Now *that's* a trademark. Something that's safe not only from people in your own field but also from people in every other field.

This brings us to the ninth of White's Irregular Rules:

The wackier your trademark, the better.

The owners of the Texas-based fast-food chain who named their multi-ingredient sandwich a *Schlotsky* were smart, not crazy. Who would dare copy such a wacky term? A word like *Kodak* is also completely wacky, that is, arbitrary or fanciful; when the camera people first used it, no one had ever heard of it.

GENERICIDE

As the Apple Computer example illustrates, even a generic word can, through proper advertising and marketing, become invested with secondary meaning that will render it at least somewhat wacky, and hence trademarkable, within a given field. This process can also go the other way, with formerly valid trademarks becoming generic. Examples: aspirin, cellophane, escalator, thermos, trampoline, yo-yo. All were once exclusive trademarks that over time became synonymous in people's minds with a specific product.

The problem of genericide produces ambivalence in the minds of businesspeople. On the one hand, they dream of their product becoming dominant in its field. On the other hand, they don't want it to become *so* dominant that its name becomes generic, and hence up for grabs by anyone. This is why, in Sanka Decaffeinated Coffee ads, Marcus Welby (also known as Robert Young) refers to "Sanka-*brand* coffee," rather than "Sanka." He's the only person in the world who says that.

This is also why, in the televised Watergate hearings, the Xerox people reportedly demanded that Senator Sam Ervin cease asking his aides to *xerox* documents. Obviously, in the Senator's mind, that word was already synonymous with *photocopy*.

CONFUSING SIMILARITY

What if your trademark isn't identical to someone else's, but quite similar? How close can you come?

The rule is, you can't use a trademark if it's so similar to an existing trademark—in appearance, sound, popular association, or anything else—that it's likely to cause confusion or error among consumers. Note that I say "likely": Someone alleging infringement of his trademark doesn't have to prove that confusion has actually occurred, or that it's certain to occur in the future. Hence, your best bet is to stay away if confusion is even a slight possibility.

Courts aren't naïve in this area. They look at the whole picture, including:

1. *Similarity of the trademarks*. You're not safe just because your trademark isn't *identical* to one already in use—for example, "*Xerocks* Photocopiers." The issue is whether the two trademarks are sufficiently similar to create a likelihood of confusion. On the other hand, the similarity has to be more than theoretical. The originator of Häagen-Dazs ice cream failed in his attempt to persuade a judge that a competing ice-cream maker's use of the name *Frusen Glädjé* infringed the Häagen-Dazs trademark by duplicating its "unique Scandinavian marketing theme." (Courts have never recognized the right of an existing scam to interfere with a new one.)

2. *Degree of similarity of the products.* Would people assume Skippy peanut butter is related to Skippy jump ropes?

3. *Degree of care likely to be exercised by consumers.* Purchasers of fine watches, airplanes, and other expensive items pay close attention to brand names; purchasers of paper clips and shoe-laces don't.

4. *Strength of the trademark.* Treat *Kodak* as if it were radio-active. The same goes for *Xerox, Schlotsky, Kaypro* (computers), *Precor* (exercise machines), and other words that have no inher-ent meaning.

5. *Manner of concurrent use.* Is the way you're using the sim-ilar trademark likely to minimize confusion, or promote it?

6. *Intent to deceive.* If you've used a trademark confusingly similar to someone else's, it's theoretically irrelevant that you may have acted innocently, rather than with intent to infringe. However, where the evidence on consumer confusion is incon-clusive, but your intent to infringe is clear, a court might, in effect, defer to your judgment, reasoning that if *you* thought confusion was likely to occur—which is why you used the of-fending trademark—then it's appropriate to rule against you.

You're not necessarily in the clear just because your trademark isn't confusingly similar to anyone else's. You also need to avoid trademarks that are:

1. *Inherently misleading.* Say you grew up in Vidalia, Georgia (pop. 10,393), and you have an abiding appreciation for the sweet onions (suitable for eating raw) that thrive thereabout. Neither this fact nor the fact that your accent and breath mark you as a native of that locale means you can use *Vidalia* as a trademark for onions you grow in upstate New York. (You'd face another prob-lem with using *Vidalia,* even if your onions were grown there. *See* "geographically descriptive" terms in subsection 3, below.)

2. *Immoral or scandalous.* Examples of trademarks (in the form of slogans) that have been held beyond the pale: *Bubby Trap,* for brassieres, and *Only a breast in the mouth is better than a leg in the hand,* for a chicken restaurant.

3. *Geographically descriptive.* These are terms like *Idaho,* as in potatoes; *French,* as in perfume; and *Southern,* as in belles. Each of these terms suggests that the product in question actually

originated in the place indicated. If your product didn't originate in one of these places, there's an obvious problem of consumer deception. Even if it did, you should probably resist using a geographically descriptive term, for the same reason you should resist using descriptive terms generally: The law wants them to remain available for use by everyone. (This is presumably why not even onion growers in Vidalia, Georgia, have been able to register *Vidalia* on the "Principal Register"—more on this below—at the Patent and Trademark Office.)

Note that some terms that appear to be geographically descriptive have been held eligible for copyright protection, because like *apple* (when referring to computers), they've acquired secondary meaning; that is, people think of them as referring to something other than a place. Examples: *Hyde Park*, when applied to men's suits, and *Dutch Boy*, when applied to paint.

USING YOUR OWN NAME

Perhaps you'd like your trademark to consist of your own name. A measure of narcissism is healthy, but is it okay from a legal perspective?

Sure. Frank Perdue built a chicken empire on his own name. Henry Ford did fine with his own name, too (although his son Edsel's experience may give you pause).

Your name isn't a *great* trademark. Undoubtedly someone, somewhere, has the same name (recall the problems encountered by the producers of Taylor wines and Stetson cowboy hats, discussed on page 182). Although courts won't let that someone exploit the coincidence blatantly, they'll be reluctant to tell him he can't use his own name at all. Still, you could do a lot worse than use your own name, especially if you get a major-league kick out of seeing it on billboards.

Registration

Registration of a trademark consists of getting it listed on either of two registers, the Principal Register or the Supplemental Register, maintained by the Patent and Trademark Office. Listing on the former confers far greater benefits—including, most significantly, putting the entire country on *constructive notice* that you're using the mark, so that no subsequent user anywhere can get away with claiming ignorance of your prior use.

Listing on either of the registers confers a number of important benefits, however, including: (1) prohibition of anyone else from registering the same or a similar mark; (2) trademark rights under various international treaties; and (3) access to federal courts for any trademark infringement action. (Federal courts are likely to have better judges and more predictable rules than state courts.)

Registration of your trademark is entirely voluntary, and even without registration, you can prevent someone from using your trademark in the same geographic region in which you're using it. You can't prevent someone from using your unregistered trademark in a *different* geographic region, however, unless you can prove (as you rarely can) that he knew of your prior use at the time he started using it.

An application to register a trademark costs $175. Amendments to applications cost $100. These fees, an application form, and a general statement of the rules are set forth in a booklet that the PTO (2011 Jefferson Davis Highway, Crystal Plaza, Building #2, Arlington, VA 20222, 703/557-3268) will send you without charge.

If it's worth your while to register your trademark, it's worth your while to hire a lawyer to handle the application. Applying on your own would be a horrific hassle, and the fact is, you probably couldn't pull it off. Neither could the average lawyer who doesn't specialize in this complicated area.

How do you find a lawyer who can handle trademark matters? Trademark lawyers and copyright lawyers tend to be one and the same, because the concepts and issues in the two fields overlap. Hence, the suggestions on finding a knowledgeable copyright lawyer (p. 181) also apply here.

How much would a lawyer charge to handle a registration? The possibility of complications from numerous sources makes it impossible to say for sure, but a ballpark figure is $1,300. This would cover the lawyer's fee, the application fee, and the cost of a standard search of existing trademarks,* but not an appeal or a response to someone's challenge to your application.

Before calling any lawyer, conduct a preliminary search on your own. Suppose you want to set up a store that delivers bouquets of helium balloons. Your first step should be to check the phone books of several large cities to get a feel for what's already out there. In the Washington, D.C., yellow pages, you'd find at least twenty companies with names like Balloon Man, Bubbly Balloons, Say It with Balloons, Inflation Station, and Laugh 'N' Gas.

Maybe this preliminary search will persuade you to abandon the idea. At the least it should help you limit your false starts in the name selection process. The easiest way to waste money in this area is to have your lawyer running back and forth to the trademark lists, each time coming up with information you could have found out on your own.

Obtaining Rights in the Trademark

Unlike the copyright area, in which a you-write-it-you-own-it rule applies, in the trademark area it's not enough simply to dream up some name or logo. To obtain rights in a mark, you first have to *use* it. Otherwise, large companies might register the thousands of trademarks their marketing and legal departments could dream up, on the theory that maybe, someday, one of those marks might come in handy.

You don't have to do much to satisfy the use requirement. Just make a sale—one sale is enough—of some item *bearing the mark*. In other words, get the mark out there in a genuine commercial context. To be absolutely safe, make a sale in *another state*, to satisfy the requirement that the mark be used in "interstate" commerce.

---

*Your lawyer will probably farm the search out to one of the companies that perform such searches all the time. Be sure to get the *extended search*, not just the *full federal search*. The latter doesn't cover the numerous common-law trademarks, that is, the trademarks that aren't registered with the PTO but that *are* in use somewhere. These have rights superior to yours in the localities where they're being used, so if you're thinking big, you want to know about them.

8. Criminal Law

What to Do If You Get Arrested •
Dealing with Police Searches •
Self-Defense •
Advice to Victims of Crime •

Almost all criminal defendants are, in fact, guilty.
ALAN M. DERSHOWITZ
Harvard Law School
(1939–   )

The terrorist and the policeman both come from the same basket.
JOSEPH CONRAD
(1857–1924)

*I recommend avoiding lawyers except when it's absolutely necessary, such
as when you're being hauled off to jail. And even then you should think
about it. You know, taste the food, talk to your prospective cellmate—
give it a chance.*
MARTIN J. YUDKOWITZ
(1954–   )

Problem: You're walking along the street one day, when sud-
denly two large men with bad breath grab you, tie you up, cram
you in the back of a car, and start taking you somewhere that,
although they haven't told you where it is, you're pretty sure
you don't want to go. Are you permitted to defend yourself?

Answer: It depends. Are the large men criminals or police
officers?

Don't get me wrong regarding police officers. Does society
need them? Indisputably.

Are many of them model citizens? Of course.

All of them? Of course *not*.

In 1985, eighty-six officers of the New York City Police De-

193

partment were arrested and charged with crimes. (There were actually eighty-*seven* arrests; one officer was arrested twice.) The most common charge was assault. Four of the arrests involved torture of prisoners with electric stun guns.

The oft-quoted British philosopher Thomas Hobbes said that without some form of police power, human existence would be "nasty, brutish, and short." The first two parts of this chapter discuss the two basic types of encounters with the police, arrests and searches, and how to minimize the chances that yours will be nasty, brutish, and *long*. The third part discusses the right of self-defense (against criminals). The fourth part offers advice to victims of violent and property-related crimes.

WHAT TO DO IF YOU GET ARRESTED

A lawyer contemplating the best advice for someone being arrested feels what flight attendants must feel when reciting their "how to minimize the splatter if we crash" mumbo-jumbo at the outset of commercial airline flights: futility. Someone being arrested, like someone in a plane doing a nosedive, has lost control of his situation. What happens to him is almost entirely out of his hands.

Almost entirely out of his hands. There's *some* legal advice worth remembering if you get arrested, although this area of law isn't like estate planning, say, in which there are things you can do now to improve your situation later. This advice becomes useful only if and when you get arrested. And it involves not so much what you *should* do, as what you *shouldn't* do.

Don't Resist

Resistance doesn't help—ever. Like squirming in quicksand, it only gets you in deeper. (Okay, if you know for sure the arresting officers are literally going to kill you, go ahead and resist. But not otherwise.)

Arresting officers can't legally use force just for the fun of it. If you resist, though, they're permitted to get nasty. Even then they're supposed to use no more force than is absolutely necessary—"force proportionate to the offense," the cases say—but who'll be able to prove you were in fact unconscious during that last clubbing?

Innocence of whatever they're charging you with doesn't legally entitle you to resist; the law affords the police a margin of error. Besides, sometimes they're acting on warrants from the local prosecutors, which means they don't know you and don't *care* if you're innocent—they *have* to bring you in.

Note that police aren't the only people who can lawfully arrest you. In most states it's legal for private store detectives or owners to briefly detain you—keep you from running away—if they suspect you've stolen property from their store. Resisting these people is no more advisable than resisting the police.

Don't Say Anything

The police, before interrogating you in jail or anywhere else from which you're not free to leave, are required to inform you of your "*Miranda* rights" (named after convicted Arizona rapist and kidnapper Ernesto Miranda, now dead from a stabbing in a bar fight).

Note that the police are required to do this only if two factors come into play simultaneously: (1) *involuntary custody*—in other words, an arrest; and (2) interrogation. Neither factor alone is enough. Thus, if police officers question you on the street but don't actually arrest you, or if they handcuff you in the back of their car (with a large growling dog) but don't actually question you, they're free to act on anything you say, even though you may have no idea of your rights.

Sometimes, even when the *Miranda*-triggering combination of factors—custodial questioning—is present, the police don't get around to informing you of your rights.

Because of this well-recognized problem ("Almost all police lie about whether they violated the Constitution in order to convict guilty defendants"—Professor Alan M. Dershowitz, Harvard Law School), I'll state them here. (If you hear them again from the police, you're twice warned.)

First, *you have the right to remain silent.* Exercise this right! Why? Because of the second element of the required *Miranda* recitation: *Anything you say can and will be used against you in court.*

At the police station you aren't legally *required* to say anything, although you should probably tell them your name (your real name—a surprising number of people claim to be Santa Claus or Ronald Reagan). The police will find out who you are sooner or later, and when you go before a judge, it'll look bad if they've had to book you as "John Doe" or "Mary Roe"— standard names for unidentified male and female arrestees. Also, when someone comes to the station to bail you out, you don't want him being told there's no one there by that name.

Whether to give the police any other information—address, next of kin, place of employment—is an open question. If your boss is going to find out about your drug arrest, would you like to break it to him personally, or have him find out from policemen who've obtained a search warrant to ransack your office?

There could be a cost to withholding such information. In many cities, if you're a first offender and the charges against you aren't too serious, you can obtain a quick release ("on citation") by showing that you have substantial, verifiable ties to the local community—a job, for example, or a spouse and kids, or membership in a church or the local Republican Club. The theory is that such ties will keep you where the police can find you if they want you. Exhibiting the slightest reluctance to provide such information, however, could preclude your release.

Stories abound of defendants who thought they might improve their positions by making *statements*—confessions—to the police, but who succeeded only in torpedoing themselves legally. This is particularly true of defendants who altered the facts of their stories to accord with their mistaken perceptions of the law.

Consider the not extraordinary case of Jay (not his real name), who was arrested for homicide. There was no question that Jay had committed the killing with which he was charged, but there was considerable question as to the events leading up to the killing. The truth, to the extent that such can ever be known by mortals, was that Jay had been walking the streets of the city when he encountered a man who, to paraphrase Jay's account, threatened him with immediate physical harm. Jay drew a pistol from his pocket and shot the man.

Jay's *story* (to the police) was that upon being threatened by the man, he ran home, grabbed the pistol, returned to the street, and shot the man. The virtue of this story, to Jay's thinking, was that it protected him from the charge of carrying a concealed weapon, a charge with which he was already familiar. In fact, as Jay learned from the public defenders, all this story did was rob him of a plausible claim of self-defense and set him up for a charge of premeditated (first-degree) murder.

Suppose, in the initial excitement of getting arrested, you spill the beans: "Okay, you've got me. I did it. The murder weapon is under the mattress." Ten minutes later, after the police have got around to "Mirandizing" you, you realize your mistake. Rats! But wait: If your confession preceded the reading of your *Miranda* rights, it's probably inadmissible in court—*unless you repeat it.*

The Supreme Court in 1985 decided a case involving just such facts. An eighteen-year-old Oregon defendant was arrested and questioned without being read his *Miranda* rights. He confessed to being present during a burglary. Later, at the police station, he was read his rights. Naturally assuming the cat was out of the bag, he confessed again, this time in writing. The Supreme Court said too bad—once you've been advised of your right to remain silent, any subsequent statements can come into evidence against you.

The lesson: *Don't say anything even if you've already said something.*

Along the same lines, if at some point you sober up in jail and realize you've made the mistake of saying something, don't *sign* anything. Once you've said something, standard police procedure is to write it up in the most damning possible fashion and ask you to sign it. Their version won't include your explanations and qualifications—"The other guy was pointing a gun at me and said, 'Prepare to meet your maker' "—points that you'd of course want to bring up at trial, but that the police will tell the jury you must have fabricated later . . . or why didn't you include them in your original statement?

Will the police become irritated if you refuse to talk to them?

A little, but they're used to it. Forget what you learned as a schoolchild about the police being your friends. If they're your friends, why are they planning to use your statements against you in court?

GET A LAWYER

How long should you refuse to say anything? Not indefinitely, like a Trappist monk. Just until your lawyer arrives; the two of you can determine together what information is appropriate to reveal. Which carries us to the next *Miranda* right the police are supposed to tell you: *You have the right to the presence of a lawyer.*

Exercise this right! It includes the right to confer with your lawyer *before* police questioning and to have him present *during* questioning. The criminal-law corollary to the first of White's Irregular Rules—"Where there's a lot of money at stake, hire a lawyer"—is:

If you get arrested, don't move without consulting a lawyer.

"Where were you at two o'clock last night?" "Do you own a shotgun?" "How well do you know Larry 'The Dog' Durkin?" Your answer to all these questions should be, "I want a lawyer," "I want a lawyer," and "I want a lawyer." Even if they're just asking your name, your answer should sound something like, "I want a lawyer my name is Al Williams I want a lawyer."

APPOINTED LAWYERS

"But I don't know any criminal lawyers," you say. "And I couldn't pay for one anyway." You're in luck: *If you can't afford a lawyer, you have the right to have one appointed to represent you—* the last element of the required *Miranda* litany. An appointed lawyer will be either a *public defender*, that is, a government-paid lawyer who represents indigents charged with criminal offenses, or a private practitioner who is willing to take the case out of the goodness of his heart (and perhaps a small fee from the government or some other source).

How poor must you be in order to be eligible for a free lawyer? There's no clear answer. Most public defenders would say "pretty damn poor." If you aren't eligible for food stamps, you probably aren't eligible for a free lawyer.

Don't assume that because a lawyer is appointed by the authorities he's not competent or truly loyal to you. As for competence, plenty of public defenders are excellent lawyers, far more knowledgeable and talented than any you could afford if you were many times richer than you are. The same is true of a number of court-appointed private practitioners, although their competence levels reportedly vary more substantially.

As for loyalty to you, keep in mind that most defense lawyers will do anything they can to get you off the hook, regardless of what they think of you personally. To them it's a game, and keeping you out of jail is like getting a hotel on Boardwalk. The famous F. Lee Bailey made his name defending the Boston Strangler—which teaches that the worse you are, the better your lawyer looks if he frees you. It doesn't matter to him that you may be a dangerous criminal, because he doesn't live near where you hang out.

GOOD NEWS, BAD NEWS

The good news is, if you can afford to hire a lawyer, you'll be permitted to have him present at any legal proceeding, no matter how minor the offense or how preliminary the proceeding. There's no downside limit on this right.

The bad news is, if you can't afford a lawyer, you can't *always* get one free. The determinant is the seriousness of the offense with which you're charged, as measured by the accompanying penalty. Specifically, if the penalty includes no imprisonment but merely a fine, you're not constitutionally entitled to a free lawyer. (The authorities in your area *could* give you one, but they don't have to.)

More bad news. There's a difference between *detention* and *imprisonment*—not one that will keep your cellmate from throwing up on you, but one that can make a difference in your right to a court-appointed lawyer. It's possible (especially if you can't make bail) that you'll be detained for days, weeks, or longer awaiting arraignment and then trial. You haven't been sentenced yet; you haven't even been found guilty—if the chief witness for the prosecution dies, they may turn you loose and leave you alone forever. The problem is, *this* jail time doesn't trigger the right to a free lawyer.

Don't Consent to Anything

> POLICE OFFICER: Things will go a lot easier for you if you cooperate. You know that, don't you?
> NEWLY ARRESTED PRISONER: Uh-huh.
> POLICE OFFICER: We've got you now. It's only a matter of time before we have all the evidence.
> PRISONER: Uh-huh.
> POLICE OFFICER: You don't mind if we search your house, do you?
> PRISONER: Well . . . you guys promise to go easy on me?

There's a wide gulf between what the police can lawfully do to you (or make you do) at their discretion, and what they can do only with your consent. For the same reason that you shouldn't *say anything* to the police before your lawyer arrives, you shouldn't *consent to anything* before your lawyer arrives.

What might the police ask you to consent to?

- Surgical extraction of something in your body.
- A search of your house or car.
- A lie detector test.
- A blood test.
- A lineup.
- Anything at all that might put you behind bars.

For some things, such as fingerprinting and photographing, the police don't need your consent, and they won't ask for it. For others, such as searching your house or obtaining a blood sample, they might be able to get what they want without your consent, by applying to a magistrate for a search warrant, but it's quicker and easier to request your permission. The police can definitely make you participate in a lineup (assuming they have some minimal basis for suspecting you've committed a crime). Without your consent, though, they may have to wait until your lawyer arrives to make sure it's conducted properly—for instance, to make sure they don't tell the rape victim to "take a real close look at Number Three."

In any event, what the police can and can't do legally is almost irrelevant once you're in their hands; if they're determined to do something, they will, and if they aren't, they won't. Your lawyer can ask a judge later to decide if it was legal. All you have to remember now is not to *consent* to it, because your consent makes it legal.

In many instances it will be clear that you're being asked to consent to something. The police will give it away by saying something like, "Do you consent to this?"

But not always. Perhaps, two hours after they've Mirandized you, they'll say, "Okay, the lie detector is ready for you." Don't assume the police wouldn't have put it that way if you had a choice; they aren't above a little trickery. Your response with respect to anything requiring your participation should be, "Do I have to do this?" If not, wait for your lawyer.

Similarly, ignore the police if they attempt to coax you with something like, "Nobody who's innocent would mind taking a lie detector test." Maybe, maybe not. Besides, who said you're innocent?

What about the police officer's comment that things will go easier on you if you cooperate? That may well be true—prosecutors make deals with prisoners all the time. But note three critical points. First, only a prosecutor can offer you a "deal" (formally known as a *plea bargain*). A police officer has no such authority. (No matter whom you're dealing with, never rely on an oral promise. Get it in writing.)

Second, your lawyer will know better than you what's the best deal you can get. Why settle for a year in jail when your lawyer might be able to bargain the authorities down to probation?

Third, don't worry that your silence or refusal to consent to something may look bad if your case ever reaches a jury. Prosecutors aren't allowed to comment on such things at trial.

You're sitting in jail. Highway patrol officers picked you up earlier for unconventional driving, and one observed that your eyes "look a little funny, like a Chinese roadmap." That and the spoon hanging around your neck led them to the conclusion that you're on drugs. Now they come into your cell and say they want a blood sample. Your mind races back to this book: *Don't consent to anything.* You throw a jab at one and a hook at the other. You go down fighting.

A good move?

To think of this book? Absolutely. Except you thought of the wrong part. The advice you should have thought of was: *Never resist.*

Withholding consent does not mean physically resisting; that's going too far. Neither does it mean merely refraining from signing a written consent form; that's not going far enough. It means protesting verbally, saying something like, "I'll go, but under protest. *I don't consent to this.*"

BREATHALYZER TESTS

In one situation withholding your consent may be more costly than yielding it. Some jurisdictions permit the police to require drivers to submit to breathalyzer or other drug-related tests, on penalty of suspension or loss of their drivers' licenses.

How do you know if that's really the choice you face? Try to call a lawyer—which of course may be difficult if you're out on a lonely highway (and too drunk to dial a telephone anyway). If the police take you into a station for testing, insist on being allowed to call a lawyer from there. If they refuse, and you decide your best bet for the moment is to take their test, resist the whiskey-based impulse to declare, "I'll take your test. I'll take any goddam test you've got." Instead, assert verbally that you're taking the test under protest. That way, if it turns out they were acting illegally in requiring you to take it, they won't be able to claim you consented to it.

THE CRITICAL PHONE CALL

You've just been arrested, and you're in the doorknob-less rear section of a police car on your way to jail. If this is your lucky day, your arrest took place in front of your lawyer, who knows just what to do in such situations and in fact is following you to the station in his car. Does anything lead you to suspect, however, that this is not your lucky day?

Shortly after your arrival at the station, you'll probably be permitted a phone call. Note that you have no *right* to this call. It's just something police normally grant.

Whom do you call, and what do you say?

Call a lawyer, if you know one, and ask him to call your spouse. Or call your spouse, and ask him to call a lawyer. Any lawyer you trust will do. If he isn't a criminal lawyer, he'll know one, or know how to find one.

If the charge is serious, there's a good chance you'll want both your lawyer and your spouse to come to the station—your lawyer to handle the legal issues and make sure the police aren't intentionally procrastinating on the paperwork, your spouse to handle the bail. (I'm using "spouse" here to refer generically to any good friend who would be willing to go out on a financial limb for you.)

There are at least two things the person you call will need to know in order to get you out: First, where are you? Second, how much is your bail?

The first of these questions shouldn't be hard to find an answer to. The police will undoubtedly be in the room with you when you make your call, so just turn and ask. Determining your bail right away might be harder.

For offenses other than, say, murder, there may well be a standard bail (or *station-house bond*) that some official at the police station can simply read to you from a chart. ("Possession of narcotics? That'll be $5,000.") If you're a first offender, you might want to await your initial appearance in court in order to get out on "personal recognizance" (also called "ROR" for "release on own recognizance")—in other words, to get out free. If you have previous convictions numbering in the double figures, you'll probably want to pay the standard bail and get out.

Be prepared to give whomever you call some indication of the nature of your offense. The police may be listening to your call, however, so don't get too specific. Don't say, for example, "I heard them mention drugs, but I don't know if they've found the you-know-what in my car trunk."

BEFORE YOUR LAWYER ARRIVES

Big-city jails typically have a public defender on duty throughout the normal working day. This means that if you're poor enough to be entitled to a free lawyer at all, you may be able to consult with him before the time of your initial appearance in court.

If you're wealthy, you may be allowed to consult with the public defender as if you were indigent. Then again, you may have to cool your heels until your own lawyer arrives.

If, rich or poor, you somehow find yourself standing alone before a judge, wing it. Look serious, call him *or her* "Your Honor," refrain from scratching yourself anywhere, and plead "not guilty." Then clam up.

PAY ATTENTION

Heads up. While you're waiting for your lawyer, try to recall all the circumstances of your arrest. Where did it take place, and at what time? Did the police have a warrant, and if so, did they show it to you (as they're supposed to)? What did they say to you, and you to them? The point is to recall anything that might help your lawyer determine whether your arrest was illegal—for example, because the arresting officers violated mandatory arrest procedures.

"What does it matter," you ask, "if my arrest was technically illegal, since the police search turned up more than enough evidence—drugs, forged checks, stolen goods—to send me to jail?" It matters enormously. If the arrest itself was illegal, it's possible that the accompanying search was also illegal, and under the Supreme Court's "exclusionary rule," illegally obtained evidence often can't be used against you at trial.

Were there witnesses to the alleged crime? If so, can you

recall who they were, or what they were wearing? You'll want your lawyer or someone else to start tracking them down immediately.

Who were the arresting officers? This is a critical question. It's not essential that you get their names, if you get their badge numbers.

Pay attention to what's going on at the police station, even as you commit to memory the details of your arrest. Suppose, for example, the police require you to participate in a lineup. How many people are in it? Are you the only albino dwarf?

Suppose, for the lineup, the police want you to put on someone else's hat, jacket, glasses, or artificial leg. Decline to wear any accessories that aren't yours, if you're given a choice; protest having to do so, if you're not.

BAIL

Bail is the term loosely used to refer to the money you're required to deposit with the authorities to guarantee that if they let you go you'll show up for your next court date. You should communicate the level of your bail to your spouse as soon as possible, because he may have to come up with old-fashioned cash. (One thing the authorities are sure to refuse is a check.)

In some states you can put up property instead of cash. The only kind of property the authorities anywhere will accept, however, is real estate; they don't like cars, stereos, coin collections, Persian cats, or anything else. The usual way of putting up real estate is by handing over the deed. Before calling your spouse, ask someone in charge if real estate is acceptable and, if so, what kind of documentation is required.

The only alternative to cash or real estate is a bond, which carries us to the subject of bail bondsmen.

BAIL BONDSMEN

A bail bondsman is a person engaged in the business of high-risk money lending. For a fee of approximately 10 percent of your bail, he'll execute (or cosign) a bail bond or undertake in some equivalent way to pay the court the full amount of your bail if you should disappear. You probably shouldn't do that, because many bail bondsmen resemble Mr. T and by all accounts employ unsavory methods of locating and dealing with errant clients.

Their public image problems nothwithstanding, bail bonds-men can come in handy, and not just for people who are too poor to make bail with cash or property. You may own Fort Knox, but if all you or your spouse can come up with over the next twenty-four hours is an American Express Gold Card, you're stranded.

How do you find a bail bondsman? Most bondsmen main-tain offices right beside the police station or courthouse, and they stay open (or at least receive phone calls) around the clock. If you don't see four or five standing nearby as you make your phone call, check the yellow pages or even consult your jailors, who may keep lists of bondsmen and their phone numbers.

THE LEVEL OF BAIL

Theoretically, the sole consideration in setting bail is the likelihood that you won't reappear at the appointed time. The judge is supposed to calculate how much money is sufficient to guarantee your appearance, either because you couldn't bear forfeiting that much to the state, or because you couldn't bear what your bail bondsman would do to you if you made him forfeit it.

Obvious factors in this calculation are the nature of the charges against you and the likelihood of your conviction at trial. Equally important are your ties to the local community. Prior convictions don't help, nor do police records showing you've jumped bail before.

At least tacitly, judges consider anything else they want to consider, including their own estimations of how dangerous you are and, more than one observer has contended, your race and social class. No doubt they also place a fair bit of emphasis on how polite you are to them. If the question of bail gets to a judge at all, it's a highly subjective process.

Note that in addition to setting bail, a judge can impose other conditions on your release. He can restrict you from the bar where the fight took place or from an entire neighborhood where drug activity is common. He can prohibit you from seeing witnesses or others connected with your case. The fact is, he can impose just about any conditions he thinks appropriate for the good of the community and the orderly administration of your case.

AFTER YOUR ARREST—THE LEGAL PROCEDURES

The first thing police do after arresting you is "book" you, that is, they record on a large blotter your name and the crime for which you were arrested. They may also record your fingerprints, several unflattering photographs, and other identifying data.

Booking is supposed to take place as soon as you walk into the police station, although it doesn't always work that way. If you're one of hundreds of people arrested at, say, a rock concert or political demonstration, the administrative backup will probably delay your turn for hours. Also, if the police for some reason take a special dislike to you, they can exhibit impressive resourcefulness in finding reasons to drag their feet.

Although the events following booking vary depending on the locality and the seriousness of the crime with which you're charged, there are three fairly standard procedures:

1. *Initial appearance.* Also called *presentment,* this takes place before a magistrate (who looks and acts just like a judge, but is paid less) shortly after your booking. Here you're informed of the charges against you and again reminded, this time on the record, of your *Miranda* rights. Also—the key event—your bail is set.

Your availability for your initial appearance, like your booking, may be delayed for reasons real or contrived. If your arrest takes place at night in a town that has no night court, for example, you may have to kill twelve hours in a cell with a drug-crazed martial arts maniac until court convenes the next morning. Some towns have neither a night court nor a *weekend* court, so if you're arrested on a Friday evening, you may have a chance to become fast friends with the martial arts maniac.

2. *Preliminary hearing.* Also referred to in some places as a

preliminary examination, a *probable cause hearing,* or a *commitment hearing,* this procedure is usually reserved for felonies and is held several days or more after your initial appearance. Here a judge (or magistrate) decides whether there is probable cause to "bind you over" for prosecution—or whether the whole thing is a crock. Those present will include the judge, your lawyer, a prosecutor, and possibly witnesses. At this point the judge might raise or lower your bail.

Don't let the word *preliminary* mislead you about the critical nature of this proceeding, which is a sort of minitrial to determine whether a full trial is necessary. A good lawyer will try to use this occasion to show the judge any holes in the prosecution's case. If he can't nip the entire matter in the bud, he'll at least discover the nature of the evidence against you and put key witnesses' testimony on the record before they decide to change it. He may also get your bail reduced. This is no time to be chintzy about getting a good lawyer.

3. *Arraignment.* This comparatively formal procedure (black tie optional) takes place any time from a few days to a number of months after your arrest. In the interim the authorities will be out talking to witnesses and performing other investigation to determine what charges they want to try to make stick. The complexity and seriousness of the case determine the length of the delay; two to three months is common.

At arraignment you're read the specific charges against you, and then you enter your plea: guilty, not guilty, or—as is permitted in most jurisdictions—*nolo contendere.* This last one (Latin for "I won't fight it") is best translated, "I'm guilty, Your Honor, but the prosecutor agreed to let me off with this if I'd spare him the trouble of proving his case."

The next step after arraignment, usually with a number of months of waiting in between, is the trial. Your lawyer can explain the trial process in detail. For present purposes just note that your entitlement to a free lawyer (if you're entitled to one at all) extends through your trial and one appeal. After that, as far as the government is concerned, you're on your own.

Grand Juries, Indictments, and Informations

In any prosecution by federal authorities and in most serious cases brought by local authorities, it's required that you be formally charged—*indicted*—by a *grand jury*. This body, composed of about twenty impartial adults selected from a cross-section of the community, superficially resembles a *trial jury* of the kind you see on "Perry Mason" reruns. Its function is different, however.

A grand jury screens prosecutorial decisions, theoretically serving as a check on overzealous government lawyers, although the process is generally agreed to be too one-sided to serve that function well. The local prosecutor recommends a case against Paolo Anastasio, putting before the grand jurors the testimony of, say, two policemen and a government informant. The grand jury then says, "Okay, Anastasio looks like he's probably guilty. Go ahead, arrest him and try him."

A *trial* jury comes into the picture later, once both Anastasio and the government have had time to put together their cases. It makes the final decision on whether Anastasio is guilty as charged.

Note that the grand jury's reviewing function can also take place *after* Anastasio's arrest. The prosecutor walks into the grand jury room and declares, "A villainous character named Paolo Anastasio has just been picked up for selling cocaine. Okay, on *suspicion* of selling cocaine, but we all know what that means." The prosecutor presents the testimony of a few witnesses (he has to have at least one) and then asks for an indictment, which he usually gets. Anastasio's arraignment takes place a few weeks later, and several months after that, his trial.

For misdemeanors (and even for felonies in a number of states), the local prosecutor may be permitted to skip the time-consuming process of obtaining a go-ahead from the grand jury and issue a charge on his own authority. Then, the charge is called not an *indictment* but an *information*—as confusing a term as the law has managed to generate.

What's the difference to you, whether you're charged by an indictment (from a grand jury) or an information (from a prosecutor)? None. I just wanted you to know what those people in pinstripes are talking about.

DEALING WITH POLICE SEARCHES

Not every encounter with police authority involves an arrest. If you're lucky, the officers may just knock on your door, flash you a search warrant, barge in, track mud on your rugs, ransack your closets, kick your dog (who has commenced gnawing on their ankles), and then leave.

How should you respond to such an intrusion (other than by having your rugs cleaned and your dog put in a body cast)? The three cardinal prohibitions discussed above with respect to arrests—*don't resist* (this means *do* unlock the door when the police knock; otherwise they'll break it down), *don't say anything*, and *don't consent to anything*—apply with equal force to searches, and for the same reasons.

Probable Cause

At the time a search is actually going on, you have no way of knowing if it's legal. The key concept with respect to the legality of searches is *probable cause:* Police can lawfully ransack any person or place if they have it. Probable cause of what? That's much debated. The term appears in the Fourth Amendment to the Constitution—". . . and no Warrants [for arrests or searches] shall issue, but upon probable cause . . ."—and presumably means probable cause to believe that a crime has been committed and that a search will turn up evidence pertaining to the crime.

Do the police officers you're dealing with have probable cause to believe they'll find incriminating evidence in your closet (or pockets, or glove compartment)? Possibly—who knows what someone has told them you've been up to? Maybe the whole thing is a terrible mistake: "The search warrant says Beechwood *Avenue*, you morons, not Beechwood *Lane*."

Must police always have a warrant before they can conduct a search? No. As with arrests, they must always have *probable cause*—the testimony of a reliable informant, for example—and if time allows, they're supposed to go to a magistrate in advance and apply for a search warrant based on that probable cause. But for searches, as for arrests, there are numerous exceptions to the prior warrant requirement, notably the "search incident to arrest" exception (to ensure an arrestee isn't carrying a weapon). In this situation, if the police have probable cause, they can search first and apply for a warrant later.

DONT RESIST

How do you know if they have probable cause? You don't, at least not at the time of the search. Usually they have *some* cause, and the question that tends to reach the higher courts is whether they had *enough* cause to constitute *probable* cause— which might not be resolved for years.

In any event, even if you're dead solid certain the courts will eventually find a lack of probable cause in your case, re- member: *There's nothing you can do about it now.*

Your response to a police search should be one of total passivity. If police are determined to look somewhere, they will, and resisting will only multiply your troubles.

DON'T SAY ANYTHING

This is no time to let down your guard. If the police aren't arresting you but just searching your house, they're not required to tell you your *Miranda* rights—a result of which is that police omissions along these lines won't serve to insulate you from the consequences of whatever you say.

DON'T CONSENT TO ANYTHING

Be careful about giving actual or implicit consent to anything when the police are engaged in a search. Suppose the police have arrested you and are taking you down to the station—in other words, they're performing a "full custody arrest," which automatically entitles them to search you from head to toe for weapons or evidence.

The search the police are permitted to make in the course of such an arrest includes not only your body and your clothes, but also the areas within your "immediate control," to prevent you from grabbing a gun or from disposing of evidence even as the arrest proceeds. But the police aren't permitted to search *everywhere*—throughout your house or wherever they've grabbed you—without either a search warrant or your consent.

So there you are in your living room—your hands against the wall, your feet spread, one officer getting to know you in a way that only your doctor knows you—when the other officer approaches the closed door to your bedroom and says, "You don't mind if I look in here, do you?" You figure he's going to do it anyway, so you shrug your shoulders and say, "Why not?"

Bad move. Your response should be, "Of course I mind if you look in there. I mind everything you're doing."

Suppose you're not being arrested at all, but you've been pulled over on the highway, and one officer says gruffly, his hand caressing his pistol butt, "Would you open your trunk, please?" Don't automatically view this inquiry as an order (unless you have a strong feeling that viewing it as anything else will get you beat up). Your reply should be, "Do I have to?" or "Are you ordering me to?" If the officer answers in the affirmative, and then it turns out he didn't have the authority to issue such an order, he won't be able to claim that the search was legal by virtue of your consent.

"Consent" comes in many forms. Suppose the police show up at your door late one night with a warrant for your arrest. You're in your bathrobe. They search you and the areas within your immediate control (a lawful "search incident to arrest") and find nothing. Then they say they're taking you downtown for questioning. You may get dressed, if you like. Dressing seems like a good idea, and not just because of the blizzard outside; the stories you've heard about sexual assaults in prison make you wish you still had that suit of armor you wore last Halloween.

As you walk to your bedroom to get dressed, the police officers following you closely, you recall something sitting in your dresser next to your underwear that you wouldn't enjoy having them see—a bag of marijuana, say. Are you on the verge of doing something that will subject the marijuana to lawful discovery by the police?

Yes! For the same reason that police may search you and the immediately surrounding areas in the course of an arrest, they may also search any place you go (closet, bedroom, bathroom) and anything you touch (dresser, overcoat, hat) before taking you in. By approaching your dresser and opening it, you're in effect "consenting" to a search of its contents. Does your bathrobe really look so bad?

A FEW WORDS ON CARS

• Police officers need neither a search warrant, probable cause, nor anything else to examine the exterior of your car or peer through its windows. The lesson: If you're carrying something in your car that you don't want anyone to see, keep it out of sight.

• Under the "search incident to arrest" rules, police are permitted to search the areas within your "immediate control" whenever they arrest you. In a car, the areas within your immediate control may include not only the dashboard and the space under the front seat, but also the entire passenger area, including the back seat and the glove compartment, if a court chooses to view the matter so broadly. The lesson: If you're carrying something in your car that you don't want anyone to see, keep it not just out of sight, but in your trunk.

• With regard to warrantless searches, the Supreme Court affords police more latitude when dealing with cars than with houses. The rationale is partly that cars tend to move around more than houses and partly that people have lesser expectations of privacy in cars.

The Supreme Court has ruled that if the police have probable cause to believe your car is carrying something illegal, they may lawfully conduct a warrantless search of every place in the car in which the object of their search might be hidden, including not only the trunk but also suitcases and other containers inside the trunk. However, the scope of their search must be limited by the nature of what they're looking for. Thus, if they have probable cause to believe you're transporting an undocumented alien, they may pull you over and immediately search your trunk, but they may *not* search your briefcase or any other container too small to conceal a person. The lesson: Nothing in your car is absolutely safe from a warrantless search, but if you're carrying something in your car that you don't want anyone to see, your best bet is to stick it in the smallest possible closable container— and keep *that* in your trunk.

• If the police stop you on the highway and decide to take you into custody, they may or may not impound your car. If they impound it, they're automatically permitted to search it and inventory its contents—to protect your property, to protect themselves from disputes over lost or stolen property, and to avoid danger from hidden explosives.

If you're carrying something in your car that you don't want anyone to see, you'd probably prefer almost any alternative to impoundment and the accompanying search. You'd happily leave the car on the side of the road, for example, or drop it at a parking lot on the way to the police station, or turn it over to a companion.

If the police don't offer any such alternative, propose one yourself. If they insist on impounding your car anyway, you can either hope they won't get around to searching it or come right out and ask them not to search it (offering to sign a waiver of claims against them for anything lost or damaged). Will such a request stimulate the police to make a more thorough search of your car than they might otherwise have made? Possibly. All you can do is go with your best judgment at the time. Stay cool.

STOP AND FRISK

You're walking along the street, by yourself, at 4:00 A.M. A cruising police car approaches you from behind. One officer rolls down his window. "You live around here?" he asks.

Now, the reason you're walking around in the middle of the night is that you're anxious about your mother's upcoming operation and can't sleep. You don't feel like talking to anybody.

You're confident that these officers don't have probable cause to arrest you, and you suspect they're just harassing you because your race is different from theirs. Two questions come immediately to your mind: First, are they breaking the law? Second, must you reply, or may you walk on in silence?

As for the first question, they're not breaking the law. A police officer enjoys the right of any citizen to address questions to other members of the public.

As for the second question, it's rarely a good idea to ignore police officers. Doing so will likely goad them into a longer, more disagreeable, and, to your irritation, entirely lawful intrusion into your life. True, they may lack probable cause to arrest you. But there's another, lesser form of detention, referred to in judicial opinions as an *investigatory stop*, for which they need nothing more than a "reasonable suspicion" that you're up to something illegal.

What circumstances suffice to give police officers a reasonable suspicion? Anything you can imagine—pacing back and forth in front of a liquor store or bank, as if casing it; driving slowly around an abandoned housing development late at night; associating with professional athletes in a neighborhood known for drugs.

Police officers have a lot of latitude in deciding what looks reasonably suspicious. In an ideal world, they wouldn't be permitted to stop someone solely because of how he's dressed, but no one would dispute that certain forms of attire—a stocking on one's head, say—go beyond the merely idiosyncratic.

Reasonably suspicious circumstances entitle the police not only to stop you, that is, detain you briefly and make limited inquiries, but also to *frisk* you, that is, search your outer clothing. Note that a frisk, also known as a *pat down*, is allowed solely for purposes of detecting weapons, not for discovering drugs or other evidence of criminal activity. (The latter would rise to the level of a *search*, for which they would need probable cause.)

So, do you answer the officers who stop you as you're out for your private, perfectly innocent stroll? Yes—because if you don't, they'll decide you're suspicious enough to deserve a frisking, and then you'll find yourself with your hands up against a wall, your feet spread, and your bad mood becoming worse by the minute. (Keep in mind that you *are* out strolling the streets at 4:00 A.M.)

You don't have to chat with the officers all night. Once you've identified yourself and told them what you're up to and where you live, you're more than entitled to say, "Unless I'm under arrest, Officers, I'm leaving." If at that point they decide to frisk you, you can either (1) put up with it and then forget about it, chalking it up as a cost of living in a semicivilized society, or (2) put up with it and then bring a lawsuit against the officers for assault and/or racial harassment. Don't overlook that both options include putting up with it.

SELF-DEFENSE

Muggers, rapists, child molesters, dog vivisectors—it's a jungle out there.

There you sit in a bar, minding your own business. A nearby drunk decides he doesn't like your looks and deliberately jostles you as he passes. You don't say anything, but you look up, annoyed. This is all the provocation he needs. He throws his drink on you and advances. On the table beside you, within reach, sit a heavy beer mug and a steak knife. Do you grab either item for self-defense? Do you use it?

The practical answer is, either find the bouncer or bartender immediately, or turn and run. Otherwise you could find yourself spending what seems like the rest of your life (along with what may in fact be your life's savings) in court, defending yourself against criminal charges (brought by the authorities), civil charges (brought by the drunk), or both.

The *legal* answer, which can get you into big trouble if you don't apply it perfectly, is embodied in the following rule: You're permitted to defend yourself with force reasonably equivalent to the force someone is using or proposing to use against you.

How much force was the drunk in this instance proposing

to use against you? Who knows? To you he looked capable of murdering you with his bare hands.

It all depends on the circumstances. The basic question is always this: Would a jury believe you were justified in acting the way you did? Because juries are unpredictable and likely to be influenced by such irrelevancies as your hairstyle, allow them plenty of margin for error.

Better yet, allow them *no* margin for error; that is, stay away from them. Litigation is no treat, even if it's litigation you're virtually certain to win.

Mistake

What if it turns out that the drunk had no weapon and that he wasn't advancing on you at all, but merely struggling to get past you on his way to the restroom? Moreover, he didn't deliberately throw his drink on you, but accidentally spilled it on you in his hurry to respond to the call of nature.

The law understands that nobody is perfect. It recognizes that some situations call for instant decisions and that omniscience is too much to expect. The question that would be put to a jury is: Did you have a reasonable basis for acting as you did?

To restate the rule of self-defense set forth above: You're permitted to defend yourself with force reasonably equivalent to the force you *reasonably believe* someone is using or proposing to use against you.

Deadly Force

A word on *deadly force*, which refers to any force likely to kill, even if it doesn't succeed. You're permitted to use it (subject to the duty-to-retreat rules discussed below)—*if* your assailant is using it against you.

What if it turns out that the mugger didn't have a gun at all and that the object in his trenchcoat pocket was a rock that he was claiming to be a gun? In other words, what if you were correct regarding his intent to use force against you, but incorrect regarding the deadly nature of the force?

Again, the question that would be put to a jury is, did you have a reasonable basis for acting as you did?

Say you've been studying oriental martial arts. This time the drunk who comes at you is small, unarmed, and wearing glasses—Woody Allen's younger brother, full of displaced hatred for his more successful sibling. You deliver a hard but nonlethal kick to his chest. He staggers backward and, in his intoxicated state, falls down, hits his head on the floor, and dies. Are you now guilty of using deadly force where the force against you was clearly of a less-than-deadly nature?

No, or at least probably not; in practice a jury would have to decide. The most likely outcome is a finding that the level of force you used was reasonable, and the man's death was an unforeseeable consequence for which you shouldn't be held responsible. The result might be entirely different, however, if you delivered more than a single blow. If the jury becomes persuaded that you were participating in an old-fashioned bar brawl, rather than defending yourself in the least violent manner possible, you might be held responsible for the man's death.

Consider here the so-called *thin-skull* rule. This rule says that if you negligently or maliciously do violence to someone who, unknown to you, has an abnormally thin skull, and this person dies as a result of your conduct, even though a normal person would have suffered no more than a bump on his head, you're responsible for that person's death.

The underlying principle: You're liable for the consequences of your actions, however unforeseeable those consequences may be. You take your victims as you find them.

Why doesn't the thin-skull rule render you responsible for the death of the man who fell down and died after you kicked him in the chest? Because the rule applies only to someone who is at fault, that is, someone who was acting negligently or maliciously. But you were just defending yourself—or so you'll have to persuade the jury.

So far the rules I've stated are, if not obvious, intuitively fair; they would command the assent of the average person on the street. But several qualifications of the rules pertaining to deadly force generate considerable controversy, and mere reasonableness won't necessarily keep you from running afoul of them.

Duty to Retreat

Some jurisdictions, more averse to the use of deadly force than others, impose on you a *duty to retreat* before allowing you to respond in kind to a potentially deadly assault.

Suppose the drunk in the bar pulls a switchblade and advances on you. You run to the wall of the bar and pull down an ornamental but razor-sharp sword, which you brandish menacingly, praying the derelict will change his mind and leave. No such luck. Blind to the danger, he continues forward. Can you run him through?

It depends on where you live. In states in the South and West, you're generally permitted to "be a man" (even if you're a woman)—in other words, to skewer away. In states in the effete Northeast and Midwest, you're generally required to retreat, if you can—to turn tail and run. The latter states want you to avoid deadly confrontations where possible, regardless of who's in the right.

How are you supposed to determine your state's rule in the three seconds before the drunk reaches you? How are you supposed to determine whether there's a rear door to the bar without turning your back on your assailant as you consult the bartender? There's no good answer to these questions, except that you're legally safe wherever you are if you get the hell out of there. That course—the one I recommend—can never get you into trouble.

Your House, Your Castle

Even some of the duty-to-retreat states allow you to stand your ground in your own house. A house is sacred, the theory goes, and you shouldn't have to sneak out the back door if you see someone crawling through a window with a gun.

Again, how are you supposed to determine the rule in your state when you need it? What are the chances that you'll remember or care what the rule is when you're making a snap judgment regarding the protection of your spouse and children? There's no good answer, but keep in mind that a shoot-first-ask-questions-later policy that kills an innocent person can be awfully hard to justify in the light of day.

If you've gone so far as to stick a gun in your closet, why not take the next step of consulting a lawyer regarding your state's rule as to when you can legally use it?

TRAPS AND SPRING GUNS

You live in a tough neighborhood—Manhattan. You work long hours, and you hate coming home at night to your dark, ground-floor apartment where there's no one present (or there ought to be no one present). Several rapes have occurred nearby in recent weeks, and you're genuinely, rationally concerned for your safety.

One day you decide to set up a spring gun—a shotgun strapped to a chair and pointed at the window, with a string connecting the window and the gun's trigger. That same night you come home and find a mangled corpse lying on the window sill, crushing your begonias.

If the deceased was your building superintendent, you're in big trouble. Even if he was an escaped felon, his loaded pistol still clutched in his insensate paw, you're in big trouble. Why? Many states have laws prohibiting spring guns under any circumstances. And even in states without such laws, you aren't permitted to defend mere property with deadly force; it's considered inherently excessive. And if you weren't present in person, what could the spring gun have been protecting except property?

Note that this rule applies to any form of indiscriminate force. Anyone who sets up a snake pit or even turns loose a hungry Chihuahua without consulting a lawyer is a high-stakes gambler.

Retaliation

A drunk has deliberately poured a beer in your lap. To add insult to injury, it was your beer. You could probably take him one-on-one, but you're a pacifist, and what you'd really like to do is rush your pants to the cleaners before they stain.

Unfortunately for you, the whole thing took place in front of your fiancée, a Southern belle with traditional notions of manhood. On the way home, she heatedly informs you that *she* was insulted by the incident, even if you weren't, and where's your backbone?

Say good-bye to her. She isn't worth going to jail for, on charges of assault and battery.

If you had responded to the drunk's provocation immediately, you might have been okay from a legal perspective. You'd probably have torn your suit coat and jammed a finger, but you'd have been within your rights of self-defense. Twenty minutes later and a half-mile away, on the other hand, you're looking not at self-defense, but at retaliation. And revenge is mine, saith the Law.

Suppose you had responded immediately, flooring the drunk with a single mighty blow. Could you then have lifted him to his feet and nailed him again, the way John Wayne used to do? No. Anything more than the minimum necessary to keep him off you is illegal. Indeed, if the drunk had followed up his beer-pouring act by running away, so that your only possible motivation in going after him would have been vengeance rather than self-defense, it's far from clear that you'd have been within your rights in doing so.

A classic situation. Your house has just been burgled, and the intruders have departed the premises only moments ago. Out your window you see them bolting down the street with your silverware. Do you run to your closet, pull out your rifle, and shoot?

No! Assuming the circumstances had been right—it was dark, the intruders were armed, retreat was impossible—you might have been within your rights in shooting *while they were inside your house*.

But now it's too late. You may not shoot as they run away. You may never use deadly force to protect mere property, which is what you'd be doing (and only arguably that) if you shot now.

May you at least go after them in an attempt to get back your silverware? That's a different question.

Recapture of Property

Sure, go after them. You're permitted to use force (*nondeadly* force) to protect your property, and the fact that someone has momentarily taken something out of your possession doesn't mean you've lost this privilege. Thus, your right to use force to protect your property includes, within limits, a right to use force to *recapture* your property.

Should you take your gun? Well, maybe, but make sure you don't use it—again, you may *never* use deadly force to protect mere property—unless someone turns on you and threatens you personally. Then you're back to self-defense.

The right to recapture property by force is to some extent a matter of timing. Courts say you're permitted to use force when you're in "fresh pursuit" of your property.

What constitutes *fresh* pursuit, as opposed to *stale* pursuit, can be hard to pin down—which is to say, the answer may depend on who your judge is. For a rule of thumb, if twelve hours have elapsed since your property was taken, don't use force. If only ten minutes have elapsed, some force may be okay. Between ten minutes and twelve hours, the answer is unclear, although as with diapers on a baby, the chances of freshness diminish with each passing minute. Unless the property in question is extremely valuable and your legal right to it beyond dispute, I strongly recommend the Coward's Rule: Don't do anything even remotely likely to result in a physical confrontation.

Defense of Others, and Citizens' Arrests

One day, outside your office window, you observe two men using a third man as a punching bag. You call the emergency police number, and a jaded voice promises to "try to get someone to look into it soon." It occurs to you that if someone doesn't do something right away, your next call will have to be to the morgue.

Go ahead—be a hero. The rule is: You're permitted to use force in defense of another person in any circumstance in which that person would be permitted to use force in defense of himself.

Suppose the scuffle outside is only one-on-one, rather than two-on-one. Also, although you're sure you heard a cry for help, at the moment the fight appears to be a draw. Can you still intervene?

Yes, but now you face a practical problem: What if you intervene on the wrong side? What if your tooth-dislodging blows land on the poor guy struggling to protect his mother's welfare check?

That's definitely a problem, and courts disagree on the answer. Some say you're not in trouble if your mistake was reasonable. Others say you intervene at your peril, that is, you're liable for damages to anyone you erroneously maul, however well-intentioned and reasonable your action. The lesson: If you're in doubt as to who's mugging whom, wait for the police.

What if nobody is mugging anybody? (An admittedly unlikely scenario.) There are still plenty of bad guys out there. May you ever use force against one of them in defense of society as a whole?

Suppose you're shopping downtown one afternoon, when from not too far away you hear the sound of a muffled explosion. An alarm bell goes off, and the next thing you know a seedy-looking man is sprinting in your direction, knocking down pedestrians left and right. You think to yourself, If this guy isn't a bank robber, I'm not Arnie Graber. Your adrenalin soaring, you hurl your newly purchased bowling ball into his stomach as he passes. That stops him, sure enough. You pounce on him and declare, "This is a citizen's arrest." Several nice-looking pedestrians of the opposite sex applaud.

A good move? Maybe. It's like intervening in a mugging, as described above: If you're right, you're a hero; if you're wrong, you're in big trouble.

The concept of a citizen's arrest isn't a fictional product of Hollywood. Indeed, in the right circumstances, it's something the law wants to encourage.

What are "the right circumstances"? The rules vary from state to state, so you're best off taking a conservative approach. Don't arrest anybody unless (1) the crime in question is serious—robbery or assault, for example; (2) it took place *in your presence* (although you don't have to have observed the actual pull of the trigger); and (3) the arrest by you is necessary—for example, the criminal is virtually certain to escape if you don't grab him. If the bank robber you've spotted has coolly seated himself at a bar and ordered a drink, resist the temptation to act out your Clint Eastwood fantasies. Call the police.

ADVICE TO VICTIMS OF CRIME

The classic case involves rape. A victim of this violent crime is in desperate need of support—emotional, medical, even financial—during the struggle to recover from the trauma. But the criminal justice system, far from providing such support or even acknowledging the need for it, has traditionally subjected the victim to further misery.

This is changing. Criminal victims' groups have sprung up around the country, often headed by people who were themselves the victims of violent crimes. If you need any form of help following a crime against you, ask around about such groups. Reportedly their services can be a godsend.

Legislatures have gotten into the act. In 1984 Congress passed the Victims of Crime Act, providing for the distribution to criminal victims' groups of millions of dollars collected through criminal penalties and fines. Most of the states—forty-four, plus the District of Columbia—have victims' compensation boards, which reimburse crime victims for lost wages, uninsured medical bills, and even funeral expenses. (Property losses generally aren't covered, nor is "pain and suffering," the category of damage that has led to a number of highly publicized million-dollar-plus jury awards.)

Some suggestions for crime victims:

• If you've just been the victim of a violent crime, do tell the police if you have a particular doctor or hospital you want to go to (assuming you aren't so critically injured that there's no time to be choosy). Otherwise you might be taken to a hospital where you're the only person who speaks English and your doctor's diploma is in an alphabet you don't recognize.

• If you've just been the victim of a sex crime, do allow a doctor to examine you to obtain evidence. This can be critical for catching the offender. Also, if the offender ends up going to trial, his lawyer will use your refusal of a medical examination to raise doubts about your story. (Feel free to insist that a friend or some person of your sex remain with you during the examination.)

• Upon discovering that someone has committed a crime against your property—burglarized your house, say—don't touch anything until the police have had a chance to take pictures, check for fingerprints, and otherwise gather whatever evidence may be present.

• If the police are holding something of yours as evidence of a crime, ask if it can be photographed and then returned to you, lest you never see it again (or not recognize it a year later because of all the mildew and rot).

• As a crime victim, it's vital that you answer questions, review photographs, attend lineups, and otherwise assist the police and prosecutors. When called upon for such tasks, however, don't hesitate to ask if they can be scheduled to suit your convenience or, when appropriate, handled over the phone.

• If you're involved in a traffic wreck (or any comparable incident) that looks as if it might wind up in court, get the names and addresses of all witnesses yourself. Don't assume from the fact that police officers are present and talking to people that they're bothering to write such information down.

9. Insurance Law

Life is a gamble, at terrible odds—if it was a bet you wouldn't take it.
                                                        TOM STOPPARD
                                                        (1937–   )

There are worse things in life than death. If you've ever spent an evening with an insurance salesman, you know exactly what I mean.
                                                        WOODY ALLEN
                                                        (1935–   )

I agree with Woody.   MARTIN J. YUDKOWITZ
                                                        (1954–   )

READING YOUR POLICY ("SELF-INDUCED NARCOLEPSY")

In order to understand what an insurance policy says, you first have to understand what an insurance policy *is*—other than unreadable, unread, and, for most people, missing. ("Hang on, I know it's around here somewhere . . . maybe the linen closet . . .")

It's a *contract*, between you and an insurance company. The basic terms are simple: You pay the company a premium, and the company pays you some amount of money back if you experience any misfortune covered by the policy. Also—what you're *really* paying for—the company's sales agents stop dropping by "just to get to know you."

Suppose you're in a car wreck. Or your playful cat Mr.

Bentley tears a seven-inch gash in your neighbor, the hemo-
philiac. If you're like most people, your first thought is, I wonder
if this is covered by my insurance. Unless the same thing has
happened before—Mr. Bentley gets around—you don't know.

How can you find out? You're tempted to take the easy
route and call your insurer, or perhaps the broker who sold you
the policy. But the better answer, which I offer as the tenth of
White's Irregular Rules, and the first in this chapter, is:

Read the policy.

There's no good way around this. If you call your insurer,
maybe the person you speak to will remember all the provisions
of all the company's policies. *Maybe* he'll remember the special
endorsements (changes) in your particular policy. *Maybe* he'll bother
to look up your policy if he can't remember what it says. *Maybe*
he'll understand what it says once he has reviewed it.

Then again, *maybe* he'll just make up an answer, erring, of
course, on the side of noncoverage.

The person who answers the phone when you call your
insurer's claims information number isn't a lawyer. He's no more
qualified to interpret your policy than you are. All he does is
spout the company line, which for obvious reasons is biased
against coverage. Presumably, since he looks at policies every
day, he can steer you to the provisions relevant to your question,
but that's about it.

To be sure, if someone at your insurer's office says a particular type of loss is covered, don't look that gift horse in the
mouth. But make a written note of the person's name, along
with the date and the number you called. Also, be sure to confirm
the title and position of the person you're talking to. If he's a
janitor, he lacks authority to bind the insurer legally.

Again, your best bet for determining whether a particular
loss is covered is to read the policy. "But I can't read all that
garbage," you say. "It would take me forever to go through it,
and I wouldn't understand it anyway."

Are you sure? There's less magic in the language of these
contracts than you might think.

This isn't to say you should never seek outside help in trying to figure out your policy, just that (1) seeking outside help shouldn't normally be your first step, and (2) you can't count on *objective* help from your insurer. For that you need a lawyer.

Hiring a lawyer to read your policy, when you could read it yourself, is an expensive indulgence. There are three circumstances, however, in which it's definitely reasonable to have a lawyer check it out.

1. *You're rich.* In this circumstance, the fact that you may not *need* a lawyer to read your policy isn't relevant to anything. What matters is that you *want* one to read it, to spare you the unpleasantness.

2. *The stakes are high.* Suppose the loss for which you want coverage amounts to tens of thousands of dollars. In this circumstance, recall the first of White's Irregular Rules:

Where there's a lot of money at stake,
hire a lawyer.

This applies regardless of the nature of the dispute, and even if you've mastered your policy from beginning to end.

3. *You've tried figuring out your policy and can't.* This hardly makes you a moron. Some policies torture you with jargon and foreign language (not to mention staples obscuring key words). Others overwhelm you with sheer length. My Aetna Homeowners Policy runs nineteen pages, with countless definitions, declarations, exclusions, conditions, more exclusions, more conditions, extensions, "special policy provisions," and more (I think).

The average policy is likely to contain the following five sections or categories of terms, familiarity with which could be helpful in figuring out your own policy:

1. *Declarations.* Usually located on the opening page, this is where you'll find certain facts you've "declared" about yourself, such as your name, address, and age. This section also states the policy period, the dollar amounts of coverage, the premium, the deductibles (if any), and other key data.

2. *Definitions.* Insurance policies routinely use lots of "defined terms," the goal being to allow the draftsperson to use a single word rather than a lengthy phrase to make an oft-recurring

point. The goal is fine, but in practice defined terms tend to produce as much confusion as clarity.

3. *The insuring agreement.* Possibly identified as "Coverages" or "Perils Insured Against," this is the heart of the contract. In a homeowner's policy this section might say, in paraphrase, "This policy covers all personal property owned by the insured, excluding his car (for which he should get automobile insurance) but not excluding his lawnmower (not even his riding lawn-mower, unless he rides it to work)."

4. *Warranties and conditions.* This section sets forth various requirements—such as paying your premiums on time, or no-tifying the insurer within thirty days of any loss that might be the subject of a claim—that you have to comply with or suffer loss of coverage.

5. *Exclusions.* Read this part with special care. Here the in-surer denies coverage of various types of losses, such as those you cause deliberately, those you cause by accident, those you cause while driving a car, those you cause while not driving a car, those you cause while breathing. . . . You get the picture.

AVOIDING RESTRICTIONS IN YOUR POLICY

Suppose your house burns down, or you slip and fall on a banana peel in a restaurant—whatever, you suffer some kind of loss for which you'd like to file a claim with your insurer. Re-viewing your policy, you eventually figure out what it says— which is, "No coverage."

Does that end the matter? Do you just curse the insurer, kick Mr. Bentley, and personally absorb the cost of rebuilding your house or treating your injuries?

Not necessarily. There are a number of ways you can avoid restrictions in the terms of your policy.

To be sure, some losses just aren't covered, and there's nothing you can do about it. Initiating a clearly losing battle just wastes your own money, clogs up the courts, and subjects you to the possibility of a countersuit.

Nevertheless, you should understand that the terms of your insurance policy aren't the final word on coverage. An insurance policy, like any contract, constitutes a sort of private law governing the relations between the signing parties. But that private law is subject to (1) interpretation by judges, who are guided by a number of well-established proconsumer principles, and (2) the higher authority of statutory law.

Consider three examples:

1. Suppose you misstated your age in your application for health insurance. You said you were thirty-nine, when in fact you were forty. You made this misstatement in a section of the application captioned "Warranties"; and warranties, a lawyer friend tells you, must be "strictly" accurate (unlike mere "representations," which need be only "substantially" accurate). Your insurer says, "Sorry, but no coverage. Our charts show that people in their forties suffer far more heart disease than people in their thirties. We'd never have accepted your application if we'd known how old you really are."

Can they get away with this?

Possibly not. A court might rule, simply as a matter of fairness in interpreting contracts, that the misstatement was trivial, that you appear to have made it innocently, and that in any event you correctly stated your date of birth. Thus, although the language of the policy, strictly construed, precludes coverage in the event of such a misstatement, you get your money.

2. Suppose you made a more substantial misstatement. You said in your application for health insurance that you had never experienced heart trouble, when in fact, seventeen years ago, you spent four days in a hospital for heart pains. Now, when you file your claim for the expenses associated with your recent heart operation, the insurance company points out your error and denies coverage. Is that the end of it?

Again, maybe not. Perhaps your doctor is more alert than you are, and in response to the insurer's request for your medical history in connection with a previous, unrelated matter, he provided all the details of your earlier heart troubles. The insurer, thereafter on notice of your misstatement, nevertheless continued to accept your premiums and in fact paid you several hundred dollars on some other claim.

In these circumstances a court might well rule that your insurer, through its continuing acceptance of your premiums and its payment of your other claim, gave up—or "waived"—its right to deny coverage. Thus, notwithstanding the strict terms of your policy, you get your money.

3. Frequently an insurer denies coverage on the ground that an insured failed to notify it as quickly as the policy requires—within thirty days, say, or "immediately"—following a fire, a wreck, or some other event leading to a loss.

Suppose you don't get around to notifying your insurer of some such event until two weeks after the deadline has passed. Could such a delay cost you everything? Possibly. But the courts in a number of states hold that noncompliance with even the most explicit deadline doesn't by itself let an insurer off the hook. These states require an insurer to show harm or "prejudice" resulting from such noncompliance; otherwise, you get your money.

Courts sometimes help insureds in a more general way, resolving ambiguities in insurance policies against the insurers. They do this partly because of the long-standing rule that ambiguity in any contract should be construed against whoever drafted it, since the drafter presumably tilted the language in his own favor at the outset. Also, they recognize that the relationship between you and your insurer is hardly one between equals. You probably got the contract on a take-it-or-leave-it basis, with zero room for negotiation.

To illustrate, suppose your health insurance policy excludes coverage of losses "arising from any preexisting condition." (Most health insurance policies do in fact exclude such coverage.) You are an epileptic. One day a seizure causes you to fall down a stairwell, breaking your spine. Did this injury "arise from" your epilepsy, which clearly constitutes a "preexisting condition"? Or would it be more accurate to say the injury arose from your fall?

Although the answer isn't assured, a sympathetic court might well focus on the uncertainty of the exclusion's applicability here and hold that because epilepsy does not, in and of itself, cause broken spines, your injury arose not from a preexisting condition, but instead from an intervening cause, the fall. And you get your money.

Consumers can often look to statutes as well as the courts for aid in avoiding restrictions in their policies. Suppose one day Fate starts dumping on you. Your company lets you go. Your girlfriend does the same, but less gently. Even your dog Gaylord packs his food bowl and hits the road. Depressed, you start seeing a psychiatrist. You submit her first bill to your health insurer. They can't deny coverage of this, you think. A psychiatrist is an M.D.

They do deny coverage, pointing out your policy's exclusion of charges associated with "nervous disorders." (This is in fact the term used by various insurers to exclude coverage of such charges. Note that if an insurance application asks about "nervous disorders" or "mental illness," you're probably expected to mention not only the most common forms of psychotherapy, but even marital counseling.) "A damn obscure way of excluding psychiatric expenses," you grumble. "I guess there's nothing I can do about it, though."

Don't be so sure. Many states—twenty-nine, by one count—*require* health insurers to cover psychiatric expenses up to a given amount—$500, $5,000, whatever the legislators thought their own spouses or kids might need. Additional states are expected to have such laws soon. These sums won't get you through a year of lie-down-on-the-sofa-and-describe-lewd-fantasies-about-your-parent-of-the-opposite-sex psychoanalysis at the rates charged by analysts working today ($80 to $100 per hour is typical). But they might get you far enough along to understand why Gaylord wanted to leave.

Another example of statutory protection. Suppose your health insurance policy has lapsed because of nonpayment of premiums—you've been out of the country, or, more likely, you just put the premium notices aside and forgot about them. Your insurer says you can renew your policy, but only at substantially higher rates.

A number of states require insurers to allow reinstatement of policies that have lapsed because of nonpayment of premiums. In these states, if you're willing to pay the overdue premiums and forgo coverage of losses that occurred during the interim, you'll be permitted to rectify your mistake, usually without an increase in premiums or other burdensome conditions.

DEALING WITH YOUR INSURER

If you're like most people who've been blessedly spared extensive contact with the insurance industry, its peddlers, and its products, you find the whole thing baffling.

With respect to life insurance, for example, there's no dearth of people willing to sell it to you—a classic example of too much being worse than not enough. But should you buy it through an independent agent or directly from an insurer? If you decide to buy through an independent agent, does he have access to every policy that's out there, or only the policies of a limited number of companies? (Only the policies of a limited number of companies—an important point to remember in evaluating his recommendations.) Should you go with a mutual company or a stock company? And within either of those categories, how do you know which company's policy is best?

The answers to these questions could fill an entire book. They *have* filled an entire book—several, in fact. A good one is Andrew Tobias's *The Invisible Bankers—Everything the Insurance Industry Never Wanted You to Know*.

But the main point to note is that these questions aren't *legal* questions. They're business or financial questions—which means you shouldn't try to get the answers from a lawyer. For help along these lines, read a book, or talk to a financial planner or perhaps an insurance agent. Reflecting this point, the following suggestions tread the borders between the purely legal matters discussed in the first two parts of this chapter and the business or financial issues just mentioned.

The Application Process

Make sure everything you say on your application form is dead solid accurate. Don't think it's okay to be *roughly* accurate, just because something strikes you as trivial, or you didn't see anything on the application characterizing your answers as "warranties" (which, as mentioned above, generally must be absolutely true). The policy itself, which (amazingly) you may not be able to obtain until you've completed your application, undoubtedly says somewhere that your application constitutes a part of the overall policy and that you "warrant" everything in it to be true.

Make sure, also, that every answer on your application is *complete*. Nothing is too trivial. If the form asks if you've had any brushes with the law and doesn't say you can omit traffic violations, list every one you've ever had. If you can't remember them all, say so: "Some parking tickets—can't remember how many. Some speeding tickets, too, although they were mostly by radar, which shouldn't count."

As for health insurance, don't assume from the fact that the insurer didn't have investigators checking up on you at the time of your purchase that FBI agents won't be sniffing around like bloodhounds if you ever make a claim.

CORRECTING ANSWERS

What if you have a heart attack between the time you file your application and the time your policy is formally issued? Most policies require you to correct answers that become inaccurate over that period. If you're on your death bed, correcting your insurance application may not rank at the top of your list of things to do. But keep it in mind.

STATEMENTS BY SALESPEOPLE

This is critical. In many states, nothing an insurance agent or broker tells you prior to signing a contract of insurance is legally binding. Suppose someone trying to sell you health insurance says, "Of course your pregnancy expenses are covered."

You buy the policy. Later, when your claim for pregnancy expenses is denied, you read the policy for the first time and discover that, sure enough, pregnancy expenses aren't covered. Is there anything you can do?

You might be able to nail the seller for fraud, if you can prove he actually made the misstatements. And you can certainly harass him by calling late at night and breathing deeply into the telephone. But as far as expanding your coverage beyond what the policy says, there's nothing you can do. "Surely," you say, "a broker can't lie like a politician about the terms of the policies he peddles." As a practical matter, yes he can. Which carries us to the eleventh of White's Irregular Rules, and the second one in this area:

> If it's not in writing, it's not covered.

Note that the law is entirely different if an *employee of your insurer* tells you of some benefit—to use the same example, "Your pregnancy expenses are covered"—*after issuance of the policy*. Then his statement constitutes an *oral modification* of the policy, even if the policy contains a provision, as it probably does, prohibiting modification except in writing. (A provision prohibiting oral modification of a contract is meaningless, because it's well established that the parties to the contract can modify *that* provision orally, and then modify anything else the same way. Lawyers who draft contracts know this, but they also know that most consumers *don't* know this.)

What about the rule just stated, that if it isn't in writing, it isn't covered? One answer is, the point of that rule is to emphasize the meaninglessness of oral statements made *before* the execution of the contract. But another and perhaps more important answer is, *put* it in writing. If an employee of your insurer says your policy includes a given benefit, and that benefit isn't mentioned anywhere in the policy, write him a letter, saying, "I sure am happy to know your company will be covering the costs of my pregnancy. What a great policy."

Make sure the employee who made the statement that got you into this game in the first place is sufficiently high-ranking in the insurance company's hierarchy to bind it legally. If the person who said your pregnancy expenses were covered is a vice-president, you're golden. If he proves to be a messenger or secretary, you're nowhere.

Consider a different kind of statement, one involving not the scope of coverage, but the time of commencement of coverage.

You call an insurance agent to ask about homeowner's insurance. He describes a policy that sounds about right, and you say you'll take it. He says, "Great. I'm putting the policy in the mail right now. *You're covered as of today.*" The next day your home is burglarized. Thank God I just bought insurance, you think. You call the agent about making a claim. For the next twenty minutes you hear an Olympic-class runaround, the upshot being that your loss isn't covered because the insurer hasn't yet accepted your application. Can you get vindication?

Maybe. The courts in some states would say you had entered into a binding contract with the insurer, so its denial of coverage constitutes an illegal, and compensable, breach. If you ever find yourself in such circumstances, your first step should be to consult a lawyer.

Periodic Review of Your Coverage

Suppose you're a happily married woman. One day you take out a $75,000 life insurance policy, naming as your beneficiary "my husband." Several years later you get divorced, and several years after that you remarry. One night at dinner your second husband casually asks who happens to be the beneficiary of your life insurance policy. You pull it out and examine it. "You are," you say.

What if, upon your death, your first husband steps forward to claim the proceeds? "I was the 'husband' she was referring to when she took out the policy," he points out accurately. "Moreover, we had an agreement. She promised never to change the beneficiary, no matter what happened to us. Besides, I paid the premiums for the first five years."

Whether a court would buy this is hard to say. But why take chances? If you experience any major change of circumstances in your life—a divorce, a remarriage, a birth, a death—go back to your insurance policies (as well as to your will) and make sure they still say exactly what you want them to say. In the example above, you could easily change the beneficiary to "my husband Arnold."

Even if nothing major has happened in your life, you should review your insurance periodically—every two years, say—and not just your life insurance. Presumably you've acquired some new possessions over the years; would your old homeowner's policy still cover everything if the place were to go up in flames? Perhaps now you can afford *replacement cost* insurance, the alternative being *actual cash value* insurance, which covers original cost minus depreciation.

Group Health Plans

These plans can be strikingly complex. Among the pitfalls you need to watch out for is the existence of choices between health-care alternatives, choices that substantially affect the extent of your coverage but that are buried in so much fine print you may not even know they're there.

Three examples:

1. *"Participating" doctors versus "nonparticipating" doctors.* Under some plans you can save a lot of money by dealing only with *participating doctors,* who become such by agreeing with the insurer to accept comparatively low fees for their services.

2. *Outpatient offices versus emergency rooms.* Some group plans offer no reimbursement at all if you visit an emergency room in a "nonemergency situation." (Why would you ever do that? Suppose you've developed a painful but nonacute earache. You call your family internist, whose nurse says, "The doctor is on his monthly trip to Rio, but he can see you for seven minutes in July." The next thing you know, you're waiting your turn in some emergency room.)

3. *Outpatient surgery versus hospital surgery.* Some plans cover 100 percent of the cost of surgery you get on an outpatient basis, but only 80 percent, say, of the cost of surgery that requires you to spend full days in the hospital.

*   *   *

Clearly, unawareness of these choices could cost you major money.
What to do? One way or another, figure out what your policy
says. Do this even if it means—God forbid—reading it.

Cooperating with Your Liability Insurer

Suppose a tree standing on your property falls and lands
on the elderly widow Jenkins. The widow Jenkins, naturally,
wants money. Your liability insurer, just as naturally, doesn't
want to give her any. The whole thing could end up in court.

Where do you stand in this dispute? Like it or not, with
your insurer. This is particularly true if the widow Jenkins is
suing you for $250,000, say, and your liability coverage goes up
to only $100,000—in other words, if you stand to lose a lot of
your own money.

Now, liability policies invariably contain a provision requiring the insured to cooperate with the insurer in opposing claims
and to refrain from harming the insurer's interests in any way.
This translates into two rules:

1. *Don't admit anything.* Suppose you come upon the widow
Jenkins lying under the fallen tree limb. She's crying in pain and
fear. Distressed by the sight, and eager to do anything you can
to ease her trauma, you blurt out, "I'm terribly sorry. This is all
my fault."

Clang! Clang! Clang! Your first remark was fine. Your second one could prove disastrous. What if a jury takes you at your
word and decides it really was your fault? Keep talking, and you
could find yourself battling your insurer, as well as the widow
Jenkins.

2. *Don't engage in settlement negotiations on your own.* This
means not only avoiding formal settlement negotiations, but also
avoiding remarks along the lines of "Heck, I'm just sick about
this. I'll pay whatever you think is fair."

Okay, you stand with your insurer. But does *it* always stand
with *you*? Consider two situations in which its interests and yours
don't coincide:

INTENTIONAL MISCONDUCT

Often a liability insurer is required by its policy not only to reimburse you for certain types of losses, but also to defend you in lawsuits connected with those losses. Suppose your cat, Mr. Bentley, mauls the widow Jenkins. Suppose, too, there's evidence indicating that you secretly hated Mrs. Jenkins, that you trained Mr. Bentley as an attack cat, and that shortly before the mauling you taunted Mr. Bentley with an old scarf of Mrs. Jenkins.

Typically, when someone's pet injures someone else, the owner's offense is that of "negligence." In this case, however, your offense appears to have gone beyond mere negligence, and beyond even "recklessness," all the way to "malice" (or "intent") in causing Mrs. Jenkins's injury.

If a jury finds that you caused her injury intentionally, rather than negligently, three things could happen: First, you could go to jail. Intentionally causing someone's injury is a crime. Second, the jury could award Mrs. Jenkins *punitive damages* (to punish you), as well as *compensatory damages* (to compensate her for medical and other out-of-pocket expenses). Third, your insurer could get out of reimbursing you for anything a jury awards Mrs. Jenkins, because *liability policies don't cover intentional misconduct*.

Now it gets interesting. Suppose the evidence against you leaks out at trial, and your lawyer, who was chosen and hired by the insurance company, sees your case slipping away. The question at this point isn't whether you're going to lose—you clearly are—but how badly. If the lawyer continues to put up a good fight and the jury finds you guilty of mere negligence, your insurer will have to reimburse you for whatever you have to pay Mrs. Jenkins, and that's that. But if the lawyer throws in the towel and lets you lose *big*, so that the jury finds you guilty of *intentional* misconduct, then your insurer is completely off the hook because of the intentional-misconduct exclusion just mentioned.

What to do? One solution is to find your own lawyer, rather than use one chosen by your insurer. Even then, however, you should pay close attention to how your case is handled. Insurance companies are great clients—they have lots of money, and they're in litigation all the time. No lawyer could fail to appreciate the benefits of cultivating a friendly relationship with one.

SETTLEMENT OFFERS

Suppose the widow Jenkins offers to settle the case for $100,000—the limit of your liability coverage. You say, "Let's take it! I wouldn't owe a cent, and I wouldn't have to endure a trial."

Your lawyer—again, someone chosen and hired by the insurance company—balks. "We should go to trial," he says. "I think a jury would let us off for less."

Do you see the conflict? If the jury does in fact let you off for less, your insurer benefits, but *you* are no better off than if you'd settled. If, on the other hand, the jury awards Mrs. Jenkins anything over $100,000, your insurer is no worse off (except for the cost of the trial) than if the settlement offer had been accepted—but you're out the amount over $100,000. Thus, going to trial can only benefit your insurer, and it can only hurt you.

Courts have witnessed this conflict so often that they've come up with rules to protect people in your position. They say an insurer defending one of its insureds must conduct the case—including evaluating settlement offers—as if there were no limit on coverage. Realistically, requiring an insurer to act *as if* something were true provides a less than absolute safeguard. So again, pay close attention to how your case is handled. If you suspect something is amiss, consult another lawyer immediately.

Public Insurance Adjusters

Suppose your house burns down. (Or up. Whatever, it's gone.) It's bad enough that you have to move in with your crazy brother-in-law for several weeks, but there's also the seemingly endless hassle associated with obtaining reimbursement from your insurer.

How do you go about inventorying and valuing your destroyed possessions? Are there limits on what you can pay (and charge your insurer) for repairs? Why is the claims adjuster being a jerk?

If you can't stand such irritants, you should consider hiring a *public insurance adjuster*. These little-known specialists, often former claims adjusters for insurance companies, are in the business of providing insurance-related assistance to people whose houses have been damaged or destroyed.

A good public adjuster will do more than fill out your claim for reimbursement. He'll help you analyze the terms of your policy, prepare an appropriately detailed inventory of lost or damaged items, obtain contractors' estimates for repairs, and negotiate with your insurer's claims adjuster (who's always working against you, no matter how fervently the insurer's ads insist he'll be on your side).

Whether a public adjuster will prove to be worth his fee— usually 10 percent (in some cities 15 percent) of the final settlement with the insurer—is impossible to predict. How well do you understand your own policy? How capable are you of inventorying your losses? How willing are you to engage in hard negotiating with your insurer's claims adjuster? (Insurers of course dislike public adjusters and say they only cost consumers money.)

To find a public adjuster, check the yellow pages under "Adjusters" or "Public Insurance Adjusters." To make sure the one you're hiring is reliable, insist on references. Also, if you live in one of the forty-plus states that regulate public adjusters, don't hire the only one in town without a license.

Lost or Damaged Luggage

People who fly a lot know that checked luggage stands a slim but still dangerous chance of vanishing into thin air. Like Amelia Earhart. There's also the problem of bags that are crushed, shredded, drenched, blown up, desecrated, defoliated, or otherwise done ill to. What's the story on insurance if an airline loses or mauls a piece of your luggage?

You should think about this *before* you travel, when there's still time to obtain enough insurance to cover whatever you're carrying. Otherwise you're taking a gamble, pure and simple, on airline competence.

To obtain insurance:

1. Check with the airline you're flying. On domestic flights, most airlines will pay for lost or damaged luggage (lost or damaged *checked* luggage) up to a maximum of $1,250 per individual. You may not get the maximum, however, unless you can prove the contents were worth that much, either by receipts or by having declared the value when you checked your bag. Before checking any bag, make a rough assessment of the value of the contents. (And for God's sake, hang on to your receipt for each bag.)

Airlines will reimburse you only for the *depreciated* value, not for the *replacement* value, of lost or damaged goods. Moreover, they won't reimburse you for just anything; roughly speaking, they insure nothing but clothes and luggage itself. They refuse responsibility for things considered "fragile" or "perishable," such as glassware or food, and things considered "valuable," such as money, cameras, jewelry, artworks, and sports equipment. You have to pay extra to insure any of these.

2. Charge your ticket on American Express. This gives you automatic coverage of $1,250; that is, up to that amount, anything the airline won't pay, American Express will pay, as well as $500 for carry-on luggage.

3. Check your homeowner's or tenant's policy to see if it covers luggage; some policies do, some don't.

4. If whatever insurance you have doesn't cover luggage, or its coverage doesn't equal the value of what you're carrying, buy more:

• From your current insurer. Most insurance companies will sell you, for example, an all-risk personal property endorsement to your homeowner's policy.

• From some other insurer. Travelers Insurance offers a Travel Insurance Pak, under which you can get six to ten days of baggage coverage in varying amounts—for example, $500 of coverage for $20, or $2,000 for $50.

• From the airline itself. United Airlines charges $1 per $100 of coverage on top of the $1,250 it provides automatically.

• From a travel agent.

Duking It Out with Your Insurer

The most likely source of disagreement with your insurer involves the scope of protection provided by the policy. If your insurer denies what you think is a legitimate claim, you have at least four options, listed below in ascending order of seriousness:

1. *Persist in demanding payment.* As often as not the problem involves a bureaucratic mix-up or a minor problem with your claim form, rather than a deliberate, carefully considered denial of coverage. No matter what it involves, though, try calling and protesting. Call several times, asking for someone higher up each time. Note the names and numbers of the people you talk to, and what each one says.

2. *Complain to your state insurance commissioner.* There's one in every state, and in some states the offices are strong and active. Describe your problem in a letter, sending copies to your insurer's legal department, its customer relations department, and—why not?—its president. While you're at it, send copies to the main newspaper in town and the local Better Business Bureau—and make sure your insurer knows you're doing so.

3. *Consider arbitration or mediation.* Arbitration constitutes a sort of minitrial, less formal than litigation (which refers by definition to a proceeding in *court*) but still adversarial in nature, with the arbitrator receiving evidence and then issuing a final ruling that both sides are required to accept. In contrast, mediation attempts to be *non*adversarial, emphasizing negotiations between the parties. The mediator serves as a facilitator, rather than a decision maker; he lacks authority to bind the parties.

Arbitration and mediation constitute well-respected alternatives to litigation. Both are far less complicated than litigation, and therefore not only faster (often requiring less than a day), but also—the bottom line—cheaper. If the amount at stake in an arbitration is great enough, you might want to hire a lawyer to handle your case (in contrast, lawyers seldom participate directly in mediation), but even then you're looking at only a fraction of the cost of doing battle in court. (Mediation is discussed at greater length in Chapter 2, "Family Law," which lists sources of mediators, as well as the address and telephone number of the American Arbitration Association.)

4. *Sue.* This is a drastic step. Before filing a lawsuit you should definitely hire a lawyer, not only to tell you if you have a plausible cause of action, but also to keep you from getting blown out of the water by the opposing counsel. Recall the second of White's Irregular Rules:

Never go one-on-one in court against a lawyer.

This is particularly true if the lawyer is one of the expensive, well-trained types that insurance companies typically hire. Experience suggests that on your own against one of these you'll stand all the chance of a cheap toupee in a high wind.

Suppose you do sue your insurer. What's your legal theory? The most obvious one is "breach of contract": Your policy is a contract, and your insurer breached it.

Another theory available in some states is that your insurer violated a statute—specifically, a statute requiring insurers to respond quickly and fairly to consumers' claims and in general to refrain from jerking consumers around.

Finally, and perhaps most important, in a number of states you can sue your insurer for "bad faith denial of coverage" or (the same thing) "wrongful failure to pay." The idea here is that your insurer not only failed to make good on its legal obligation, but that it did so *knowingly,* with the goal of either escaping payment altogether or at least postponing payment so as to collect interest on the owed money for as long as possible. If you win on this theory—this is the beauty of it—you can get not only the money you should have gotten in the first place, but also potentially enormous "punitive damages."

What good does knowing this theory do you, since you can't take advantage of it unless you go to trial—and if you go to trial, you'll have a lawyer who'll already know about it? The first of these premises isn't correct; one way of indicating your seriousness in the initial stages of pressing your claim is to write a letter to your insurer's legal department making explicit reference to the insurer's "bad faith" and "wrongful failure to pay." These are legal buzzwords, which the legal department will recognize and likely respond to with appropriate concern. In any event, they'll realize they're dealing with a sophisticated consumer, someone who didn't just drive into town yesterday on the turnip truck.

10. Wills

Death never takes the wise man by surprise; he is always ready to go.
JEAN DE LA FONTAINE
(1621–1695)

I have nothing. I owe much. I leave the rest to the poor.
FRANÇOIS RABELAIS
(c. 1483–1553)

CLIENT: *"What happens if I die?"*
LAWYER: *"What do you mean 'if'?"*   Old joke, told by
MARTIN J. YUDKOWITZ
(1954–   )

WHO SAYS YOU NEED A WILL?

You may live forever; only circumstantial evidence suggests you're not immortal. But what if your reservations in the hotel of life should be unexpectedly canceled? Come on, there's a chance. Shouldn't you have a will?

Probably—but not necessarily.

There are at least two situations in which you don't need a will. First, you don't care who gets your property when you die. Second, you don't *have* any property.

Consider the second of these situations first. You've just graduated from Yale. You feel like a million dollars. But you also owe about that much on your college loans. You live in a semi-furnished apartment, and your only possessions consist of a

246

windup alarm clock, a stereo with one working speaker, and some funny cigarettes that cost more than the other items combined.

In these circumstances, do you need a will? It would empower someone to step in and bury you, pay your bills, and rummage through your room to confirm that the above-listed items are in fact all you own. But that's hardly a great reason to spend money you desperately need.

Consider the other situation. You're a ninety-year-old oil tycoon. With the returns on just one of your gushers outside Tulsa, you could buy Albania. But your wife and friends have long since died. And you haven't spoken to your children since they began voting Democratic. (You wouldn't *mind* if your children got some of your money—indeed, it would probably turn them Republican—but you aren't willing to go out of your way to see that they do.) Furthermore, you don't believe in charity.

In these circumstances, why would you pay a lawyer one nickel to prepare a will? You'd sooner pay a lawyer *not* to prepare one, so you wouldn't have to fool with reading it.

There's another and better reason you might not want to pay for a will: You already have one. The state legislature has written it, it's in the statute books, and it says where your property will go if you should die *intestate* (which isn't as painful as it sounds, although you shouldn't bring it up at cocktail parties).

To be sure, a legislative will doesn't do everything you'd like a will to do, especially if your *estate*—whatever property you leave behind when you die—is sizable. In particular, a legislative will doesn't name an *executor* to inventory, value, and transfer your assets; thus, a court will have to appoint someone to perform these tasks—possibly someone you've never heard of, and someone you wouldn't trust to feed your fish while you're out of town. Furthermore, a legislative will doesn't relieve your executor of the standard requirement of posting a bond against possible mistakes or fraud. The cost of complying with this requirement will ultimately come out of your estate, and it will almost definitely exceed what you'd have paid for a will.

Nevertheless, your property will go *somewhere* when you die. Hence, assuming you're not troubled by the shortcomings of legislative wills, the question you need to consider is, would you prefer that your property go somewhere else? Note that this is one of the rare instances in which *your* law—the law according to O'Malley—can override that of the legislature.

The majority of people in this country die without wills (other than legislative wills). Abraham Lincoln died without a will. Why?

Who knows?

But *I* don't have a will. If I should go around the Far Turn tomorrow, everything I own would go to my parents, or maybe to my parents and brothers. I'm not married, I have no children—that's where I'd *want* it to go.

True, it might take longer and cost more to get there than if I had a will. But the extra time wouldn't matter—none of my heirs is in immediate financial need—and the extra cost wouldn't be much. Your situation may be similar.

Virtually all states give the property of an *intestate* (that's you if you die without a will) to the spouse and kids, or maybe to the spouse, parents, and siblings. The division is fifty/fifty, one-third/two-thirds, or one-quarter/three-quarters—it varies. If you have no living spouse, kids, parents, or siblings, your property will go to your grandparents, nieces, nephews, cousins, or other remote kin. Each state has its own rules, but basically they all start with those closest to you—by blood, not marriage (except for your spouse)—and move out from there.

"Well," you say, "I *hope* that's what would become of my things if I were to die without a will. I hate to think the legislature would be fool enough to give them to my boss or landlord."

Exactly. The legislators weren't trying to be jerks in writing these laws. They were trying to be helpful. They were trying to give your property to the people you would have given it to if you'd thought about it.

"Hold on," you say. "I don't doubt that they were *trying*. But what if they didn't succeed? I want to be absolutely sure of where my property is going."

Not unreasonable. Perhaps, for example, you want all your property go to your husband, and none to your parents, who don't need it and would just use it to make your husband miserable, because he drives a motorcycle and they never liked him in the first place. Perhaps, if all your wealth is tied up in your house, you want everything to go to your husband, and none to your grown children, because to give your children anything would force your husband to sell the house and move.

How can you be sure?

If you're determined to keep the lawyers from getting one nickel, you could check a write-your-own-will handbook, if one exists for your state. (Call a few bookstores, or the local bar association.) You might be able to track down the answer in a local law library, although that's a hard route; even if you manage to find the right statute, you might not be able to make sense of it if English is your only language.

Consulting a lawyer for such information would cost you next to nothing. The conversation would go something like this:

YOU: Where would my property go if I died intestate?
LAWYER: Are you married?
YOU: No.
LAWYER: Any children?
YOU: No.
LAWYER: Brothers or sisters?
YOU: One of each.
LAWYER: Your parents alive?
YOU: One of them is.
LAWYER: In this state your property would go to————.

If the law will eventually get your property where you'd want it to go, a will might serve no purpose (beyond the limited one of getting it there somewhat faster and more cheaply than it would have got there otherwise).

Note that I say "might" serve no purpose. Consider a fictional individual whose property includes, say, an ocean-view mansion in Malibu, a chauffeur-driven Rolls-Royce, three hundred custom tailored turbans, and a securities portfolio worth $50 million. This swarthy, accented man, known to his friends as Muhammad, also has a wife and one son, each of whom he wants to receive one-half of all his possessions if he should die before they do.

Muhammad doesn't want to pay for a will. One afternoon he has his chauffeur drive him to the U.C.L.A. law library. There,

with the aid of a bespectacled first-year law student, he deter-
mines that under California law his property would go one-half
to his wife and one-half to his son if he should die intestate.
Elated, he decides he doesn't need a will.

Is Muhammad making a big mistake?

Two days after his trip to U.C.L.A., Muhammad suffocates
in an avalanche of turbans in his walk-in closet. What happens
to his possessions?

Muhammad's wife, with the aid of a lawyer, petitions the
local court to be appointed the "administrator" of Muhammad's
estate. At her request, Muhammad's scrupulously honest accountant compiles an inventory of all Muhammad's holdings,
down to the last turban, and pays off all minor debts. Then he
takes care of the taxes: (1) a whopping federal *estate tax*—Uncle
Sam's last shot at the departed; (2) a comparatively small state
inheritance tax (which is actually imposed not on Muhammad
himself but on Mrs. Muhammad and Muhammad, Jr., for coming into all that money); and (3) depending on the state in question, a local estate tax, similar to the federal estate tax, except
usually smaller.

The whole process takes a year or two. Mrs. Muhammad
and Muhammad, Jr., are in no rush, however, because they have
major-league bank accounts in their own names. And they hardly
notice the sizable cost of posting a bond, as required in connection with the administration of so large an estate. Eventually
they get the still sizable remainder of Muhammad's property
and live happily ever after.

That's *one* ending to the story. Consider another.

No sooner have Mrs. Muhammad and Muhammad, Jr., gone
into mourning than an enterprising reporter discovers that the
priest who performed Mrs. Muhammad's marriage to Muhammad was in fact not a priest, but a Hollywood actor practicing
to replace Bing Crosby in the remake of *Going My Way*. The
marriage wasn't valid under California law, and "Mrs. Muhammad's" entitlement to anything from Muhammad's estate is dubious. (It appears that the entire estate might end up in the hands
of Muhammad, Jr., who never got along with his mother and
might well leave her penniless.)

Moreover, Muhammad's scrupulously honest accountant (you

never believed that part anyway) issues a report showing that Muhammad's stock portfolio is worth less than a million dollars and doesn't include a single share of that IBM stock Muhammad always boasted about to his friends. "If only Muhammad had listened to me," the accountant laments as he boards a jet to Geneva.

Finally, two wills surface, both allegedly written in Muhammad's own hand. One gives everything to Muhammad's personal secretary, a full-figured blonde who wears halter tops and leather miniskirts. The other gives everything to an Amoco mechanic who once gave Muhammad a free tow when his Rolls-Royce had a flat and Muhammad was short on cash. The litigation over these wills appears headed for the year 2000. Meanwhile, neither Mrs. Muhammad nor Muhammad, Jr., has a penny to live on.

Bizarre? Large sums of money trigger *lots* of bizarre occurrences—which leads us once again to the first of White's Irregular Rules:

> Where there's a lot of money at stake,
> hire a lawyer.

In this area of the law, saying "hire a lawyer" is equivalent to saying "get a will," because that's what any lawyer in his right mind would advise someone with a lot of money to do. Disaster seeks out large sums of money, the way pigeons seek out newly washed cars. (And it doesn't have to be anything near $50 million.)

Could the problems that arose in the second Muhammad scenario have been obviated by a will? Probably. First, if Muhammad had executed a will mentioning Mrs. Muhammad by name ("To Doris . . ."), the validity of their marriage would never have become an issue. The intestacy statute may give your property only to your relatives (if there are any), but *you* can generally give your property to whomever you please.

Second, if Muhammad had left a will including comprehensive who-gets-what provisions, the accountant might have been harder put to make off with Muhammad's stocks undetected. Rarely does a will list all one's possessions, but it can.

In any event, Muhammad's discussions with a lawyer about the terms of a will would surely have touched on the scope of his wealth, thus putting the lawyer in a position to cry "Foul" when Muhammad's estate proved to be so small. This is one reason you should periodically update your will—every two or three years, say, or after any major event, such as a death or divorce.

Third, the existence of a clearly valid will would surely have discouraged Muhammad's secretary and the Amoco mechanic from their attempted scams. There's no way to guarantee that fraudulent wills won't surface, but an authentic will, properly prepared, can usually overcome a fraudulent one.

Three More Points on Whether You Need a Will

CHILDREN

If you have a child, it's critical that you have a will indicating who should get custody of him if you should die. The last thing a parentless child needs is to have his relatives fighting it out in court over his custody. Courts have the final say over this issue, but a provision in your will constitutes a strong recommendation and will usually carry the day.

For full protection along these lines, it's imperative that your spouse's will have a parallel custody provision. If you should predecease your husband, he would get custody of the child— which is presumably fine with you except that, your own will's custody provision would lose all effect.

Custody isn't the only child-related issue your will should address. If you're planning to leave your child any substantial property—$100,000, say—your will should appoint someone to serve as *guardian* or *conservator* of that money until the child reaches legal adulthood. Otherwise a court will appoint someone for you. The court might appoint your husband, but you can't be sure of that. And even if it does, your husband, as a court-appointee, might well have to incur the expense of posting a protective bond.

One more reason you need a will if you have a child: A

child's arrival on the scene can dramatically alter the story on who would get what in the event of your intestate death. Perhaps, before your child made his appearance, everything you own would have gone to your husband—an arrangement you were happy with then, and one you'd like to keep.

But the intestacy law in your state may provide that half or more of your property goes to the child, who when he eventually gets full control of it might use it to go to medical school or—and this is your lurking fear—might give it to the Moonies. Why chance it? With a will you can make sure it all goes to your husband—or perhaps half to your husband and half to your child, but with your child's half being held in trust until he reaches some specified age.

TIMING

A will that's clear, and clearly valid, will speed up the transfer of your property upon your death—a little or a lot, depending on the procedures in your state and the size and complexity of your finances. If you care not only where your property goes, but when it gets there, a will is a good investment.

ESTATE PLANNING

If you're a person of any means—and for these purposes, ownership of a small house constitutes "means"—any lawyer you consult about a will is sure to suggest that you do some *estate planning*, that is, take advantage of one or more of the various devices—primarily tax-avoidance and tax-postponement devices—legally available for conserving the property you leave behind when you die. Note the reference to "when you die"; here's the connection with wills, which play a prominent though not exclusive role in determining what happens to your property when you die.

Estate planning is discussed in greater detail in Chapter 3, "Taxes." The point to note here is that given the interrelation of wills and estate planning, the time to start thinking about the latter is when you start thinking about the former.

GETTING A WILL

There are two ways to get a will: (1) have a lawyer prepare one for you, or (2) prepare your own.

Having a Lawyer Prepare Your Will

If you get irritated at the thought of paying good money for a thin sheaf of paper covered with mumbo-jumbo, remember that preparing wills is something God created lawyers to do. Mechanics repair carburetors, plumbers clear drains, and lawyers prepare wills.

There's much to be said for having a lawyer prepare your will. It's far easier than preparing your own, you'll sleep a tad better, and it won't cost much anyway.

Regarding the cost, it's axiomatic in the legal profession that no one gets rich writing wills. They're so easy to produce that the market won't bear a high price, and even the most ostentatious consumer wants only one. If your possessions aren't unusually complicated or, more important, what you want to do with your possessions isn't unusually complicated, there's no reason you shouldn't go to one of the giant, bulk-process legal clinics, where you could probably get a serviceable will for under one hundred dollars. Even at a traditional firm, a simple will shouldn't cost more than several hundred dollars.

Do you need a specialist to prepare your will? As a rule, no. There are so many standard form books in this area that half the work consists of just filling in the blanks. Paralegals could do it. Paralegals *do* do it.

A word of caution: What I'm talking about here is getting a will, not estate planning. A will says who gets what when you die. If you're into spendthrift trusts, charitable foundations, and generation-skipping transfers, then it's *not* just a matter of filling in the blanks, and *not* just any lawyer can do it.

Preparing Your Own Will

Preparing your own will isn't a great idea. It's too easy to trip over some technicality of local law. Besides, if you're so broke that you can't afford the minimal cost of getting a will at one of the giant clinics, you may not need a will at all.

Nevertheless, I'll try to coach you through it. Hey, this book delivers.

1. *Equipment.* Write your will in ink, not pencil, and write it on paper, not your home computer or the dust on your stereo speaker (although by all evidence the dust will be around indefinitely).

2. *Writing.* Write your will out longhand—no typing. And use cursive, not printing. This is a pain, but in a handful of states it may help you out. The idea is that such a *holographic* (handwritten) will is capable of being authenticated as *your* will, even without witnesses, because your handwriting is presumably more distinctive than the lettering of your IBM Selectric.

3. *Label and opening recitation.* At the top of the first page of your will write the word *Will.* That should make it clear enough. You also need an opening sentence. You'd think it would be enough if you said, "This is my will." But you should probably dress it up a bit:

> I, Maxwell Plum, known to my friends as "Skip," of the City of Atlanta, County of Fulton, and State of Georgia, being of full age and sound mind, and knowing the nature of my property and the natural objects of my bounty, do hereby make and declare this to be my last will, and I hereby revoke any and all prior wills and codicils.

4. *Who gets what.* The body of your will says where you want your property to go. For example: "I give my stereo to Mel Brooks, and my dog Gaylord to Gene Wilder." Be specific, using last names. Also, note the following:

• No matter how many favors you've ever done Gene, he doesn't have to accept Gaylord. Gene may *hate* Gaylord. Or, at the time of your death, Gene may have died—causing what lawyers refer to as a *lapse* of the gift. Both problems can be solved by listing alternative recipients. For example: "If Gene doesn't want Gaylord or isn't around to take him, then to Mel. If Mel doesn't want Gaylord or isn't around to take him, then to the National Institutes of Health."

• There are countless ways a specific bequest can be used up, destroyed, or otherwise lost, causing an *ademption* of the gift. But just as the problem of lapse can be remedied by listing alternative *recipients,* ademption can be remedied by listing alternative *bequests.* For example: "I leave my bonsai trees to my daughter Lisa, but if none of them is alive at my death, then I give Lisa my stereo. If my stereo isn't working at the time of my death, then I give Lisa $10,000."

• What if, in the above example, you've already given Lisa the bonsai trees before your death—raising the problem of *satisfaction?* (Only for lawyers is that a problem.) Do you want Lisa to get anything else? Your will could provide, "No gift I've made before my death shall be deemed to *satisfy* any bequest in this will. If any attempted bequest of specific property fails because the designated recipient already has such property, I direct my executor to make a substitute gift of money equal to the value of such property."

• Suppose you have three beloved former college roommates, each of whom, according to your will, is to receive one of your three beloved Hawaiian shirts. Shortly before your death, your cat, Bentley, gets ahold of two of them (your shirts), raising the problem of *abatement.* Who gets the remaining good shirt? You can avoid this problem by specifying the priority of your gifts.

• Perhaps you want to leave your entire estate to the first two of your three sons, the third being a Methodist, or a thespian. You're worried, however, that some lawyer will persuade a court that you simply overlooked your third son. Your best bet in this situation is to be brutally explicit: "I intentionally give nothing to my no-count third son, Jake."

5. *Your executor.* This is critical. Your will should name an *executor,* someone you consider sufficiently responsible and trustworthy to be in charge of putting your who-gets-what pro-

visions into effect. An executor generally has no powers that aren't specifically provided for in the will, so you should state that your executor has full power to sell or otherwise dispose of your property as he believes best. Depending on how much you trust your executor, you might also grant him the powers to borrow money or mortgage your property; put your property (temporarily) in his own name; distribute your estate among your beneficiaries at such values as he thinks appropriate; contest, settle, or abandon claims by or against your estate; and hire lawyers, accountants, and any other advisers he thinks he needs.

6. *Closing recitation.* Right after the who-gets-what provisions of your will, and right before your signature, insert a paragraph describing what's going on:

> In witness hereof, I have signed this will, which consists of this page and the [two] preceding pages. I have initialed each unsigned page in the top left margin, in the presence of the undersigned three persons, who have, at my request and in my presence and in the presence of each other, acted as my witnesses, this——day of——, 19——.

7. *Signature.* Sign your full name (and print it under the signature line). Make sure your signature gets on the same page as the closing recitation. Place it just *before* the witnesses' signatures (and their attestation clause), but *after everything else.* This means no P.S.s; if you think of something you want to add later, do the whole thing over.

8. *Initials.* Place your initials in the top left margin of every page except the page bearing your signature.

9. *Date.* Place the date beside your initials on each page, as well as in the space indicated in the closing recitation. Spell out the name of the month—"August 2, 1953"—rather than using just numbers—"8/2/53."

10. *Witnesses.* It's not enough just to sign your will; you have to have people watch you do it.

• Get three witnesses. Most states require only two, but a few require three, and you want to play it safe.

• Your witnesses should be at least twenty-one years old.

In some states it's okay if they're only eighteen, but again, you want to play it safe.

• Your witnesses should be sane. Don't use the lady next door who lives with forty-seven cats, or the guy upstairs who gets an odd look in his eyes when someone lights a match.

• Your witnesses can't be *interested*. Don't use anyone who might have a stake in how your will comes out—your parents, your siblings, your cousins, or the spouses of any of these. Also, avoid anyone who might be charged with having an undue influence over you—your boss, lover, landlord, or doctor.

• Your witnesses should sign the document in front of each other and you, *after* personally watching *you* sign and initial it. In other words, get all four of you together at once, and then do it—first you, then each of them.

• Each witness should print his name and address *under* his signature, and place the date immediately *beside* (to the right of) his name. This is getting picky, but you might as well use the conventional style.

• Your witnesses' signatures should be preceded by the word *Witnesses*, along with an *attestation clause* explaining the obvious. For example:

Witnesses

We, the undersigned persons, each being at least 21 years of age, hereby state that on this date we watched Maxwell Plum sign this will, which consists of [three] handwritten pages and which he declared to us to be his last will. He signed it in the presence of all of us together, and he requested us to witness his signature of it. Each of us signed it at the same time in his presence and the presence of each other. We declare that we believe Maxwell Plum to be of sound mind and memory.

11. *Changes.* Suppose, ten years down the road, you want to make a change in your will (called a *codicil*—how could your lawyer justify charging you so much for a mere "change"?). Fine. But don't simply insert new names, numbers, or words. Repeat the entire process, with witnesses and everything, to ensure compliance with the most stringent requirements of any state.

For the same reason, never leave an erasure or crossing out in any part of your will; once you've gone around the Big Bend, how is a court to know *you* made that erasure, rather than your shifty roommate, the primary beneficiary of the altered version?

Three Things You Can't Do in Your Will

DISINHERIT YOUR SPOUSE

Suppose you and your wife—call her Nancy—haven't been getting along. You decide you'll disinherit her. You tell your lawyer to include in your will a provision leaving her a nickel, so you can have the last laugh.

Your lawyer scowls. "You can't do that," he says. "That is, you can do it, but a court won't enforce it."

"It's my money," you protest. "Can't I do whatever I want with it?" No. Most states guarantee a spouse some portion, usually one-third to one-half, of everything the other spouse owns—the so-called *forced share.* All you can do in your will is give Nancy *more* than her forced share, assuming you and she haven't signed a prenuptial agreement. (See Chapter 2, "Family Law.")

"Even if Nancy earns more as a big-time corporate lawyer than I've ever earned as a clerk-typist?"

Yes. If this intrusion on your testamentary freedom galls you, take comfort in the knowledge that most states have brought their laws into the twentieth century: If Nancy dies first, *she* can't disinherit *you.*

This doesn't mean either of you should throw in the towel on trying to make the other miserable. If you attempt to disinherit Nancy altogether, she may get one-third to one-half of your estate (assuming a court doesn't throw out the entire will as invalid). But if you write no will at all, Nancy may get *everything.* In legalese, Nancy's *intestate* share (you die with no will at all) may be greater than her forced share (your will purports to leave her nothing).

Is there any way around this forced share? Two approaches spring to your resourceful mind. First, go for a divorce right now. That way Nancy won't be entitled to a spouse's forced share when you die, because she won't *be* your spouse when you die. Second, give away some or most of your property right now, all but what you need to live on, so somebody else will own it when you die.

Bad news: It's unlikely that either approach will work—which brings us to the twelfth of White's Irregular Rules, and one that applies in virtually all areas of law:

Don't get fancy without a lawyer.

Getting divorced tends to be a fancy matter. Ask anyone who has done it. It can be moderately simple if everybody is cooperating, but what are the chances Nancy will be cooperating if you're trying to do her out of a share of your property? Furthermore, you may live in one of the eight *community property* states (discussed below), where a spouse is deemed by law to own one-half of all property acquired by either spouse during the marriage (with certain exceptions). The bottom line: See a lawyer.

As for giving away your property to deprive Nancy of her interests in it, some courts would call this a "fraud on the law." You're in trouble if it's apparent that what you're trying to do is what you're trying to do. Again, see a lawyer.

GIVE PROPERTY TO YOUR
GREAT-GREAT-GREAT GRANDCHILDREN

Perhaps you'd like to do something nice for your remote descendants. Leave them a piece of land. According to the *Rule Against Perpetuities,* which every state has in some form or other, you can't do that. The rule says that except in certain charitable and commercial circumstances, no one should be able to control a given patch of turf for that long.

What this centuries-old rule says, specifically, is:

No interest in property is good unless it must vest, if it vests at all, not later than twenty-one years after some life in being at the time of creation of the interest.

If these words make sense to you the first time around, you have great potential as a lawyer. Law students spend long hours mastering them.

Don't worry about this rule unless you have an appetite for the arcane. Check with a lawyer as to whether a bequest you're contemplating passes muster under it. As a general guideline, leave your property to someone who's alive when you're preparing your will, or to the *children* of someone who's alive when you're preparing your will.

Note an exception to the Rule Against Perpetuities for gifts to charitable trusts—for example, "I give $10 million in trust to the Harvard University Medical School, to fund a fellowship for research into the causes of cancer." The reason for this exception is simply that the law wants to encourage charitable giving. There's no law, by the way, that says a charitable trust may be set up only in a will. You could set one up today. It's your best shot at immortality.

PROHIBIT YOUR CHILD FROM MARRYING SOMEONE OF ANOTHER RACE

Suppose your neighbor is a blond, blue-eyed Texas belle. She's president of the local chapters of the Daughters of the American Confederacy, the Daughters of the American Revolution, and the Daughters of the Morons Who Stayed Behind at the Alamo. In her will she'd like to leave everything "to my boy James Earl, unless within one year my daughter Betty-Jo divorces that [insert ethnic slur]. If she does, then to Betty-Jo, but it should go back to James Earl if Betty-Jo ever marries another one."

You are rightly appalled. Can she do this?

No. It's *against public policy*—the term judges apply to something they find so offensive that they just aren't willing to let anyone get away with it. If a will tries to induce someone to do something that's illegal or extremely tacky, a judge may wipe out the offending provision and possibly the entire document.

Your neighbor asks, "Why can't I use my property to encourage my daughter to marry someone I approve of?" She can, but not through her will. Enforcing a will calls into play the

powers of the courts. And courts aren't in the business of pro-
moting such objectionable ends.

CHALLENGING SOMEONE'S WILL

There you sit in your windowless office, mired in the drudg-
ery of your insurance business, when a call comes in. Your fabulously rich Uncle Eldon, ninety-three years old, has just died.

All *right!* you think. You never liked your Uncle Eldon.
Nobody did. But you and your three brothers went to great
lengths to stay on good terms with him. He had to leave his
fortune to somebody.

Two days later you and your brothers meet at a law firm
downtown for the reading of Eldon's will. A pompous, gray-
suited man in his fifties introduces himself as the head of the
firm's trusts and estates department. After perfunctory condo-
lences, he opens a large envelope, withdraws a white, legal-size
document, and commences to read. The preliminaries go on
interminably. You drum the table with your thumbs. " 'Sound
mind,' my ass," you mutter.

The reading halts. The lawyer glances around. Then he re-
sumes reading. You can't believe your ears. Uncle Eldon has left
one-third of his fortune to your brother Arnold, one-third to the
Anti-Vivisection Society, and one-third to someone identified as
"Rabbi O'Malley." You become nauseous and eye the lawyer's
Persian rug maliciously.

What now? you wonder. Do you just go home, kicking
yourself for all the time you wasted sending Uncle Eldon cards
and presents on his birthday?

Assuming the superficial validity of the will—Was it properly executed? Was it Uncle Eldon's only will? His *last* will?—
there are three general bases for challenging its substantive terms.
The rules in this area vary from state to state, and in any state
it's hard to overcome a presumptively valid will. Hence you
should consult a lawyer if you think you smell something fishy.

1. *Incapacity.* Was Eldon senile? Plenty of people at ninety-

three are. What was his connection with the Anti-Vivisection Society? Did he have any unusual relationships with his pets?

It's not enough that Eldon thought he was Napoleon, if he left a perfectly valid will. That might be relevant if his will purported to leave one of you the Louisiana Purchase, but the question a judge will ask (unless Eldon was *completely* out of it) is whether Eldon's particular delusions affected his awareness of his assets and the "natural objects of his bounty."

There's a lesson here for the opposite situation, where you're getting *more* than you might ordinarily expect, rather than less. If you know that someone elderly or a tad eccentric is leaving you something of substantial value, persuade him to meet with a lawyer or psychiatrist—someone with no stake in the will and no obligations to you—so that in the event of a lawsuit there will be someone who can testify that your benefactor understood what he was doing.

2. *Fraud.* The possibilities here are endless. Might your brother Arnold have lied to Eldon, telling him you and the other brothers had married outside the faith? Do you have any suspicions about this "Rabbi O'Malley"?

3. *Undue influence.* This murky concept refers to anything that undermines the free will of the testator (Uncle Eldon) and substitutes the will of another. Did Arnold, who happens to be a lawyer, help Eldon draft his will? Is Eldon's psychotherapist a director of the Anti-Vivisection Society? Any close relationship between the testator and a beneficiary of his will can raise questions.

If a friend ever comments that you'd be tickled pink to see what he's leaving you in his will, and you suspect his generosity to you will irritate someone else, don't just sit back hoping for the best. Persuade your friend to meet with a lawyer or some other outsider, to establish on the record that the arrangement is aboveboard. If you happen to be your friend's priest, doctor, or therapist, this is especially important. At the least, don't help draft the thing, and don't serve as one of its witnesses. Distance yourself from it.

PROBATE

The first thing you need to understand in connection with avoiding probate is, what *is* probate? Once you've got that down, you can decide for yourself whether you want to avoid it. Right?

Technically, *probate* is the process of "proving," or determining the validity of, your will in court. As generally used, the term also includes the administration of your estate, that is, the process (once the validity of your will is established) of inventorying your assets, valuing them, and getting them where they're supposed to go—to your beneficiaries, to your creditors, to Uncle Sam (*not* in that order).

"But what the hell does a *will* do," you ask, "if not get my property where I want it to go?" A reasonable question. The answer is that merely ordering something to be done doesn't automatically get it done.

Problems can arise from countless sources to keep your property from going where your will directs it to go. First, someone has to *find* your will—you won't be around to say, "It's in the top drawer, fellas." Then someone has to look it over closely to make sure that's really your signature on it.

Furthermore, what if more than one will surfaces? Or somebody says you were insane or defrauded when you wrote your will? With regard to that provision donating your "stocks" to Duke University, did you mean to include the funds in your money market account?

"Okay," you concede, "the fact that I've written and executed a will doesn't mean there's no work to be done after my death. Hence the rigamarole of probate. Why, then, should I want to avoid it?"

Because it can take a long time. Weeks, maybe months, possibly years may pass between when you die and when your beneficiaries obtain full control over what you wanted them to receive. To be sure, if your will is uncontested, your witnesses' signatures can be readily verified, and your estate is uncomplicated and not subject to state or federal estate taxes, the process might move quickly.

But there are countless potential sources of delay. In some

jurisdictions a notice of probate has to be given to all heirs, creditors, and other possibly interested parties. This notice may have to be published in newspapers, and there may be a mandatory waiting period for responses. If someone disputes the validity or interpretation of your will, lengthy negotiations and even a full trial could ensue. Finally, for purposes of determining who gets how much out of your estate, there's the task of locating, inventorying, and valuing your assets—the notorious burdensomeness of which is reflected by the fact that your estate tax return isn't due until nine months after your death.

Note that the probate avoidance measures to be discussed below won't necessarily *eliminate* these potential sources of delay. For example, the notice to interested parties will presumably be required regardless of such measures (in those states where it's required at all). But anything passing *outside* probate should reach its new owner *unaffected* by these sources of delay—and hence more quickly than it otherwise might.

There's another reason to avoid probate: In some states it can cost a bundle. There are always fees connected with court or administrative agency proceedings. And whoever handles the process—your executor—usually takes a share of the estate. In New York, at present, this share is legally set at 5 percent of the first $100,000 of assets, declining gradually to 2 percent of anything over $5 million. How ready are you to give that up, especially after all the effort you put into securing one extra percentage point on your IRA?

A Word on Executors

Can you name a family member—your husband, say—as your executor? You figure he knows more about your finances than anyone other than you. Also, since he's the main beneficiary of your will, you don't care what he charges (although for obvious reasons he probably won't charge anything). The answer is, Sure you can. If your estate is small, uncomplicated, and doesn't involve taking immediate control of a business he isn't familiar with, why not?

What if, on the other hand, your estate is large and complicated? Can you name a personal friend as your executor—

your old college roommate, say—who has a fair bit of business experience and would undoubtedly be willing to handle the job for a pittance?

Again the answer is, Sure. You can name anyone you like. If you don't name someone, the probate court will name someone for you—who'll then be called an *administrator*, rather than an executor. (To complicate the nomenclature, the feminine versions of these terms are *executrix* and *administratrix*. If this Latin gets on your nerves, feel free to substitute, as many courts do, *personal representative* for any of the above terms.)

Your old roommate might prove to be a great executor. Before naming him in your will, however, consider three points: First, he doesn't have to accept the position. So talk with him about it in advance.

Second, even if he feels too guilty to decline the position, you're doing him no favor by asking him to take it. Serving as an executor often involves woeful amounts of tedious, complicated paperwork, and if he fouls up anything, he could find himself in serious trouble. (Often he'll be required to furnish a bond to protect the estate from his own missteps.) An executor has to make countless hard judgments regarding the valuation and distribution of estate assets, and not infrequently he has to endure ugly family disputes over property.

Third, handling an estate of any size is *so* complicated that your old roommate will have to hire a lawyer, accountant, or some other professional as a consultant or "co-executor" in any event. Dealing with local probate authorities and the IRS simply requires more expertise than nonprofessionals tend to have.

Keep the foregoing in mind if you ever find yourself designated as the executor for someone else's estate. In that event, do three things: First, consult a lawyer. It'll cost the estate a little extra, but c'est la vie—or, in this case, la mort.

Second, resist the impulse to borrow money from the deceased's estate, even if circumstances suggest that it would be entirely reasonable—for example, no one else needs the money, you have every intention of repaying it at a better-than-market rate, and you and the deceased used to loan each other money all the time. (Borrowing money while in such a "fiduciary" capacity is what got John Zaccaro, husband of 1984 Democratic vice-presidential candidate Geraldine Ferraro, in such hot water and no doubt cost the Mondale-Ferraro team votes they could ill afford to lose.)

Third, inform the IRS (on its standard form) that you'll be acting as executor for your friend's estate. (Do this *after* you've consulted a lawyer.)

Assume now that you're the deceased. Who minds the store while your executor is rummaging through your papers, tallying your possessions, and paying your bills? Who feeds your dog? Who milks your cows?

Your executor handles all this, too, although often by delegation rather than personally. (What does he know about cows?) He takes at least nominal control of everything.

If you care about those you'll be leaving behind, you want your executor to be the right kind of person. Bank officials—stodgy, boring, sober—make fine executors. So do lawyers. They know what needs to be done, and they understand how meticulously it needs to be done. (Note that you could name both a family member *and* one of these people, who could serve together as co-executors.)

There's another reason lawyers and bankers make good executors. When you die, the last thing your spouse and children will need is to have to conduct a missing-person search to locate your executor. Lawyers and bankers are always easy to *find*. Like faithful dogs, they don't wander much. And when they do go somewhere, they leave forwarding addresses. That's just the kind of people they are.

This is why it's a good idea to let a lawyer or banker—ideally, the very one who's going to serve as your executor—*hold* your will. Upon your death, one call will send this person or someone from his office scampering to the probate court with your will, commencing the probate process immediately.

"What?" you say. "Let someone else hold my will?"

Well, what else are you going to do with it? Wad it up in the thumb hole of your softball mitt? You don't want it to remain hidden forever. Which carries us to another important matter.

Not infrequently someone puts his will in a bank safe-deposit box. Not only does he tell no one it's there, but for maximum safety, he hides the key where absolutely no one can find it. Great. Forty years after his death, when his children are in their seventies, his will finally emerges.

Note another potential problem. Because your executor is someone named in your will, his authority to put your affairs in order and distribute your property commences . . . when you die? No. Not until your will is formally validated. But what about the days, weeks, or months in between? How are your children and aged parents, for whom you were the sole source of support, to survive meanwhile?

Realistically, if there's money available and your dependents need it, there shouldn't be any problem. A number of states allow immediate distribution to a deceased's spouse and children of certain types of property, such as the deceased's wages due, bank accounts, and car. But why take chances? You can ensure that your dependents are adequately taken care of by establishing separate bank accounts in their names or by any of various other arrangements, *if* you think about the problem in advance.

Back to Probate—and Avoiding It

At the outset, note several sets of circumstances that might obviate the need to avoid probate. First, you may die in penury—virtuous, but poor as a churchmouse. Some states dispense with probate in cases involving "small estates"—for example, those consisting of personal property worth less than $10,000.

Second, you may die in one of the handful of states that allow "probate in the common form," which refers to a quick, informal proceeding without the usual time-consuming notice to all possibly interested parties. Under this form of probate, the will is "proved" by the oath of someone such as the estate's executor.

Third, perhaps you hang out with people who don't know or don't care about the law of probate and who therefore may be inclined simply to walk in and take over your assets when you die. This is hardly unheard of. Estate administration doesn't commence automatically; someone has to initiate the process.

Whole books have been written on the four basic ways to avoid probate. That's overkill: The three simple ways are so simple that there aren't many details to master, and the one fancy way, *inter vivos* trusts, discussed below, is so fancy that you'll need the help of a lawyer anyway.

GIFTS

If you give away something while you're alive, you won't own it when you die. Hence, it won't constitute part of your estate and therefore won't have to go through probate. (What about the federal gift tax? You can give your spouse an unlimited amount of money, and anyone else up to $10,000 per year, without owing any gift tax.)

LIFE INSURANCE

Suppose you're dirt poor except for an enormous life insurance policy. It's crazy, you know, but you get wildly excited at the thought of your death triggering the movement of $250,000.

If the policy names you as the beneficiary (which is certainly permissible, as odd as that may seem), the money will be paid into your estate and sit there until probate is completed (and until estate taxes have been paid on it). But suppose the policy names your daughter as the beneficiary. Then the money will go directly to her, without passing GO and without being held up in probate. (If you've retained certain "incidents of ownership" in the policy, such as the power to cancel it or change its beneficiary, the money might be subject to the federal estate tax. Even so, it would still escape probate.)

Note that certain other types of "benefits payable," such as Social Security and worker's compensation benefits, can also escape probate by being made payable to someone other than yourself.

JOINT OWNERSHIP OF PROPERTY

Suppose you want "your" house (title is in your name) to go to your wife when you die. Fine. One way to accomplish this is to put it in a *joint tenancy*—which has nothing to do with an apartment tenancy. It's a form of co-ownership that means your wife automatically—and immediately—gets the place when you die (and vice versa). (Let's get technical. A joint tenancy between two people who happen to be married to each other is generally called a *tenancy by the entirety*. If the two people are just friends, even if they fool around a lot, it's called a *joint tenancy*.)

In legalese, a joint tenancy gives each of you a *right of survivorship* in the property, which means the property never goes through probate. Your wife gets it—and could sell it, if she wants—the minute after you die, or at least after filing a death certificate or complying with other minimal requirements.

Another benefit of holding property jointly with your *spouse* is that people to whom either of you owes money *individually* can't take the property, by lawsuit or otherwise. They can break your kneecaps, but they can't get title to the property. (See Chapter 2, "Family Law.")

Realistically, no one is going to throw your wife out of the house or refuse to let her drive the car pending completion of probate. Still, a joint tenancy is a wonderfully easy way to avoid the potential hassle and expense of probate with respect to certain types of property—most commonly real estate, but also cars, stocks, bank accounts, and safe-deposit boxes. (These types of property typically come with papers on which you can specify the nature of your ownership.)

Setting up a joint tenancy doesn't cost much, if anything. It's usually just a matter of scribbling a few words on the title papers, something along the lines of: "To be held by———[Husband] and———[Wife] as joint tenants [tenants by the entirety], with right of survivorship and the other incidents of that estate, and not as tenants in common." (A *tenancy in common* is a form of co-ownership that doesn't carry a right of survivorship.)

The more explicit, the better. This is especially true with respect to joint bank accounts. People often casually refer to a two-person account as *joint*, without really intending to create a right of survivorship. When opening a *true* joint account, it can't hurt to add to the papers a sentence such as: "It is our intention that the funds in this account be treated as jointly owned with right of survivorship, that they *not* be included in the probate estate of the first of us to die, and that such funds become solely the property of the survivor of us."

There are several drawbacks to joint tenancies you should be aware of. First, putting property in a joint tenancy means giving up exclusive control of something that would otherwise be yours alone.

Second, the right of survivorship can result in unintended disinheritance. Suppose you and your husband, who have two children, place the bulk of your wealth in a joint tenancy. Then your husband dies. Everything becomes yours. You remarry. You and your second husband place the bulk of your wealth in a joint tenancy. Then you die. What do your children by your first marriage inherit from you? Nothing—not even if you have a will that says they should get everything. The right of survivorship gives it all to your second husband.

Finally, in certain situations, especially those involving people of substantial wealth, holding property in a joint tenancy can yield adverse estate-tax consequences. This subject is sufficiently complex that if you're concerned about your estate taxes, you should consult an expert before placing anything really valuable in a joint tenancy.

A word on "community property." If you and your spouse live in one of eight quirky states (geographic states), you don't need to put your property in a joint tenancy. This is because all *marital property*, that is, everything acquired by either of you during your marriage, is *already* in a form of joint tenancy.

The rules vary even within the community-property states— Arizona, California, Idaho, Louisiana, Nevada, New Mexico, Texas, and Washington—but the idea is that all such property is considered by the law to be co-owned by both of you, with two exceptions: (1) property acquired by either of you before marriage, and (2) property acquired by either of you through inheritance or gift, whether before or during marriage.

What's the significance of the community-property system for your will? If you live in one of these states, at least half of all the property you acquire during your marriage will automatically go to your spouse if you should die first, regardless of who actually paid for the property and *regardless of the terms of your will.* (Note that your spouse's interest in the property attaches at the moment you acquire it. Hence, you can't sell more than a half-interest in it even one day later without your spouse's permission.)

INTER VIVOS TRUSTS

The last device for avoiding probate is a *trust*, or to toss in some Latin for good effect, an *inter vivos* ("among the living") trust. This means a trust you set up now, while you're alive, rather than one you set up through your will, which becomes effective only when you're dead.

You can't see a trust. It exists only on paper. You could think of a trust as a relationship involving people in three distinct roles (although one person can play more than one role).

Take a simple example. The three players are you, your five-year-old nephew Alexander, and your banker, Mr. Banker. You have $50,000 that you want to make sure is available for Alexander's college education.

You (the originator or *settlor* of the trust) give the $50,000 (the trust *corpus* or *res*) to Mr. Banker (the *trustee*) under a simple contract providing that he and his fellow trust officers at the bank hold and invest the money for the next ten or fifteen years, and then pay it out when Alexander (the *beneficiary*) needs it for college. (As for the contract itself, most banks have standard forms lying around, but for anything beyond the simplest arrangement you should get input from a lawyer.)

What does Mr. Banker get out of this arrangement? A small, standard percentage of the $50,000.

What do you get out of it? Peace of mind.

"That's fine," you say, "but I don't want to turn over all that money to my bank's trust officers. I'm better at investing than they are. Besides, I may change my mind."

No problem. Name *yourself* as the primary trustee, and Mr. Banker as a mere backup trustee. You can do this. Now you're wearing two hats: You're the trust's settlor and also its trustee.

Feel free to give yourself a *life interest* in the money, that is, provide that the money should remain available for your own use and benefit for as long as you live, and *then* become available for Alexander's use and benefit. Now you're wearing *three* hats:

You're the trust's settlor, its primary trustee, and its initial beneficiary. You have control over the money now (as primary trustee), and you can spend some or all of it on yourself (as the initial beneficiary).

What if you lose all the money in the stock market, so that there's none left for Alexander? Too bad. He can apply for a scholarship.

What if you decide Alexander isn't college material? No problem. You can change your mind about the whole thing, so long as you've provided in the trust papers that the trust is "revocable" (the law usually assumes the reverse—that it's *irrevocable*—unless you say so).

What happens if you, the primary trustee, should die? Who then has the authority to hold the money for Alexander? Mr. Banker, whom you've named as your backup trustee, and his fellow trust officers. And that, indeed, is the whole point: A bank, whose continued existence is more certain than yours, can make things happen for Alexander after you're gone.

Does this arrangement sound too complicated for you? Suppose your worldly possessions consist of one wrinkled suit and the $2,000 you found under the bench you slept on last night. You'd like your wife to have whatever remains of that $2,000 after you're gone, but you can't bear the thought of visiting a lawyer to set up a trust.

In this situation you should consider a *Totten trust,* named after a 1904 New York case that validated a trust arrangement based on a regular savings account. All you do is put your money in such an account, listing it in *your* name but "in trust for" your *wife.* You can withdraw some or all of this money, as you wish—which is why this arrangement is sometimes called a *tentative trust.* But if there's any left when you die, your wife gets it.

You don't need a lawyer for this. Just walk into any commercial bank and ask about Totten trusts, or "in trust for" accounts, or "Payable on Death (P.O.D.)" accounts, or perhaps "savings account trusts." You'll have to fill out a form or two, and then you can leave. (It wouldn't hurt to notify your wife of the arrangement so she'll know to ask for what remains in the account once you're gone.)

11. Death and Dying

Of all the wonders that I yet have heard,
It seems to me most strange that men should fear;
Seeing that death, a necessary end,
Will come when it will come.　　　　　　**WILLIAM SHAKESPEARE**
　　　　　　　　　　　　　　　　　　　　　　　(1564–1616)

"I think I'm gonna live forever.
Dyin' ain't on my list of things to do."　　　　**MERLE HAGGARD**
　　　　　　　　　　　　　　　　　　　　　　　(1937–　　)

The difference between "brain death" and regular death is that with the
latter you can't always get a job in the post office.
　　　　　　　　　　　　　　　　　　　　MARTIN J. YUDKOWITZ
　　　　　　　　　　　　　　　　　　　　　(1954–　　)

As discussed in the preceding chapter, it may or may not be necessary for you to prepare a will in order to clear the decks for your inevitable pushing off from mortal shores. There are other measures both prudent and humane, however, that everyone would do well to take in connection with death.

This chapter doesn't suggest you can *remedy* death, in the sense of avoiding or abolishing it. It doesn't even suggest you can come to know much about death, although sitting through several days of congressional speeches may give you a fair notion of Eternity. The subject of this chapter is *preparing* for death, including in certain circumstances exerting control over the time and manner of its occurrence, especially on behalf of the one

274

person in the world over whom you alone have, or you alone *ought* to have, the legitimate power of life and death: yourself.

The first part of this chapter discusses the "right to die," including the nature and function of living wills and durable powers of attorney. The second part also discusses living wills and durable powers of attorney, focusing on whether adopting one is a good idea for you. The third part discusses the grim but critical issue of what to do with your body following your death. Finally, the fourth part briefly discusses funerals.

THE "RIGHT TO DIE"

Death is the subject of our darkest nightmares. Most people attempt to cope with it by denying its existence. Of those who are forced by outward circumstances or irrepressible realism to acknowledge it, none but those in severe pain anticipate it with anything but resignation, at best. More often, dread.

The existence or prospect of severe pain—the classic case being that of a terminally ill patient confronting the misery and indignity of spending his last months on earth drugged, immobile, away from home, and attached to miraculous medical machines as warm and personal as an automatic bank teller—presents the peculiarly modern question of a person's right to exercise individual control over the time and manner of his death. Presenting this question in an even more difficult form is the circumstance of someone so near death as to be incapable of feeling any pain at all, or—more difficult yet—of expressing his preference as to how and when he would like to meet death.

The so-called right-to-die controversy is replete with hard questions, social and political. The immediate question for you personally, however, is what you can do now to maximize your individual control over the time and manner of your death.

At the outset, note that as long as you're conscious and rational, you needn't worry about measures you might or might not have taken *previously* to indicate your preferences as to the time and manner of your death. *Previous* indications of preference are important only if for some reason you're unable to indicate your *current* preferences.

As long as you're conscious and rational, you can say, "Wait a minute, fellas. I'll take your morphine and anything else you have to kill the pain. But keep that machine away from me." And by and large the doctors, nurses, and hospital authorities will comply. They may not *like* complying, because they tend to rate themselves solely in terms of lives prolonged. But if you're the one dying, who cares what they like?

You couldn't always obtain compliance in this manner. As recently as 1984, some Los Angeles doctors who had connected a seventy-year-old man to a respirator when one of his lungs collapsed refused to disconnect the device, although the patient repeatedly begged them to do so. The patient was dying from emphysema, heart disease, cancer, and more. He was in considerable pain. Still, he was fully aware of the nature of his pleas.

The dispute went to court. Some seven months later, before the lawsuit was resolved, the patient died of kidney failure. Only posthumously did he receive vindication, as the California Court of Appeals ruled that a competent adult patient has a constitutional right to refuse medical treatment, even if the consequence of such refusal is almost certain death.

The court said a competent adult could refuse *medical* treatment, meaning such things as surgery, radiation, and the use of respirators, kidney machines, and other artificial life-prolonging devices. There remains an open, fringe-of-the-law question about whether one can also refuse food and water. At least two courts, the Supreme Court of New Jersey and an intermediate court in California, have held that intravenous feeding is no different from the use of respirators and other artificial life-support equipment, and therefore such feeding may be discontinued in certain circumstances. (The California case involved a twenty-eight-year-old female quadriplegic suffering from crippling arthritis and severe cerebral palsy. The court emphasized that a refusal to be force-fed, even if it hastens death, does not constitute suicide, which in any event is not a crime in California or any other state.*) In other states, the very statutes that au-

---

*What *is* a crime is directly helping someone else to commit suicide.

horize the disconnection of life-prolonging equipment expressly
prohibit the withholding of food and water.

What can you do now to maximize your individual control over
the time and manner of your death?

There are at least two devices by which you can maximize
such control: (1) living wills, and (2) durable powers of attorney.
Both are effective, the latter more so than the former. Although
courts have ruled that these devices aren't the only legally effective means of asserting your rights along these lines, they're
far surer and safer than any of the alternatives.

Living Wills

A *living will*, referred to in some statutes as a "declaration"
or "directive," is typically a simple, one-page document stating
that if you should become terminally ill and unable to express
your current preferences, you hope your doctors and family will
permit you to die as naturally and expeditiously as possible,
without administering medical treatment to prolong your life
artificially. It requests, in other words, that they let you go when
your time comes. (Typically, it also requests that they keep you
clean, comfortable, free of pain, and as dignified as your condition permits.)

Are living wills legally effective? Generally, yes—although
since it's not always clear when a terminally ill patient has gone
beyond the point of consciousness and rationality, it's not always
clear when a living will becomes legally effective.

In 1976 California passed the first "right to die" or "death
with dignity" statute authorizing living wills, and now equivalent laws are on the books in thirty-five states plus the District
of Columbia—a number that will undoubtedly increase even as
this book goes to press. These laws are far from uniform, however. The most accurate statement might be that each of these
jurisdictions has *some* form of statute making *some* form of living
will legally binding in *some* circumstances.

The living-will movement has been around for a number of
years, but it drew major impetus from the famous 1976 Karen
Ann Quinlan case, in which a New Jersey court authorized the

father of the permanently comatose Ms. Quinlan to remove her
life-support devices (in consultation with the hospital's "ethics
committee" or similar body). Unexpectedly, Ms. Quinlan sur-
vived, still comatose, almost ten years following the disconnection of these devices. But the ruling in her case nevertheless
contributed greatly to the socially monumental principle that in
some instances, to state the proposition in its baldest form, death
might legitimately be preferred to life.

How can you determine your state's law pertaining to living
wills? How much would a lawyer charge you to prepare one?

To determine the law in your state, call or write Concern
for Dying (250 West 57th Street, New York, NY 10107, 212/246-
6962), a national membership organization with approximately
250,000 members. Concern's personnel will provide you with all
the information you could want. Its philosophy toward dying-
related issues is apparent from its stated goals: "To protect patient autonomy in regard to treatment during terminal illness;
to prevent the futile prolongation of the dying process and need-
less suffering by the dying."

As for how much a lawyer would charge for the preparation
of a living will, there's no need to find out. Concern for Dying
will send you an adequate model living will for no charge.

Other possible sources of information and assistance in this
area include:

• *The Society for the Right to Die* (212/246-6973) was once part
of Concern for Dying and still maintains offices at the same
address. The Society's views on dying-related issues are essentially the same as those of Concern for Dying, and it too provides
model living wills. It also publishes a booklet titled "Handbook
of Living Will Laws." Since these laws generally contain model
living wills within their very provisions, you could use this booklet to prepare a living will suitable in just about any state.

• *The American Association of Retired Persons* (1909 K Street,
N.W., Washington, DC 20049, 202/872-4700), a national membership organization with approximately 19 million members, is
committed to assisting the elderly through educational and legislative efforts. Its publications include: (1) *It's Your Choice: The
Practical Guide to Planning a Funeral*, (2) *The Essential Guide to Wills*,

Estates, Trusts, and Death Taxes, and (3) *The Over Easy Foot Care Book.*

   • *The Hemlock Society* (P.O. Box 66218, Los Angeles, CA 90066, 213/391-1871), a national organization with approximately 10,000 members, is viewed by some as the most radical of these organizations. It favors "the option of active voluntary euthanasia for the terminally ill," meaning not just the withholding or discontinuance of life-prolonging medical treatment, but also the active assistance of those seeking "self-deliverance." Hemlock's publications include: *Commonsense Suicide: The Final Right* and *Let Me Die Before I Wake—Hemlock's Book of Self-Deliverance for the Dying.*

However you obtain your living will, don't just stick it in your files or a safety deposit box; publicize it. Send a copy to your doctor, your lawyer, and responsible members of your family. Do you know anyone at *The New York Times*? Keep extra copies on hand, and take one with you when you travel. The goal is to be sure that when a decision arises as to whether to resort to extraordinary measures to keep you alive, at least one of the persons present knows of your wishes. To avoid later conflicts, it's extremely helpful to inform your family of your plans and elicit their full support.

What's wrong with living wills? Nothing, inherently. But quirks—shortcomings—in the laws of various states raise problems you should know about. Some states require you to file your living will with a local court. Others require you to "reaffirm" your living will periodically, as by placing your initials on it each year. While these requirements are easy enough to find out about, many people just never get around to complying with them.

   Finally, and downright peculiarly, the laws in some states, such as California, say your living will is valid only if executed *after* you've been diagnosed as terminally ill and then *notified* of that fact, the rationale presumably being that you can't really know the kind of treatment you'd want as a terminally ill patient until you've become one. What good this law will do you if you're rendered comatose by a stroke, car wreck, or some othe: sudden event is hard to imagine.

Durable Powers of Attorney

Consider first a "regular," as opposed to a "durable," powei of attorney. Like a living will, it's usually a simple, one-page document. Its function is to convey to a given person, your *agen* or *attorney-in-fact*, the power to make binding legal decisions or your behalf.

A *durable* power of attorney gives your agent the authority to make legal decisions for you at a time when you're incapable— or people think you're incapable—of making such decisions foi yourself. My own durable power, for example, gives my brother (who happens to be a lawyer but for this purpose needn't be) the power to tell doctors to refrain from imposing their life-prolonging, misery-prolonging measures on my body if I should become terminally ill and unable to tell them to get the hell away from me on my own. The term *durable* derives from the fact that this species of power of attorney, unlike a regular power, doesn't lose its legal effectiveness in the event of your incapacity; on the contrary, it's at that point that its legal effectiveness kicks in.

Among the advantages of a durable power of attorney over a living will is that a durable power obviates the need to antic-ipate every contingency that could arise during your incapacity. You're free to provide for as many specific contingencies as you like, but if you have confidence in the judgment of your attorney-in-fact, you can simply turn over to him the power to make all necessary decisions in light of existing circumstances, and then forget about it.

The authority conferred by a durable power of attorney need not be *limited*, that is, confined to one or a few specific areas, such as the administering or withholding of medical treatment. It can be *general*, empowering your attorney-in-fact to execute documents, pay taxes, buy or sell property, and otherwise take any action he thinks appropriate.

Not only can a durable power of attorney be as broad as you want it to be, but it can say anything you want it to say, express your preferences in any direction. Regarding life-prolonging medical treatment, for example, a durable power is as good for protecting your right to *have* such treatment as for protecting your right *not* to have it. (In contrast, a living will is nearly always written—and may even be statutorily required to be written—to *withhold* life-prolonging medical treatment.) If you're determined to use up every second allotted to you on this planet, even though when your durable power takes effect you may not know what planet you're on, you can provide in it that you want your doctors to keep you alive no matter what.

Another advantage of a durable power of attorney over a living will is that the former can take effect when you're incapacitated *temporarily*, as well as when you're incapacitated terminally. Recall that in 1985, just before President Reagan went under anesthesia for eight hours in connection with colon surgery, he signed over the powers of the presidency to Vice-President Bush. Quite appropriately for the president of the United States, he wanted someone to have the power to make decisions on his behalf during even that brief period of incapacity.

A durable power lets you do the same thing.

Suppose your problem isn't that you're terminally ill, but that you've become senile or otherwise mentally incapable of looking after your affairs. Here, too, a durable power can be invaluable.

What happens in this situation if you *haven't* executed a durable power of attorney? Assuming you're fortunate enough to have a friend or relative who cares about you, this person can go into court, present the evidence of your senility, and request the appointment of a "conservator" (or "guardian"—the terminology varies from place to place). If the judge grants this request, the person appointed (not necessarily the person who initiated the proceeding) becomes responsible for handling all your affairs—possibly for a sizable fee to be paid out of your pocket.

A properly drafted durable power of attorney can achieve the same result, but with two big advantages: First, it ensures that your attorney-in-fact is someone of your own choosing. Second, assuming you've named as your attorney-in-fact someone who is clearly disinterested and rational, it minimizes the chances that anyone will initiate a proceeding to challenge his judgment regarding whether you in fact need a conservator and, if so, who it should be. Such a proceeding has the potential, especially if you're wealthy, to degenerate into a bitter courtroom brawl. A sad example of this involved the protracted battle for control of Groucho Marx and his assets when the great comedian went into mental decline.

One further advantage of a durable power of attorney is that unlike a living will, which merely *expresses* your wishes, a durable power names someone to *enforce* your wishes. Suppose you've become comatose as the result of a car wreck. Your chances of recovery are estimated at zero, and the only open question is whether you'll be allowed to die quickly or instead kept alive on a respirator for several more months.

Would a living will provide the answer, requiring your doctor to disconnect the respirator and let nature take its course? Yes, technically. But doctors don't like being pushed around by lawyers, and especially not by little pieces of paper prepared by lawyers. Even assuming your doctor knows about and understands your living will, there's a good chance he'll read it, crumple it up, and toss it in the trash can.

So much for your living will.

Suppose, on the other hand, you've adopted a durable power of attorney. It names as your attorney-in-fact your old college roommate, Todd. When word of the car wreck reaches your family and Todd, they all rush to the hospital to see you and meet with your doctor. Putting his cards on the table, your doctor says you're dead in every meaningful sense of the word. He requests permission to disconnect your respirator. Todd tearfully nods his head in assent. He is startled to hear your elderly parents dissent. "Absolutely not," they say. "When God wants our boy, He'll take him." Todd begins to understand why you didn't name either of them as your attorney-in-fact.

Grimacing inwardly, Todd speaks up. "I'm terribly sorry, but I'm in the odd position of having to discharge a responsibility Irving gave me several years ago." He pulls a folded sheet out of his breast pocket. "This is a durable power of attorney. I've read it closely a number of times, including today on the way to the hospital. It couldn't be clearer. Irv insisted that in this very situation he wanted to be allowed to die. He felt it was his moral duty."

Your parents are momentarily stunned. Your mother, who knows a little about law, reads the document and then takes your father aside. They come back looking resigned. Your doctor has the hospital's lawyer go over the document. Everyone agrees that it's legally binding and that the decision regarding the respirator lies with Todd. Expressing his regrets to your parents, Todd gives the doctor the go-ahead. Observing from Up There, you make a note to do Todd a favor your next time around.

Every jurisdiction in the country (except, amazingly, Washington, D.C.) now authorizes durable powers of attorney. The easiest way to get one is, as with living wills, to contact Concern for Dying, which offers model forms for every state. You might also get an adequate form from a local medical or health organization.

Should you consult a lawyer? It's not essential if your durable power is to be limited to medical decisions, although even then it wouldn't hurt. On the other hand, if your durable power is to be general, giving your attorney-in-fact power over your personal and financial as well as medical affairs, it's probably wise to consult a lawyer to make sure your goals are properly stated. The cost shouldn't exceed $150 and might well be closer to $20.

SHOULD YOU DO IT?:
LIVING WILLS AND DURABLE POWERS OF ATTORNEY

Unlike living wills, which are consistently written with the one substantive goal of refusing life-prolonging medical treatment, durable powers of attorney have no inherent function other than to make sure someone of your choice has the immediate authority to make legal decisions for you in the event of your incapacity. Given the clear value of this function, a durable power *in some form* is indisputably worth having.

But this doesn't answer the primary substantive issue, namely, should you, by either device, refuse life-prolonging medical treatment in the event of your terminal incapacity? This issue can be examined via two basic questions: Why do it? and Why *not* do it?

Why Do It?

There are two primary arguments—one objective, one subjective—for refusing life-prolonging medical treatment.

1. *The cost.* The objective reason involves the staggering, possibly seven-digit cost of keeping a terminally ill patient "alive." Try to imagine yourself in Karen Ann Quinlan's circumstances—indefinitely comatose, with no hope of recovery. If some percentage of your medical costs were to come not out of your insurance but out of your bank account, what would be the economic consequences for your family? And even if insurance were to pay the whole tab, how often could society bear such massive consumption of medical resources—drugs, machinery, hospital space, nurse-time, doctor-time—by someone with no prospect of a conscious, meaningful existence?

2. *The guilt.* The subjective reason involves guilt. Not yours—you'll be way beyond that—but that of your family.

Suppose the worst: You're not merely comatose, but *brain dead,* that is, your heart continues to pump, so that your body tissues remain healthy, but your gray matter yields only a flat line on the electroencephalograph. A dozen medical experts agree that your chances of recovery are zero. You're unlikely to survive nine more months, and in order to last even one month you'll have to stay in a special unit of a modern, big-city hospital, supported by no fewer than three wildly expensive machines, with around-the-clock care and monitoring.

The doctors tell your husband you should be allowed to die—which they say they could accomplish quickly and painlessly by disconnecting any one of your life-support machines. This would not only free up the machines for patients who have some chance of recovery but also spare him the economically disastrous burden of sustaining you over the upcoming months. No less important, it would allow him to get on with the critical process of grieving your loss.

Your husband, nevertheless, is tortured by guilt. He feels he would be betraying you by letting you go.

Consider whether he might have been spared some of this agony if you had previously indicated, via a living will or durable power of attorney, that in such circumstances you would want to be allowed to die. Consider whether he might have been comforted upon being reminded that the decision he faces isn't whether to prolong your *life*, but whether to prolong your *dying*, with all its attendant suffering and cost.

Why Not *Do It*

There are four primary arguments for *not* refusing, that is, for tolerating the imposition of, life-prolonging medical treatment.

1. *The possibility of pain.* Withholding *life-prolonging* medical treatment in no way implies withholding *pain-relieving* medical treatment. Indeed, most living wills and durable powers of attorney expressly request that treatment be provided to whatever extent necessary to keep the patient free of pain, as well as clean, comfortable, and as dignified as his condition permits. The fundamental goal of living wills and durable powers is to *relieve* suffering, rather than permitting it—worse, forcing it—to continue.

2. *An aversion to death.* For most people the very subject of death provokes anxiety. They can't bring themselves to *think* about it, much less *prepare* for it. Without question, life is generally preferable to death. But with respect to a terminally ill patient, the term *life* may be inapt. Only if your definition of life includes a human body supported by a marginal heartbeat (frequently an electronically sustained heartbeat) does the life of a terminally ill, perhaps comatose patient remain extant and superior to whatever lies beyond.

3. *The possibility of mistake.* If you authorize the withholding of medical treatment, how do you know the doctors won't let you go before you're really out of the picture? How do they

know you're terminally ill, rather than just having a real bad day?

The basic answer to these questions is that doctors don't disconnect respirators, withhold medication, or otherwise throw in the towel on a patient where there's even a tiny possibility of recovery. Only where there exists "medical certainty" of non-recovery will life-prolonging treatment be withheld. Medical certainty is an admittedly difficult concept, but even the skeptical would likely agree that in *some* circumstances—where the odds against recovery are one million to one, to take an easy example—it could be said to exist.

Perhaps you have a fantasy that just as the doctors are about to pull the plug on your heart-lung machine, you'll sit up, look around, and say, "Hi, guys. What's everybody staring at?"

It hasn't happened yet.

4. *Religious opposition.* None of the three major Western faiths—Judaism, Catholicism, and Protestantism—opposes withholding medical treatment from terminally ill patients. These groups are so large and diverse, to be sure, that you could undoubtedly find dissenters within each. Still, given that no *major* group in the Western religious tradition opposes such withholding of medical treatment, it seems that anyone who would cite divine authority in support of his gut-level opposition to it overestimates the channels of communication between his gut level and the divine.

DISPOSING OF YOUR BODY

Neither less grim nor less important than the subjects addressed above is the subject of what will become of your body after your death. Bear shudderingly with me.

There are arguably two parts to "you" after your death: your body, on the one hand, and your spirit (or soul, or essence, or whatever you want to call it), on the other.

What becomes of the latter isn't a legal matter (not that lawyers concede they don't *know* what becomes of it). What becomes of the former, however, is a legal matter. Moreover, it's entirely within your control, assuming your wishes are expressed prior to your death.

There are two categories of options for dealing with your body: useful options, and not-useful options. Which options fall into which category isn't hard to figure out.

Burial and cremation are foremost among the not-useful options. They aren't harmful—especially cremation, which takes up no space in the ground. From a social perspective, however, that's the best you can say about either of them. (This is definitely not to say that memorial services and other opportunities for grieving are valueless.)

What are the useful alternatives? There are two: donating your "living" organs for transplant, and donating your corpse to a medical school.

Organ Donation

At last count, over 8,000 Americans were awaiting organs for transplant. According to a recent survey, however, only 17 percent of Americans carry organ donor cards. In other words, most Americans are going to the grave with organs that could mean the difference between life and death for others.

The way to become an organ donor on your own volition (it's always possible that your next-of-kin will make you one when you're in no position to be consulted) is to carry in your wallet a credit-card–size "organ donor card." (Mine bears the ingenious label "Organ Donor Card.") Such a card, which will generally have to be signed by you and witnessed by two other people, states simply that you're willing to donate some or all of your organs upon your death. (You can specify individual organs that you can't bear to part with.) Don't worry that carrying this card will subject you to physical danger; no one has ever had an organ extracted while he was asleep or just not paying attention.

A nonmandatory but invariably helpful step is to inform your family of your intent to list yourself as an organ donor. An organ donor card is legally binding, so if your family should attempt to have it nullified in court, they'd probably lose. As a matter of practice, however, doctors and hospital administrators won't attempt to override the wishes of a patient's family. The moral: Don't leave anything to chance. *Inform your family, and persuade them to go along.*

What portions of your body can you donate? Not only major "organs," such as your heart, lungs, liver, kidneys, and pancreas, but also "tissues," such as your skin, bones, and corneas.* As for your eyes, don't assume they aren't usable just because you wear glasses thick enough to stop bullets. The only part of the eye now being transplanted is the cornea, and your corneas could be in excellent condition even if you're literally blind.

As for the logistics of an organ's voyage from donor to recipient, consider what's likely to happen if a prospective donor suffers brain death in a small town in northern Idaho, and the most suitable recipients of his two surviving organs reside in other states. The story depends, first, on which organs we're talking about. Hearts and livers are able to survive so briefly outside the body—roughly six and twelve hours, respectively— that sheer transportation time precludes transplants to recipients in remote places. In contrast, kidneys can survive for as long as seventy-two hours and hence can go just about anywhere.

Similarly, hearts and livers are surgically harder to transplant than kidneys. The U.S. medical centers technically capable of transplanting hearts and livers number 56 and 33, respectively, whereas those capable of transplanting kidneys number 173.

Now, suppose the organs that appear suitable for transplant from the donor in Idaho are his heart and kidney. The doctors attending him there are general practitioners and have never performed an organ transplant. Moreover, they have no idea where they might find suitable recipients for the organs. They are likely to proceed as follows:

First, assuming they know of no transplant facility in Idaho, they call either the United Network for Organ Sharing (UNOS),

---

*For these purposes, *organs* are those body parts that a hospital will accept only if your heart is pumping right up to the moment of procurement, the point being to ensure that they're "alive" and healthy. (An implicit corollary is that your "death," for purposes of organ donation, must be "brain death.") In contrast, *tissues* are those body parts that a hospital will accept regardless of what your heart is up to.

based in Richmond, Virginia, or the North American Transplant Coordinators Organization (NATCO), based in Pittsburgh, Pennsylvania. UNOS or NATCO identifies for them the closest medical facility—a major Seattle hospital, say—whose staff includes *transplant coordinators* (nonphysician transplant specialists). This facility immediately dispatches one of its transplant coordinators to examine the deceased and confirm that his organs are in fact suitable for donation.

If the transplant coordinator finds the organs suitable, he attempts to match them with recipients anywhere in the country. To place the heart, he calls NATCO, whose computers provide essential data on patients needing heart, lung, or liver transplants. Having identified a suitable recipient, he arranges for a team of surgeons trained in heart transplants to come to the donor's hospital, remove the heart, carry it back to the recipient's hospital, and there perform the transplant.

To place the kidney, the coordinator follows much the same procedure, having the kidney removed from the donor almost simultaneously with the removal of the heart. Instead of calling NATCO, however, he calls UNOS, which for historical reasons has what amounts to a monopoly on data pertaining to patients in need of kidneys.

This scenario illustrates a point worth noting if it ever occurs to you that listing yourself as an organ donor might somehow jeopardize your health—in particular, that if you should reach a state of marginal health, some doctor might let you go prematurely in order to obtain your organs for transplant to someone else. *The doctors attending you won't be the same doctors attending the prospective recipients of your organs.* Your doctors won't know the transplanting doctors, most likely will never have heard of them, and certainly won't have acquired any familiarity with or personal interest in their patients. Thus, your doctors will have no allegiance to anyone but you, no stake in preserving anyone's life but yours.

Mightn't they crave the glory associated with a daring transplant, or simply welcome an opportunity to practice their surgical technique? It wouldn't matter: A donor's doctors aren't allowed to be part of the transplant team.

There's another reason you shouldn't worry. Consider what

makes a given doctor look good, what accomplishments generate the respect of his colleagues and, more important, referrals. Certainly *not* a record number of organs procured from patients who expired under his care. That's just not a distinction a doctor wants.

Some additional facts about organ donation:

• You needn't mention your plans regarding organ donation in your will. It's just not necessary.

• Organ donation needn't affect standard funeral arrangements. The organ removal process is neat and sterile; it doesn't disfigure the body.

• It's illegal for you or anyone else to be paid anything in connection with the donation of your organs.

• Donating all or part of your body is consistent with mainstream Western religious thought. Some small groups, notably very traditional Jews, do have problems with this.

• If you change your mind about donating your organs, all you have to do is tear up your organ donor card.

• There are many sources from which you can obtain a free organ donor card and additional information, including: *UNOS*, P.O. Box 5303, 2024 Monument Avenue, Richmond, VA 23220 (800/446-2726 or, in Virginia, 800/552-2138); *The Living Bank*, P.O. Box 6725, Houston, TX 77005 (713/528-2971); *The American Council on Transplantation*, P.O. Box 9999, Washington, DC 20016 (800-ACT-GIVE).

Donating Your Body to a Medical School

Much of what I've said about organ donation applies as well to the donation of your body to a medical school:

• There's a real need for it.

• Mainstream religious thought supports it.

• You needn't mention it in your will.

• You should carry a "body donor card," which often will be identical to or even part of an organ donor card. You can obtain such from any medical school.

• If you change your mind about donating your body, all you have to do is tear up your body donor card.

• It's illegal for you or anyone else to be paid anything in connection with the donation of your body. On the other hand, no one will be charged anything—which is more than you can say about burial or cremation. Are you averse to saving your family thousands of dollars?

What medical schools usually do with deceased persons' bodies, referred to as *cadavers,* is supply them to first-year medical students for intensive anatomical study. (Organs and tissues are sometimes used for medical research.) For purposes of full disclosure, I should point out that cadavers don't come out looking the way they looked when they went in. This is hardly less true with respect to cremation and burial, however.

This last point is worth focusing on by persons who feel an aversion to organ or body donation on what might be called aesthetic grounds. To state the point explicitly, cremation represents the ultimate form of obliteration. And burial differs only with respect to the speed of the process. Morticians' claims notwithstanding, the most any casket can offer is temporary protection, not indefinite preservation. This is true even of so-called sealer caskets, which come with rubber gaskets around the edges.

It says a lot about the undertaking industry that sealer caskets often carry warranties providing for replacement should one of them "fail." Any mortician who promotes a casket on this basis is a soulless reprobate attempting to prey on the bereaved, because who would ever check to see if a casket had "failed"?

What happens to a cadaver when a medical school is through with it? It's cremated. Some schools will return the ashes to the family, some won't. Some inter the ashes in a plot specifically designated for body donors.

A minor logistical difference between organ donation and body donation is that for the latter you're encouraged to make advance arrangements with a specific medical school. The benefits of advance arrangements are largely for you and your family—for you, to allow you to select the school you're most interested in helping; for your family, to spare them from having to think about such things at the time of your death.

Note that schools won't accept a body if any major organ has been removed. Neither will they accept a body that has undergone embalming or an autopsy, or if the deceased was suffering from widespread cancer or an infectious disease.

What if you've made arrangements to give your body to a school on the East Coast, but you suffer an unexpected demise while camping in Montana? It's not cheap to ship a body across the country; airplane passengers complain if they have to sit next to one, even in the smoking section. And most medical schools will accept the cost of transporting bodies only within their immediate areas. If you should die in a remote place and your next-of-kin don't want to fly your body back at their own expense, they can make alternative arrangements with some other medical school nearby; the originally intended recipient school will relinquish its claim to the donation.

FUNERALS

There are a number of issues worth addressing in connection with funerals, but virtually all are practical or financial, rather than legal. Two helpful, readable guides to the myriad issues that you may someday face in connection with the death of a relative or friend, and that you ought to face as soon as possible in connection with your own death, are:

Ernest Morgan's *Dealing Creatively with Death: A Manual of Death Education and Simple Burial* (1984), 156 pp., $6.50 (Celo Press, 1901 Hannah Branch Road, Burnsville, NC 28714, and also available from the Continental Association of Funeral and Memorial Societies, 2001 S. Street, Suite 530, N.W., Washington, DC 20009, 202/745-0634). This book offers not only much practical information, but also humane discussion of various philosophical and psychological issues relating to death. It describes the growing and invaluable role of *hospices*, which provide health care for the terminally ill, generally on an outpatient basis and generally focusing on the family as the primary source of care and comfort.

Thomas C. Nelson's *It's Your Choice—The Practical Guide to Planning a Funeral* (1983), 118 pp., $4.95 (Scott, Foresman and

Company, 1900 East Lake Avenue, Glenview, IL 60025, and also available from the American Association of Retired Persons, discussed in the first part of this chapter). This highly practical book discusses everything from hearses to pallbearers to cremation urns.

The following points should be emphasized:

1. *Dealing with a deceased's body immediately after his death.* If you can't or don't want to donate a deceased's body or organs, you may need time to figure out what you do want to do and then to make the necessary arrangements. Where to keep the body meanwhile?

If the death occurred at a hospital or nursing home, you may be able to leave the body there. If not, you can buy time by having it picked up and carried to a funeral home. You'll be charged for this service, but you might find it worth the price in order to avoid a decision that could prove costly or emotionally unsatisfying later on. Note that you're *not* thereby committed to using that funeral home for further services (assuming you decide to use a funeral home at all).

2. *Choosing among funeral or memorial service options.* If you're in charge of someone's funeral or memorial service arrangements, don't let anyone tell you there's any particular format you have to follow or any particular feature you have to include. Suit yourself—emotionally, aesthetically, financially. If you want advice, get it. Otherwise, ignore your neighbors. Ignore your priest, rabbi, or minister. Above all, ignore the funeral home director.

3. *Planning your own funeral or memorial service.* As generous a gift as you could ever make to your friends and relatives is preplanning the events to follow your death. Recognizing your mortality in this manner may not be the most pleasant task around, but you do your loved ones no favor by leaving it to them to speculate, in their sadness and guilt, over "what dear old Woodrow would have wanted." *Tell* them what dear old Woodrow would have wanted, down to the last detail: "I want five eulogies, all humorous, none lasting more than five minutes, and none to be given by ministers or lawyers. Champagne should be served, before and after. Domestic."

Don't be overly modest in your proposals. People will need an opportunity to grieve your loss.

Index